MANAGEMENT IN HUMAN SERVICE ORGANIZATIONS

MANAGEMENT
IN HUMAN SERVICE
ORGANIZATIONS

MARC L. MIRINGOFF

Macmillan Publishing Co., Inc.
New York
Collier Macmillan Publishers
London

Macmillan Publishing Co., Inc.
866 Third Avenue, New York, New York 10022

Collier Macmillan Canada, Ltd.

Library of Congress Cataloging in Publication Data

Miringoff, Marc L
    Management in human service organizations.

    Includes index.
    1. Social work administration—United States.
I. Title.
HV85.M57 1980   658′.91′361   79–15694
ISBN 0–02–381780–1

Printing: 1 2 3 4 5 6 7 8   Year: 0 1 2 3 4 5 6

For my father, Hyman Miringoff, whose life symbolized that there can be perfect harmony between the heart that cares intensely and the mind that knows what needs to be done.

PREFACE

Toward the end of the 1960s, perhaps with the assassinations of 1968, a sense of resignation became a part of our national mood; somehow events seemed to have drifted beyond our control. During the past decade, this sentiment has intensified, and as a nation, we have retreated from our problems, maintaining that they are too large and too pervasive. In an effort to control *something*, we have turned our concern from the problems themselves to the inadequacies of past solutions. We have found many of those solutions to be unwieldy and ineffective, particularly in the field of social welfare. Recent initiatives in the field have focused almost exclusively on coordinating, streamlining, dismantling—in short, controlling—the programs and policies of the past. The term now used to describe this process is management.

Management, as it is applied to social welfare, can and should achieve far more than the control of resources; it needs to be used to enhance the benefits to society which social programs can bring about. After the recent proliferation of material decrying programmatic failure, opposing government spending, and questioning the efficacy of American social welfare itself, it is time to consider approaches which can lead to success rather than to retrenchment. What is needed is a way of analyzing how programs actually function at the level of implementation—the human service organization; how they succeed and how they fail. It is upon such a perspective that effective human service management can be built; the kind of management which can sustain and improve American social welfare.

From a personal perspective, this book has been a difficult endeavor. How does one integrate the humanitarian intent of social programs with the hardnosed process of analyzing and running an organization? How does one blend compassion and pragmatism into a workable concept of human service management? Inevitably, there must be a balance between the energy of idealism and the necessity of result. After observing the functioning of a significant number of human service organizations, both in the voluntary sector and at the federal, state, and local levels of the public sector, I feel that such integration is difficult to achieve. My hope is that this book will contribute to the development of a concept of human service management which is much needed if the delivery of effective human services is to continue to be a goal of American society.

Marc L. Miringoff

ACKNOWLEDGMENTS

There are many people whose ideas and encouragement have been important to me. I shall mention but a few. My mother, Helen, whose perspective has taught me the most about organizational functioning; my wife, Marque-Luisa, assistant professor of sociology at Vassar College, whose ideas and insights are present on every page; my brother Lee, assistant professor of political science at Marist College; and sister-in-law Nancy, a social worker at Wassaic Development Center, who reviewed the entire manuscript several times and whose suggestions were invaluable; my close friend Sandra Opdycke who made an enormous contribution to both the ideas and their presentation; my colleagues at the Graduate School of Social Welfare at the State University of New York at Albany, particularly Professor Max Siporin for his vital support and valuable suggestions, Associate Professor William Roth for some important perceptions, and Associate Professor Steven Pflanczar for his concept of systems analysis; my research assistants Elizabeth Boden and Lisa Ernst for their careful and tireless effort; the students who have taken SSW 626 over the last four years and have guided me on points of content, focus, and clarification; Donald Newman, dean of the School of Criminal Justice at The State University of New York at Albany, who gave encouragement when it was very much needed; Ken Scott, senior editor at Macmillan, who made this book possible, and Nancy Ciolino, production editor, who made sure that it continued to be possible; finally, Peter Edelman, former Director of the New York State Division for Youth, who delivered just the right message at just the right time.

CONTENTS

MANAGEMENT IN HUMAN SERVICE ORGANIZATIONS

Chapter ONE

THE NEED FOR HUMAN SERVICE MANAGEMENT

THE SOCIAL WELFARE INSTITUTION

The social problems facing America are extensive. Some of these problems affect all sectors of the population, others touch only specific groups; many are potentially threatening to everyone. Taken together, such problems as child abuse, alcoholism, mental retardation, poverty, marital and family breakdown, unemployment, violence, and drug abuse deeply affect the well-being of society.

Within the last one hundred years, the United States has developed a significant social welfare institution designed to confront these and similar problems.[1] Before the 1930s most social programs were conducted under private, nongovernmental auspices. In 1932, the New Deal administration of President Franklin Roosevelt initiated the beginnings of a national social welfare institution. The early programs of the 1930s dealt almost exclusively with the problem of economic insecurity. Since that time, the social welfare institution has dramatically expanded; it now strives to confront a great variety of social problems.[2] Yet the growth and acceptance of social welfare, both as an idea and as an institution of society, has not always been easily achieved.[3]

Social welfare has been greatly influenced by two fundamental attitudes periodically exhibited by people in the United States: one is compassion, the other pragmatism. The development of the social welfare institution in this country has been characterized by periods dominated first by one and then the other of these attitudes. Generally, initiatives made during a period of expansion are severely scrutinized during a subsequent time of contraction. The 1930s and the 1960s were periods of expansion, whereas the 1950s and 1970s have brought contraction. Even during periods of contraction, however, there appears to be a consensus about the humanitarian intent of social welfare; that some services need to be provided to the mentally ill, the disabled, the poor, and so on. The criticism has generally been focused on the *conduct* of these programs and at their lack of a demonstrable outcome in serving significant numbers of the population.[4] That is the pragmatic side. Certainly when social welfare programs are perceived to yield such visible results, they enjoy long-term support. An entire coalition, built around the Social Security Act of 1935, which established Unemployment Insurance, Social Security, and other measures, changed American politics; remnants of that coalition are still powerful today. The same is true of such measures as Medicare in the early 1960s. It appears, however, that other innovations such as the Economic Opportunity Act of 1964, which initiated the "Great Society," have not enjoyed sustained public support, chiefly because they were generally viewed as lacking effectiveness.

The concern for accountability and beneficial results is a compelling one.[5] It stands as a major consideration for those who support social programs as a means of alleviating social problems and human suffering. This is the case because attention to accountability and outcome can produce programs that not only aspire to help those in need, but truly "work," and can be shown to work.

Another factor, strongly influencing the movement of the pendulum between compassion and pragmatism, is the availability of economic resources for social welfare. The phrase "but where will the money come from" echoes from the largest federal offices to the smallest neighborhood program. Clearly, we are living in a time of diminishing resources. Traditional liberal economics in the United States has assumed that financial support for social welfare can be derived from general economic growth, stimulated through government spending. Hence, the government "primes the pump" and the resulting economic expansion provides the fiscal basis for expanded social welfare.[6]

Significant new resources for the social welfare institution, then, can be available through significant growth in the economy. An alternative approach is the redistribution of resources for social welfare.[7] Resources, in effect, can be reallocated from other parts of the private or public sector to help support social policy and programs. This is possible by shifting priorities in the federal budget, from defense to social welfare, for example, or through taxation, from the private sector.[8]

The first of these two options, social welfare funded through economic growth, is likely to accumulate more long-term, on-going support than the second, although this is very much affected by socioeconomic conditions. What does appear clear, however, is that although some new resources may be available for social welfare, *significant* new expansions are unlikely under present conditions, or in the immediate future. In fact, general cutbacks are more likely. Zald notes

> First, I think, it is apparent that there will be no large-scale re-distribution program. Second, the major crisis in our welfare program is likely to come in the area of female headed households. If the recent trend does not soon abate we can expect an extraordinarily high demand for services in this area. Third, new programs will be so tailored that they minimize the explicit re-distribution effect. Fourth, large and costly new programs will be trimmed so that they only affect the most desperately needed parts of the population. Fifth, labor intensive social welfare services will find it increasingly difficult to be funded, especially since they so rarely show the benefits their initial advocates proclaim. Thus, many labor intensive programs will be found serving the middle class who can afford them rather than the very poor who will depend upon government funding for them. Finally, in the overall priority of things the welfare state in western industrial countries will be in low gear.[9]

The future of the social welfare institution, then, lies not only in programs that work but also in those that can be conducted within the general constraints of fiscal resources. In short, the development of human services in the coming decade will come not through major increases of funds but through more effective and efficient use of current resources. Proponents of social welfare need to accept an orientation and philosophy that can merge compassion and pragmatism in the *conduct* of social programs. This is required both from the point of view of the public and from the perspective of those who are served by social programs. There is little compassion in ineffective programs.

THE HUMAN SERVICE ORGANIZATION

The social welfare institution is the sum total of the resources, policies, programs, and technical knowledge devoted by society to social welfare. The point at which these elements merge to confront social problems is the *human service organization*. The human service organization is the "front line" of the social welfare institution. It is at the organizational level that humanitarian intent can be translated into effective result and it is there that programs ultimately succeed or fail. It is at the organizational level, too, where the social welfare institution is closest to its public, and most vulnerable to criticism and attack. In the final analysis, it is the functioning of the human service organization that can determine the strength and survival of the social welfare institution.

A human service organization has been defined as "an organization whose primary function is to define or alter a person's behavior, attributes and social status in order to maintain or enhance his well-being."[10] An important element distinguishing human service organizations, then, is the nature of the intended outcome, or the organizational product: to alleviate a human or social problem through change in an individual or group of service recipients. For the purposes of this book, human service organizations are divided into two types, *the delivery organization and the planning organization*. The human service delivery organization is charged with the actual provision of service directly to a specified client population. The human service planning organization does not actually deliver the service itself, but functions to plan, administer, fund, or coordinate human services within a specified region or domain of responsibility.

Delivery organizations are usually designed in one of two ways; the first as a deliverer of *one* type of service to all age groups of recipients. Examples are mental health agencies, employment services (or manpower programs), health care centers, and recreation facilities. The second kind of delivery organization provides services to a specified clientele: youth services, services for the elderly, child and protective services, services for the poor, and so on. Here the service may be multiple (mental health and employment and recreation), but the recipients are specified. *The Encyclopedia of Social Work* provides the following list, which furnishes examples of many of the human services:[11]

Child Welfare
 Adoption and foster care
 Day care
 Institutional care
 Preschool services
 Residential treatment

Crime and Delinquency
 Institutions
 Probation and parole
 Treatment and prevention

Disability and Physical Handicap
 Services for the chronically ill
 Visual and auditory services
 Vocational rehabilitation

Family
 Family planning
 Family service agencies
 Marital counseling

Health Care
 Ambulatory care
 Hospital care
 Genetic counseling
 Mother and child health
 Public health

Housing
 Services for low-income housing
 Relocation

Income Maintenance
  Social security
  Public assistance
  Unemployment insurance
  Workmen's compensation
Labor
  Vocational guidance
  Employment services
Mental Health
  Counseling
  Mental retardation
  Alcoholism services
  Institution and residential care
Migration and Resettlement
Nursing Home Care
Protective Services
  Adults
  Children
Recreational Services

The organizational structure of agencies delivering these services is often characterized by several groupings of personnel. First, there are the service providers themselves, often professionals. These may include nurses, physicians, social workers, psychologists, employment specialists, recreation workers, and other specialized personnel, depending on the kind of service being provided. Next, there are supervisory personnel whose major function is to guide and oversee the work of the service providers. Thirdly, there is a group of what might be termed support staff, composed of clerical personnel, maintenance personnel, and so on. In residential organizations, there is generally an entire staff of attendants who provide custodial care for the patients. Finally, there are those who perform the managerial tasks—these compose the subject of this book.

The delivery organizations often relate to the planning organizations on a hierarchical basis. For example, a county or local department of mental health will be funded through a state department of mental health. The major human service planning organization in the United States is, of course, the Department of Health and Human Services (HHS, formerly HEW) in Washington, D.C. This agency has responsibility for large numbers of human service programs ranging from public welfare and mental health to aging and child development. Other federal-level departments are responsible for other human services, such as the Labor Department in the area of Manpower programs, Agriculture in Food Stamps, the Department of Housing and Urban Development in public housing and Model Cities (now Community Development), and the Department of Defense in the area of social services for military personnel.[12] There are similar kinds of organizations at regional (multistate) levels. For example, HHS divides the country into ten regions, each of which contains a variety of program components in many different policy areas.

Planning organizations also exist in the governments of all 50 states, and are characterized by a great multiplicity of organizational arrangements. Each state, because of a different history, political climate, level of funding, and governmental structure, has developed a different arrangement in the organization of its human services.[13] Some states combine several human service areas into one organizational structure, others have specialized organizations, and some states do not have state-level organizations in some human service areas. Some states are divided into multicounty regions for the provision of some services. In this case the state-level organization might establish a number of regional offices to help plan and coordinate local services.

In addition to federal, multistate regional, and multicounty regional systems, many local and metropolitan areas maintain organizations or organizational components that relate to human service planning. New York City's Human Resources Administration is a comprehensive human services agency representing an "HHS"-type structure on a metropolitan level. In Illinois, the Cook County Department of Public Aid in Chicago may be more significant than some of the state-level human service organizations.

The question that needs to be asked in regard to the human service organization is: To what degree is it achieving the actual alleviation of social problems; how effective is it? The implicit assumption from the public's perspective is that a drug abuse program, for example, alleviates drug abuse, a program for the elderly is expected to help the elderly, and a mental hospital treats the mentally ill. But how many of the activities in a given organization actually achieve their intended result? How much funding and organizational energy and resource is wasted or utilized in the pursuit of other goals, ranging from merely controlling patients to gaining advancement for individual members of the organization? The Department of HHS in Washington is designed to pursue the goal of quality in health, education, and welfare. But how many of its activities actually achieve something in these areas? This is of vital concern not only for the recipients of service but also because it is what the public *expects* these human service organizations to do. It is when the activities and pursuits of human service organizations do not contribute to the alleviation of social problems, that the social welfare institution is weakened.

It is impossible, of course, to know with a high degree of specificity the degree to which service goals are being met and human problems alleviated by human service organizations. The problems of measurement and the portrayal of demonstrable results are endemic to organizations which service people. Profit and loss sheets are difficult to conceive. Yet even the most partisan proponent of the human services would not argue that the human service organization, in general, is as efficient and effective as it needs to be, nor that from the perspective of the public and the service recipient, anything less than a significant degree of service effectiveness is a serious problem with profound implications. The point is: we need to do better.[14]

THE NEED FOR A NEW PERSPECTIVE IN HUMAN SERVICE MANAGEMENT

All human service organizations carry out at least some managerial activities. There is the need to prepare budgets, to represent the organization to entities such as boards or political bodies, to secure and dispense funding, to attend to personnel, to keep fiscal records, to establish consistent organizational procedures, and to settle staff disputes; in short, the organization must be maintained. These and similar activities constitute *main-*

tenance management and are essential to the survival of any formal organization.

A smoothly functioning, efficient human service organization with successful maintenance management, however, is but a *prerequisite* to effective service. Such an organization does not necessarily help clients nor alleviate social problems nor contribute to the survival and development of the social welfare institution. The fact that an organization is efficient in its operations does not mean that it is effective in its provision of service. A human service organization that devotes a disproportionate amount of managerial time, energy, and commitment to maintenance may lose its capacity to provide service effectively. In order to help ensure effective service, an additional managerial capacity is necessary, which complements maintenance management; this can be termed *service management*. Service management is responsible for the quality, substance, and effectiveness of the organization's service product. As such, it is a managerial perspective that confronts the question: "Is this organization, as a whole, providing service that works?", to accompany the question (of maintenance management) "Is this organization efficiently maintaining itself?" A verse from a civil rights song went: "Keep your eyes on the prize, hold on." This message should shape service management, the prize being the provision of effective service.

Service management views organizational activities, structures, practices, relationships, and dynamics in terms of their *effect on the quality of service,* and concentrates on making each contribute to the enhancement of that quality. Yet, such management is rare in human service organizations, where maintenance predominates. This is the case for several reasons, one of which is conceptual. Unlike England, for example,[15] where there is an established concept of "social administration" supported by a firm intellectual tradition, the United States lacks a unifying concept of human service management. One reason is that in the United States, the concepts of "management" or "administration" have evolved separately from social welfare and human service provision, and are drawn mostly from the world and theory of business. Hence, as social welfare has grown, there has been an increasing recognition that management is needed, but such management has often been perceived, even by its own practitioners, as an activity almost divorced from the quality of service itself. In this view, management is concerned almost exclusively with an organization's maintenance and political functioning; the quality and substance of the service provided is seen to lie outside the purview of management.[16] Hence managerial measures of efficiency and budgetary concerns have often been viewed by service practitioners as being counterproductive to service delivery.[17] Managers have often viewed themselves as possessing a generic skill, applicable to most any organization and only loosely related to the actual service "product." In short, in the absence of a well-conceived notion of "social management," the human services have tended to adopt existing managerial concepts created in other spheres of endeavor.

Maintenance management can often predominate because it is more tangible, more concrete and more measurable than service management. It is far easier to count numbers of forms, or physical resources, or funding, than to assess service outcome, determine what in the organization could enhance it, and to bring about that enhancement. Furthermore, the recent growth in the number and complexity of human service organizations has required a concomitant growth in the effort expended to maintain them. Hence, maintaining coordinative, procedural, and financial interrelationships diverts managerial effort from the consideration of actual service quality.

In the day-to-day functioning of a human service organization, it is often not difficult to perceive the dominance of maintenance over service management. The following questions may be helpful in assessing the balance in a given organization:

1. Is much of management concerned with "paperwork?"
2. Do the concerns, objectives, and activities of management seem divorced from those of the service providers?
3. Is there a component of the organization charged with considering such issues as: "Where do we want our services to be in five years?"
4. Is there any mechanism for the evaluation of service results?
5. Is each year's budget essentially a repetition of the previous year's, with little or no attention to program results or changing circumstances?

6. Are staff members hired, fired, or appraised on the basis of factors other than their capacity to provide service?
7. Has the organization assumed a professional responsibility for educating the surrounding community about the relevant social problems and the services available?
8. Is advancement in the organization based primarily on successful service achievement?
9. Is the interaction between a planning organization and the delivery organizations of its network characterized to any significant degree by the issues of quality of service?
10. Is there an organized, systematic assessment of the organization's functioning to determine how it affects the quality of service?

Improvement in service management is essential if the multitude of human service organizations composing the social welfare institution are to enhance the quality and effectiveness of their service. A new perspective and approach is needed in human service management that will emphasize service more and maintenance less, in both concept and application. Such an approach requires that the functioning of the human service organization be carefully analyzed in terms of *how that functioning affects the quality of service;* the analysis must be followed by the establishment of managerial initiatives for making the necessary changes.

This book endeavors to contribute to the development of the concept and application of service management. Although maintenance management is also covered, the tasks of maintenance are de-emphasized because this subject has been covered in other works. Maintenance is considered primarily in the context of its relationship to service management and to program effectiveness. For it is effectiveness and not maintenance that needs to be viewed as the ultimate purpose of human service management.

In presenting the concept of service management this book addresses two questions: (1) What are the significant dynamics inherent in the functioning of human service organizations that underlie its day-to-day activities and serve to explain the quality of the service outcome; and (2) What are the purposes and objectives of a concept of management that is designed to improve service effectiveness? The first of these questions is addressed in Part I of this book, *Analyzing the Organization;* the second is covered in Part II, *Managing the Organization.* The first question requires a systematic framework for analysis that (a) identifies the significant organizational factors; (b) indicates their possible range of variability; (c) demonstrates how they relate to one another; and (d) can show, in its totality, how organizational functioning can bring about varying patterns of effective service. Such a framework needs to be sufficiently concrete to provide organizational insight and sufficiently generalized to provide application to varied organizational situations. In order to be of use in evolving a concept of service management, the framework must reveal the patterns of functioning that underlie an organization's daily activities and make clear which patterns encourage and which obstruct effective service. In short, in order for service management to become a reality, it is necessary that the manager understand the elements that act and interact or make an activity such as the preparation of the budget move either toward or away from contributing to service effectiveness. Hence, the framework will attempt to indicate how generic processes present in human service organizations, such as decision making, goal setting, the use of authority, and the utilization of professional expertise (technology) combine to compose the essential dynamics of service effectiveness.

It is a major contention of this work that analyzing these processes and their interrelationships in specified ways can provide a picture of how organizational functioning affects the quality of service, and that such analysis can also indicate how management can improve the quality of service. Hence, the framework can be an instrument of human service management.

Part II of the book does not indicate all of the tasks of management, but does point out the objectives and purposes of management given the concepts provided in Part 1. For example, it points out what needs to be achieved and avoided in such management functions as staff development, program evaluation, community relations, and budgeting in order to bring about more effective service. Part II also considers the strategies of management in carrying out these functions. Specific applications of management to the planning organization are also considered as are the implications of human service management for the future of the social welfare institution.

In the last analysis, the strength of the social welfare institution is built upon the degree to which its human service organizations can deliver effective service. Policy pronouncements can emanate from the highest levels of the national intent, but if the organizations charged with the actual implementation of that intent function in such a way as to make service impossible, then policy is rendered ineffectual. This book, therefore, is intended to serve practitioners and students of human service management, whether their background and perspective be derived from social work and social welfare or from the world of business management and public administration. Both of these areas are currently involved in the management of the social welfare institution, and both have impact on the quality of care in the social welfare institution. The book is designed to contribute to scholarly endeavor as well. The subject of human service management and its role in increasing the effectiveness of services has received far too little scholarly attention from those writing in the field of social welfare.[18] Yet the task of developing a sound base of theory and knowledge upon which human service management can be practiced is a difficult one. It is hoped that this book can contribute to such deliberation.

NOTES

1. Samuel Mencher, *From Poor Law to Poverty Programs: Economic Security Policy in Britain and the United States* (Pittsburgh: University of Pittsburgh Press, 1967). See also Clair Wilcox, *Toward Social Welfare: An Analysis of Programs and Proposals Attacking Poverty, Insecurity and Inequality of Opportunity* (Homewood, Ill.: R. D. Irwin, 1969), for an excellent description of the social welfare institution with particular emphasis on income maintenance programs.
2. David G. Gil, *Unraveling Social Policy* (Cambridge, Mass.: Schenkman Publishing Co., 1973); Neil Gilbert and Harry Specht, *Dimensions of Social Welfare Policy* (Englewood Cliffs, N.J.: Prentice-Hall, 1974); Alfred J. Kahn, *Social Policy and Social Science* (New York: Random House, 1973).

3. For varying views on the social welfare institution see Morris Janowitz, *Social Control and the Welfare State* (New York: Elsevier Scientific Publishing Co., 1976) and David G. Gil, *The Challenge of Social Equality: Essays on Social Policy, Social Development and Political Practice* (Cambridge, Mass.: Schenkman Publishing Co., 1976).

4. Public opinion polls consistently show, for example, that while the population will support statements such as "the government should help the poor," they often oppose specific programs such as public assistance due mainly to perceived inefficiency, corruption, etc.

5. Emmanuel Tropp, "Expectation, Performance, and Accountability," *Social Work*, vol. 19, no. 2, March, 1974, pp. 139–48; Edward Newman and Jerry Turem, "The Crisis of Accountability," *Social Work*, vol. 19, no. 1, January 1974, pp. 139–147; Marvin L. Rosenberg and Ralph Brody, "The Threat or Challenge of Accountability," *Social Work*, vol. 19, no. 3, May 1974, pp. 344–350.

6. For a lucid introduction to the dynamics of government spending, see Robert L. Heilbroner and Peter L. Bernstein, *A Primer on Government Spending* (New York: Random House, 1971) or John Kenneth Galbraith, *Economics and the Public Purpose* (New York: Houghton-Mifflin, 1973), especially pp. 307 ff.

7. Lester C. Thurow, *Poverty and Discrimination* (Washington: Brookings Institution, 1969).

8. For a discussion of tax reform proposals to support social welfare, see Martha N. Ozawa, "Taxation and Social Welfare," *Social Work*, vol. 18, no. 3, May 1973, pp. 66–76.

9. Mayer Zald, "The Future of the Welfare State," *Social Service Review*, vol. 51, no. 1, pp. 121–22.

10. Yeheskel Hasenfeld and Richard A. English, eds., *Human Service Organizations: A Book of Readings* (Ann Arbor, The University of Michigan Press, 1974), p. 6.

11. *Encyclopedia of Social Work*, 2 vols. (National Association of Social Workers, Washington, D.C., 17th ed., 1977).

12. Sheila B. Kamerman and Alfred J. Kahn, *Social Services in the United States: Policies and Programs* (Philadelphia: Temple University Press, 1976), see especially, Appendix: "Social Welfare in the American Community."

13. For a presentation of the organization of many of these services, see *Public Welfare Directory 78/79*, vol. 39 (Washington, D.C.: American Public Welfare Association).

14. Sar A. Levitan and Robert Taggert, *The Promise of Greatness* (Cambridge, Mass.: Harvard University Press, 1976).

15. Joyce Warham, *An Introduction to Administration for Social Workers*, rev. ed., (Atlantic Highlands, N.J.: Humanities Press, 1975); Sidney Zimbalist, "A Comparison of Social Welfare Values: A Systematic Approach," *Social Work*, vol. 23, no. 3, May 1978; Richard Titmuss, *Social Policy* (London: Allen and Unwin, Ltd, 1974) and *Commitment to Welfare* (New York: Pantheon Books, 1968), *Introduction to Social Administration in Britain* (New York: Hillary House Publishers, 1969); R. G. S. Brown, *The Management of Welfare: A Study of British Social Service Administration* (London: William Collins, 1975).

16. For example, Harold F. Gurtner, *Administration in the Public Sector* (New York: John Wiley and Sons, 1977) and Barry M. Richman and Richard Farmer, *Management and Organizations* (New York: Random House).

17. For a clear-cut example of why management can be feared by practitioners, see Murray Gruber, "Total Administration," *Social Work*, vol. 19, no. 5, September 1974, pp. 625–636.

18. Edward Schwartz, "On Macro-Social Work: A Practice in Search of Some Theory," *Social Service Review*, vol. 51, no. 2, June 1978, pp. 207–27.

PART I

Analyzing the Organization: How the Human Service Product Is Derived

Understanding the process by which the functioning of a human service organization affects its service product is a prerequisite to effective management. In Part I, the human service organization is considered with regard to both its internal functioning and the influence of that functioning on its organizational environment. In presenting a systematic framework for analyzing a human service organization, a perspective involving input, throughput, and output is utilized. The input constitutes resources emanating from the organization's environment, which the organization requires in order to provide a service product. The throughput is concerned with the manner in which the organization utilizes these resources. The output represents the organization's service product. A comprehensive analysis of the functioning of a human service organization must take into account the dynamic interrelationship of these three factors.

Chapter TWO

THE INPUT:
The Human Service
Organization and Its Resources

In order to begin to assess systematically the functioning of human service organizations, consideration must be given to the kinds of raw materials, resources, or inputs that are required. All formal complex organizations utilize what can be called *maintenance resources,* which include funding, equipment, supplies, a physical plant, and so forth. These resources are necessary to ensure the survival of an organization. A human service organization, however, because of the uniqueness of its organizational product, requires a second kind of resource. This can be termed a *service resource,* which is derived from the existence and availability of a specific type of expertise designed to alleviate the given social problem with which the organization deals. It is this kind of resource that forms the basis and ultimately determines the effectiveness of an organization's service product. Without sufficient service resources an organization cannot deliver an effective service product, despite the presence of an adequate quantity of maintenance resources.

The procurement and efficient disposal of maintenance resources is the basis of maintenance management. The procurement and overall effective application of the service resources constitutes service management. The management of maintenance resources, as noted in the introductory chapter, is a subject that has been extensively explored, particularly in the areas of business and public administration. An integrated and developed concept of the management of service resources, on the other hand, has received little attention. Hence the emphasis throughout this work is on service resources and their management. Maintenance resources are considered in the context of their effect on service outcome. The ultimate purpose of human service management is to promote and enhance effective service, therefore efficiency and maintenance must be viewed as a means to that end, rather than as goals in themselves. The chapters that compose Part I therefore provide a framework designed to address the following question: What are the significant factors operating in human service organizations that determine the ultimate quality of the service product?

THE SERVICE RESOURCE

The State of a Human Service Technology

A useful concept that helps to clarify the notion of a service resource is a human service technology,[1] which may be defined as the sum total of the knowledge, procedures, and techniques that, when applied in a given human service field, will yield consistent, desired, and predictable results.[2] Charles Perrow, an organizational analyst, has developed several criteria for what may be considered a model of a highly developed human service technology:

1. Some knowledge of a nonrandom cause-and-effect relationship is required, that is, the techniques lead to the performance of acts which, for known or unknown reasons, cause a change under specific conditions.
2. There is some system of feedback such that the consequences of the acts can be assessed in an objective manner.
3. It is possible to secure repeated demonstrations of the efficacy of the acts.
4. There is an acceptable, reasonable, and determinant range of tolerance, that is, the proportion of the successes must be estimated, and even though the proportion might be small, it is judged high enough to continue the activity.
5. The techniques can be communicated sufficiently so that most persons with appropriate preliminary training can be ex-

pected to master the techniques and perform them under acceptable limits of tolerance.[3]

Taken together, these criteria represent an ideal technology in the highest state of development. Such criteria are useful as standards for assessing the state of a given technology at a given time. Technologies may approach all of these criteria, in which case they are highly developed; they may manifest few or none, in which case they are minimally developed; or they may reflect varying degrees of development.[4] To understand the concept of human service technology it is therefore important that it be viewed as a *continuous* variable or factor.[5] The important consideration is not *whether* a technology is present but *to what degree* it is present, making it a continuous variable. It is a rare human service in which no technology whatever is present, and an equally rare situation in which a human technology is *fully* developed. This continuous concept can be visualized as follows, with most, if not all actual human service technologies falling between the two poles.

The State of a Human Service Technology

Highly
Developed

Minimally
Developed

Every organization employs some kind of technology in order to execute the functions it is designed to carry out. In a manufacturing plant, technology is typically tangible in that the process of assembling the elements results in a concrete product, be it clothing, automobiles, or toothpaste. This kind of technology is generally characterized by a high degree of routinization.[6] Once the operational system is in place, the tasks become clear, the causative relationships apparent, the process highly repetitive, and the product standardized. Some technologies are so perfected that human input becomes marginal. The spaceflights are a good example. Rather than being commanded, as in much science fiction, by a human being who acted often by instinct and, in crises, quickly developed and applied a new theoretical breakthrough, the spaceflights were dominated by a computerized technology that left little to chance. So routinized became the technology that the excitement, for television audiences, became increasingly diminished as the number of flights increased.

The technology of human service is quite different.[7] What actually occurs between a patient and a therapist in a mental health setting, or a social worker and a client in a drug abuse program, a worker and a trainee in a manpower training program, or a caseworker and a public assistance recipient in a social services program constitutes a technology characterized by elements that are difficult to control.[8] Unlike the highly routinized technology of manufacturing, which deals with inanimate objects, human service technology concerns changes in human beings and is therefore far less tangible and definable. Nevertheless, the product of a human service organization is its service effectiveness, and technology represents the vital component that constitutes the necessary raw material ultimately leading to the formulation of that product.

Although there has been some research linking technology to other aspects of organizational functioning, there has, unfortunately, been little work attempting to analyze and compare different human service technologies.[9] Great differences in technological development are apparent. Health-related technology, particularly surgery, is relatively more developed in its techniques and specialized procedures than is community organization, for example, which has only progressed to the point of descriptive categories of professional functioning and the development of role models for practice.[10]

The degree of development of a given human service technology used by a given human service organization is a crucial factor in the eventual quality of its service. If little is known about a particular human service problem and how to treat or alleviate it, then it will be difficult for a human service organization to function in a consistent, effective manner, no matter how efficient it may be, how much rhetoric surrounds its initiation, or how much public support it may command. What is achieved can most probably be attributed to serendipitous and inconsistent techniques.

The first factor, then, in understanding how the ultimate quality of the service product of a human service organization is determined, lies in the state of development of the technology that the organization employs. In order to understand the service resources available to the organization, the manager must understand the capabilities and limitations of the given technology. The manager must consider, for example, the following kinds of questions concerning the technology:[11]

1. Is the technology exacting and routinized?
2. Is it abstract and intangible?
3. Are advances and modifications in the technology frequent?
4. Is there concrete evidence of its efficacy and effectiveness?
5. Are its elements easy or difficult to measure?
6. Are its elements easily communicated?[12]

None of these, nor similar kinds of questions that serve to help clarify the nature of a given human service technology, have ready answers. But without an approach and consideration to these kinds of questions, it is difficult to perceive how a human service manager might proceed in enhancing the service product of an organization.

The Degree to Which Human Service Technology Is Possessed by Practitioners

The state of development of a human service technology does not, in itself, constitute a service resource. There may, in fact, exist a technology at a sufficiently high state of development to provide some degree of effective service, but if a sufficient number of practitioners who are trained to utilize it are unavailable to a given organization, the technology itself is of little use in actual service delivery. Therefore, the *possession* of the technology by practitioners who are available to the organization becomes an important factor. The focal points for technological development and training are the human service professions and their educational institutions. In graduate schools of social work, for example, the technology of social casework, which is practiced in a great variety of human service settings, is taught to future professionals. To what degree is the state of the technology actually transmitted to these students?[13] Clearly, factors are present in an educational process that can cause the nature of what transpires to be less than adequate, thereby adversely affecting a future practitioner's preparation and ultimately reducing his or her technological possession.[14] This issue is primarily an educational one, but it has a significant effect on the level of practice that takes place in human service organizations. If the educational institution can transmit most of the technological elements, or a framework through which these elements can be assembled by future practitioners, then the eventual quality of service in the organization in which these practitioners eventually practice is maximized. Of course, the acquisition of technology by no means ends in school and much is acquired "on the job," but the educational process can provide the basis of professional identity and socialization that depends largely upon the acquisition of technological knowledge and skill.

As in the case of the state of technology, it is unlikely that a practitioner of human services will possess no degree of technology, nor is it likely that he or she would possess such knowledge to the point at which there is no opportunity for further development. Therefore, the degree of possession is clearly another continuous variable.

The Degree to Which Human Service Technology
Is Possessed by Practitioners

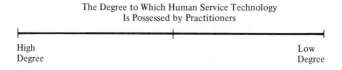

High
Degree

Low
Degree

Thus the second factor involved in understanding how effective service is derived is the degree of technology possessed by the practitioners who provide the service. A human service manager needs to consider the following kinds of questions:

1. Is a profession involved in the technology? Do the formal educational credentials relate to a significant degree to the actual carrying out of tasks? Does the profession have different gradation levels and do these levels relate significantly to the possession of ability?
2. Does the knowledge on which the technology is based include different formalized schools of thought, and are

there controversies in the field? Are such schools and controversies manifested by the practitioners of the organization?

3. Can the degree to which the technology is possessed be determined and evaluated? Are standards of assessment part of the profession? Is an assessment on the level of training and the nature of the professional background available?[15]

It is *both* the state of a human service technology and its possession by practitioners, then, that provide the basis for understanding the service resources of a human service organization. In understanding how an organization derives its product, therefore, the human service manager needs to understand these two factors in the context of a given organization. A knowledge and assessment of these "raw materials" that compose the service resources of the organization is a necessary step in understanding the totality of how the service product is produced.

The availability of service resources thus constitutes the input in the process culminating in a service product. This process, at this point, can be viewed below.[16]

Taken together, these two input factors indicate whether

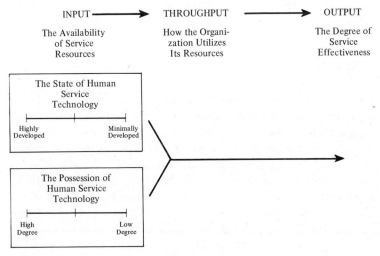

FIGURE 2–1

a human service organization has at its disposal a relatively *maximal* or *minimal* degree of service resource availability. The nature of this input is clearly vital to the rest of the process. If, for example, the input tends to be minimal, this will profoundly affect the throughput and output in a negative way from the perspective of service quality. If the input is relatively maximal, the throughput process and the output will probably be enhanced with a resulting increase in service quality. These dynamics are considered in greater depth in the following chapters.

One final word about human service technology and its possession: It can be argued that in human service organizations the nature of the technology is not always manifestly clear. "What works" and attains the desired result may not always be apparent either to those rendering or those receiving the service. Hence, a patient or client might "feel better" or experience enhanced social functioning without knowing exactly what it was in the course of treatment that produced this outcome. Although this is often true, and some of the important aspects of the technology may be latent rather than manifest, these aspects nonetheless constitute the elements that serve to bring about the desired effect. An important goal in the development of human service technology, therefore, may be to help make these latent aspects more manifest, so that they become more easily communicated between practitioners. Be that as it may, the technology, manifest or latent, is the core of human service.

SUMMARY

The practice of human service management needs to be based on a comprehensive and ongoing assessment of a human service organization's product—service to meet human needs. It is important to analyze the process by which this product comes about, and to understand how the quality of service is affected by the organization. This chapter has been concerned with an important aspect of this process, the organization's resources. Two kinds of resources are required by a human service organization. The first can be viewed as maintenance resources; these include funding, a physical plant, and similar materials. The efficient procurement and dispersal of these resources constitutes maintenance management. The second kind of resources, which composed the principal concern of the chapter, are service resources. The service resource contributes most directly to the quality of the service outcome. The procurement and efficient utilization of this resource constitutes the process of service management.

The service resources available to a given human service organization represent the input in our framework, and can be understood through the concept of human service technology. Human service technology has been defined as the sum total of the knowledge, procedures, and techniques that, when applied in a given human service field, will yield consistent, desired, and predictable results. The state of the technology utilized by a human service organization is clearly an important factor in understanding how the quality of service is derived. It is a factor that varies between minimal and high development. The human service manager must understand the nature of the technology and its capabilities and limitations. The second factor is the possession of the technology by practitioners. A highly developed technology might exist, but without practitioners who can utilize it and who are available to the organization, this technology will be of little benefit to service delivery. Like the state of technology, the possession of technology also varies among practitioners.

It is through the understanding of these two factors, which compose the service resource, that the human service manager can begin to understand how the effectiveness of service is derived, in the context of the functioning of a human service organization.

NOTES

1. I am most indebted to the work of both James Thompson and Charles Perrow for their examination and conceptualization of the concept of technology; most particularly to Perrow for his concept of technology as an independent variable.
2. Marc L. Miringoff, "Incomplete Technology and Organizational Dynamics of a State Mental Hospital," *Administration in Mental Health*, vol. 3, no. 2, Spring 1976, p. 133.

3. Charles Perrow, "A Framework for the Comparative Analysis of Organizations," *American Sociological Review*, vol. 26, no. 6, p. 854.

4. For a concise discussion of technology in an organizational context, see James B. Thompson, *Organizations in Action: Social Science Bases of Administrative Theory* (New York: McGraw-Hill Book Co., 1967), pp. 14–24.

5. Claire Selltiz, Lawrence Wrightsman, and Stuart Cook, *Research Methods in Social Relations* (New York: Holt, Rinehart and Winston, 1976).

6. Routinized technology is, of course, possible in human service organizations as well. See, for example, Jerald Hage and Michael Aiken, "Routine Technology, Social Structure and Organizational Goals," *American Sociological Review*, vol. 14, no. 3, pp. 366–376.

7. For an extensive bibliography including technology as it applies to human services, see Jack Rothman, *Planning and Organizing for Social Change: Action Principles From Social Science Research* (New York: Columbia University Press, 1974), pp. 189–192.

8. Much has been written on the effectiveness of such technology, particularly under the general heading of "social casework." See, for example, Joel Fisher, "Is Casework Effective: A Review," *Social Work*, vol. 18, no. 1, January 1973, pp. 5–20, for a review of this literature. Also see Katherine M. Wood, "Casework Effectiveness: A New Look at the Research Literature," *Social Work*, vol. 23, no. 6, November 1978, pp. 437–460.

9. Charles Perrow, "A Framework for the Comparative Analysis of Organizations," *Administrative Science Quarterly*, vol. 32, no. 2: 194–208; David J. Hickson, D. S. Pugh, and Diana C. Pheysey, "Operations Technology and Organization Structure: An Empirical Reappraisal," *Administrative Science Quarterly*, vol. 14, 1969, pp. 378–397. See also Hage and Aiken, op. cit.

10. See Irving Spergel, *Community Problem Solving*, Chicago: University of Chicago Press, 1969, ch. 6; and Murray Ross, *Community Organization: Theory and Principles*, 2d ed. (New York: Harper and Row, 1971).

11. Applying these questions to actual human service technologies, as in mental health, social services, or drug abuse service, will help to concretize the concepts.

12. See Carol Meyer, "Frameworks and Knowledge: The Content of Social Work Practice," *Social Work Practice*, 2d ed. (New York: The Free Press, 1976); and Ernest Greenwood, "Attributes of a Profession," *Social Work*, vol. 2, no. 3, July 1957, pp. 45–55.

13. Martin Bloom, "Analysis of the Research on Educating Social Work Students," *Journal of Education for Social Work*, vol. 12, no. 4, Fall 1976, pp. 3–10.
14. Werner W. Boehm, "Social Work Education: Issues and Problems in Light of Recent Developments," *Journal of Education for Social Work*, vol. 12, no. 1, Winter 1976, pp. 20–27.
15. Neil Gilbert and Harry Specht, "The Incomplete Profession," *Social Work*, vol. 19, no. 6, November 1974, pp. 665–674; Amitai Etzioni (ed.), *The Semi-Professions and their Organization*, New York: Free Press, 1969; William Bell, "Obstacles to Shifting from a Descriptive to an Analytical Approach in Teaching Social Services," *Journal of Social Work Education*, Spring 1969, pp. 5–13.
16. For the definitive presentation of Systems Analysis, see Talcott Parsons, *The Social System*, New York: The Free Press, 1952.

Chapter THREE

THE THROUGHPUT:
How the Organization Utilizes
Its Service Resources:
Decision Making

Many human service practitioners, particularly those who are relatively new in the field have adverse reactions to organizational and bureaucratic constraints that impede their ability to apply their technological skills. Yet it is rarely possible to apply the technology of a human service directly and completely to a social problem and client. The organization may come between the service provider and consumer, and place constraints and limitations on the use of service resources.[1] This is true, of course, in other kinds of organizations as well. Consider the most famous practitioner of the technology of crime-solving, Sherlock Holmes, who, in an unencumbered manner, was able to apply the technology of his trade (with a keen sense of both cause and effect and nonrandom occurrence) directly to the crime at hand. In contrast, his counterparts from Scotland Yard are continually portrayed as conducting routine, rather uncreative, standardized investigations (the terms themselves connoting bureaucratic rather than service needs). The Scotland Yard agents are functioning for the benefit of the organization and its needs as much as responding to the intricacies of the crime, with always far less dazzling results than Sherlock Holmes.

Whether an organization in its internal or throughput functioning helps or hinders the application of human service technology to the social problem and clientele with which the agency is involved is a vital factor in determining the quality of service. This issue may be posed as follows: Does the functioning of a given human service organization tend to co-opt or optimize its service resources; does it, in fact, make full use of the human service technology available to it? This is an important issue for the human service manager because whatever the level of resources available to the organization, they need to be optimized in order to bring about effective service.

How, then, does the manager examine the organization's throughput functioning to assess the degree to which these resources are being utilized? It is a difficult question. We must turn to an examination of the process of organizational functioning in order to develop an approach that can be utilized by the manager to help the organization evolve a better quality service product.

Three factors, present in all human service organizations, require attention: *decision making, organizational goals,* and the use of *authority.*[2] An ongoing examination of these three factors can help the human service manager determine how the organization's functioning affects the use of resources and, in turn, helps determine the ultimate service product. It is important to understand that our analysis of these throughput factors reflects their interdependence. Their relationship is circular, with changes in one affecting changes in the others.

A major activity, conducted at many levels throughout a formal organization, is the process of decision making, which is the subject of this chapter. Decisions are made in meetings, in groups, and individually, both formally and informally. The sum total of these decisions is extremely influential in determining the procurement, control, and utilization of resources and, therefore, the internal and external functioning of a human service organization. The important question, for our purposes is: *How does decision making affect the utilization of service resources in human service organizations?*[3]

Because organizational decision making is a human endeavor, those factors that underlie the making of decisions encompass a wide variety of considerations. Decisions are not always based on the most rational, objective, factual, or professionally oriented assessment of a given situation.[4] Individuals or groups may press for particular outcomes because they *believe*

Analyzing the Organization

(on value or ideological grounds) that it is the "right" approach. The motivation for a specific stance in decision making may also reflect the desire of some members to gain the advantage over other members of an organization, over contending groups, departments, or service components. Friendships or personality clashes, as well, may be of long-standing duration within an organization and may exert a major influence over important decisions.[5] Individuals often will couch their proposals or reactions in service-oriented terms, although their actual intent may lie elsewhere.[6]

If all organizational decisions directly affecting the service product were anchored in objective assessments of that organization's capacity from the perspective of *service alone*, then the quality of the service outcome would be furthered as a natural by-product. Since this is obviously not the case in the real world of most human service organizations, it is important to delineate and assess those factors that interrelate in decision making, and which ultimately determine the effect of decision making on service effectiveness. This chapter considers three such factors and their interrelationships: capability elements, value elements, and political elements.[7]

Capability Elements in Decision Making

The service capability of a human service organization is the sum total of the service resources that *that specific organization* possesses at a specific time. In short, it is the degree to which practitioners of a given human service organization can utilize and apply the available technology within a given organizational context. It is not what organizational members think *should* be achieved; it is what, in actuality, *can be* achieved. Capability elements vary between organizations that function in the same service area. The state of a human service technology and the degree to which practitioners working in a field possess that technology define the parameters of service capability that are possible in a given human service field. However, within these parameters the service capability of specific organizations will differ, because some organizations have greater opportunities to tap resources than do others. The capability of a single human service organization can itself vary, influenced by a variety of factors of internal functioning. The variance in capability is a crucial factor, which should be objectively assessed, on an ongoing basis within any organization; yet little scholarly work has been done in the field of social welfare to derive standards, mechanisms, and processes for facilitating this assessment.

In the context of decision making, it is the capability elements that are most crucial to the human service manager, for it is these elements that embody the service resources of the organization. As decisions are made, however, capability elements may give way to other elements such as value and political.

Value Elements in Decision Making

A sense of values is deeply woven into the human service tradition in the United States. Much social progress and reform has been initiated, at least in part, because of the belief that it was just and moral. The history of the social welfare institution in this country has often been shaped by leaders who enunciated or symbolized certain strongly held values. Values often provide the motivation for those who are involved in the delivery of human services. Each human service profession, psychiatry, psychology, social work, and nursing, for example, has a set of professional values and ethics to which its practitioners are expected to conform, a set of standards to strive for, and a set of ultimate goals to achieve.[8]

Many value systems stress a common set of human needs and a commitment to service in confronting and alleviating these needs. Operationalized, however, at the level of service delivery and in the context of an organization, the realization of these values is often difficult to achieve. Value elements are often confused with capability elements. What needs to be done, or should be done, is often confused with what actually *can* be accomplished. When decisions reflect values that do not accurately encompass realistic assessments of capability, this can ultimately have negative effects on the service product of an organization.

Values can be generated from both inside the organization

Analyzing the Organization

and from the organization's environment. Many environmental factors can influence and shape the values of those who work in a human service organization. The norms of the community in which the organization is located, the attitudes and beliefs of client groups and other environmental bodies can interact with the values held by organizational members to form the value elements of a given decision-making process. An organization is never closed to the value influences of its environment.

Value elements, even more than capability elements, are both difficult to discern and to assess. Because they are ethical statements and not empirically verifiable, value elements can be the basis of the most intensive kind of conflict. Yet values as well as capability elements play a large role in the decision making of human service organizations.

Political Elements in Decision Making

Political elements involve such considerations as power, position, gain, loss, advantage, control, and survival.[9] Unlike considering a given decision in the light of "What can we actually accomplish?" or "What is right?" and "What conforms to our convictions?" the political elements involve such considerations as "What will the organization gain by this move?" "What will it lose?" "Who will complain?" "Who will be happy?" "What leverage do we have?" or "Can we afford to hurt X at the expense of Y?" The organizational perspective is often overshadowed by the individual point of view: "What will I lose if I go along with this?" or "Will this help me get the position of assistant director?" Political elements frequently determine agency policy: "We have to do this because the politicians insist," or "This service is needed but agency Y is already in that business, and we can't afford to overlap."[10]

It is a rare organization in which such political elements do not exert a profound influence on the functioning of organizational decision making, whether they originate inside or outside the organization.[11] In fact, many experienced participants in human service organizations will observe that no matter how lofty the values that guide a person, or how precise that individual's expertise, the ability to carry out service goals is based more on one's political ability than on the strength of one's convictions or the depth of one's knowledge.

Capability, Value, and Political Elements: The Interplay

The interplay of capability, value and political elements underlies the dynamics of many kinds of decision-making processes. The capability considerations involved in the development of a military weapons system, for example, are routinized and exacting. The technology might include the procedures necessary for constructing a missile, determining its trajectory, calculating its impact, and so forth. All of this is contained within the purview of a knowledge base, presumably a part of the technology of defense. After the system is assembled and is in place, many decisions remain, such as, at whom should the missiles be pointed? This question is beyond the realm of defense technology; it is a question of values or politics. Do we aim the missiles at Cuba or at England? The Cuban system of government reflects values that are at odds with those of the United States, whereas England is more compatible, more within our own tradition. Political considerations are obviously important as well. The gains and losses vis-à-vis allies and enemies of developing a particular weapons system can be the determining factor in the decision-making process rather than either values or technology. In this military example, the interrelationships of capability, political, and value elements illustrate that, despite the presence of a highly developed technology, the process is characterized, or even ultimately determined, by other factors.

Another example regards the War on Poverty of the 1960s. One consideration in the establishment of this set of social programs was a particular set of values. The presence of poverty in the United States was deemed wrong, and the suffering that it brought was believed to need alleviation. Government therefore should intervene to help the poor. A sense of social justice was present among those who formulated these policies and many of their values found their way into the rhetoric of the period. Yet political considerations, as well, were extremely influential in the decisions that initiated the War on Poverty. One political consideration involved the building of future support for the Democratic party. Quite aside from the moral intent of these programs, leaders of the Democratic party felt that much could be gained from the enactment of the War on Poverty programs. There was interest in rebuilding and extending the New Deal coalition that had formed the basis of the Democratic party. The new poverty policies could reach a different population and help convert them into Democratic voters just as the New Deal had done previously. A clear, long-term, political gain was, therefore, perceived.[12]

Many writers have analyzed the War on Poverty from a capability viewpoint and found it lacking.[13] Apparently, the questions "Why should we solve poverty?" and "What do we gain through this program?" proved more compelling than "How do we solve poverty?" In the eyes of one key participant, the decision-making process leading to the formulation of the actual programs was marked by considerable confusion.

> *Interviewer:* What is your general assessment of the level of conceptualization, the level of analysis that went into the formulation of the Bill (The Economic Opportunity Act of 1964)?
> *Respondent:* Not much. What it was at that stage was a parlor game.[14]

Did the programs that came to constitute the War on Poverty, Head Start, Community Action, and Neighborhood Youth Corps actually reflect the highest current state of technology for solving poverty? Here again, political factors heavily influenced the capability elements. It is possible from a capability perspective that massive job creation or income redistribution, or tax reform would have been more appropriate to the goals that were established and would have proved far more effective in alleviating poverty. But such approaches were ignored for political reasons. As one member of the group which formulated the programs observed:

> Policy-making people never have time to look at the longer run issues; they can't afford to look at the longer run problems because the policy people are confronted with doing something about the present situation or there is going to be political repercussions. So you deal with the present and don't look to the future—anyway by the time you get to the future you've got a program that deals with the past.[15]

Consider a further example. A department of welfare of a large city conducts a study of its low-income population in relation to public assistance eligibility in order to determine to what extent the department is meeting the needs of the poor. The study is conducted under the auspices of staff whose values reflect the desire to help those in financial need to the optimal extent. The results of the study indicate that a full 17 percent of the city's population is eligible for welfare but is not receiving it. If those eligible for, but not receiving, assistance were to become recipients, the welfare rolls would increase by a full 21 per cent. From a political perspective, even the proposal of such an addition would cost both the agency and the individuals involved to a great extent, yet the capability for solving the problem was certainly available and the values did dictate the alleviation of the suffering of people in need who are eligible. Under a different political climate, one far more favorable to welfare, the situation might become quite different. The value and the capability elements would then probably play a far greater role in the decision-making process. Obviously, in this case, the interplay of the three elements would cause a complicated and difficult set of decisions requiring a keen balance.

One important key to understanding the functioning of a human service organization, then, is to recognize the action and interaction of capability, value and political elements in the decision-making process, both with regard to individual decisions and with patterns of decisions that evolve over time. These decision-making activities occur not only in formal meetings but on a daily basis, both formally and informally, individually and in groups. The sum total of these decisions represents much about what the organization is and what it is doing with regard to the degree of application of its technology.[16]

Of the three, it is capability that maintains the focus of concern, because, as noted, capability most directly reflects the technology and the organization's ability to provide service—and the provision of service is the organization's reason for being, its justification as part of the social welfare institution. The key point lies in the juxtaposition of capability elements to value and political elements. Ideally, values should guide capability; they should determine the ends and philosophies toward which capability is directed. Values dictate that the mentally retarded should receive service in a humane and effective manner. Capability can bring this about. Politics should represent a means through which capability can be realized. A capability-directed decision must often contain political aspects in order for it to be realized. The program for the retarded may require a political "touch" in order to be implemented and sustained. A functional juxtaposition among the three elements, however, cannot exist all the time; when it does, it can be referred to as a *congruent* mix of elements. Congruency often does not exist in decision making, and value or political elements become the objective and/or motivation of decision making. When this occurs, the pursuit of these elements can come to dominate decision making and displace capability elements. From our perspective, this *noncongruence* is a dysfunctional mix of decision-making elements, dysfunctional for the application of technology. As with the factors discussed in Chapter Two, congruency and noncongruency represent polar outcomes in decision making. Most decisions or patterns of decision making fall somewhere between the two. This can be shown as follows:

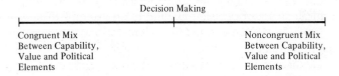

Decision Making

| Congruent Mix Between Capability, Value and Political Elements | Noncongruent Mix Between Capability, Value and Political Elements |

The key to how decision making affects the organization's utilization of its service resources thus lies in the degree of congruency that characterizes both individual decisions and overall patterns of decision making. If there is a high degree of noncongruency, then decisions are dominated by political and value elements and the overall utilization of service resources becomes less significant. Service resources are not necessary in carrying out political or value-oriented objectives. It is only where *capability is the fundamental concern* that *service resources and considerations of technology become the essential ingredient.*

At this point a simple relationship between the input and the throughput can be demonstrated. If the availability of service resources (the state and possession of technology) tends toward the maximum, then there is more capability present in any given organizational decision-making process. With the increased strength of capability, congruent decisions become more possible. Obviously, with little or no availability of service resources, capability lessens: politics and values become far more significant in decision making, and noncongruence is the likely result. These relationships will be discussed in more detail in Chapter Six.

The ability to be sensitive to congruence and to be able to recognize it in the context of organizational activities is not easily attained. However, decision making occurs continually and its effects on the organization's use of resources and ultimate product is highly significant. Understanding the dynamics of decision making and its effects is therefore a necessity for the human service manager. It provides the manager with a framework by which he or she can continually assess the process of decision making. Rather than merely concentrating, in a meeting, for example, on the details of the immediate task at hand, or the personal characteristics of those present, the manager can understand the effects of the decision itself on service resource utilization and the quality of service outcome. This analysis of the dynamics allows judgments to be made which carefully consider all elements of decision making in an attempt to maximize congruence. In some cases, political elements may be represented by one individual or a group in the organization. Others may be more inclined toward capability and often represent that perspective. Negotiation may be necessary in order to come to a decision. Such decisions may either enhance or impede congruence, depending upon the manager's skill. The manager may also want to select the composition of staff meetings, task groups, and other decision-making bodies on the basis of his or her perception of who represents which elements, how strongly, and how a given combination of organizational members can be brought together to maximize congruence.

CASE ILLUSTRATION—DECISION MAKING

The Situation

The recent trend in the country in community mental health is what has been called "*deinstitutionalization.*" Essentially this concept is based on the premise that more effective mental health care can be provided in a community environment, rather than in a state mental institution. Efforts have thus been made to move patients out of the state hospital and into smaller facilities located in communities and neighborhoods in order to provide an atmosphere for the patients that more nearly approximates normal everyday life. In this way, the patient is less alienated and will, it is hoped, have much to gain from integration with community life. The success and benefit of this policy of deinstitutionalization are yet to be fully evaluated, but it has created in many communities the kind of human service decision-making problems that are evident in this example.

The setting for this case example is a county in a large northeastern state, in which the movement for community mental health is comparatively highly developed. As in other parts of the country, the primary responsibility for community mental health services in this state lies with local-level government—in this case, the county. Hence, the opening of community mental health centers, the planning and coordination of mental health services and agencies throughout the county, and the final responsibility for mental health care lies with the county department of mental health and with its director. The county department is directly responsible to the county executive and to the county legislature. The one important exception to this is the operation of the state hospital, which is located in the county and comes under the jurisdiction of the *state* department of mental health. Deinstitutionalization of patients, then, requires optimal cooperation between the state and the county departments of mental health, in order that the transition of patients from the hospital to the community can be made under the best possible circumstances. In effect, the patients are shifted not only from one facility to another but from the jurisdiction of one governmental level to another. In this case, both the county department and the state were in agreement as to the soundness of the concept of deinstitutionalization in its benefit to the patients, but implementing the concept has presented problems nevertheless.

At a given time, the state began to release patients into different communities throughout the county. They were placed in a variety of residences ranging from small family care homes to large proprietary adult homes, to boardinghouses of varying types. As is often the case, with changes in social policy, the initiation of this program received little general community attention. As the numbers of patients and the number of neighborhoods in which they were placed increased, the situation became problematic. There developed a growing resentment toward the community placements on the part of those living nearby. There was a fear of the patients and of possible incidents and economic concerns about property values. These negative reactions intensified, bringing a series of local (township and small metropolitan levels of government) ordinances against further patient placement. The issue became a major one for the county.

The chief recipient of the pressure and controversy was the county director of mental health who had always been a strong advocate of community mental health and deinstitutionalization. With the pressure of the community and of the county legislature building, and with the very continuity of the program threatened, some kind of action was required—a major decision of policy was needed.

For the purposes of presenting the case example, let us imagine that the director calls a meeting of key members of the department for the purposes of resolving this problem. Those present include the director, a psychiatrist, who has the final responsibilty for the decision; the assistant director (Phil), who has a Master of Public Administration degree and serves as the top staff to the director; the chief of social services, a social worker (Harriet) with a Master of Social Work degree and long experience who heads the largest clinical program in the department; and a board member (Susan), a member of the community who is actively involved in the promotion of mental health. These four people convene to arrive at a decision about deinstitutionalization.

DIRECTOR: I'm calling this meeting today because we are faced with a very serious problem with deinstitutionalization. As you know there has been a great deal of pressure on the department from the community, the legislature, and the state department of mental health about deinstitutionalization. The community and legislature want to stop it, the state wants to intensify it. We're in the middle. I feel at this point that what we've tried to achieve with deinstitutionalization is going to be threatened if we don't do something. We need some change in the policy, and we need a basic decision about what that change needs to be.

BOARD MEMBER: I think that what you're saying is that you're retreating from the concept of community mental health, and the idea of getting patients out of the hospital. And if that's what you're saying I have concerns about it. The board has believed in what you're doing and in the principles of community mental health. I understand political pressures, but if something is right, I don't feel we should compromise basic principles.

ASSISTANT DIRECTOR: Look, unfortunately, we live in a world of reality and of political necessity. And I'm sorry to be blunt, but if the policy costs the department too much, we're just going to have to modify what we're doing.

CHIEF OF SOCIAL SERVICES: I want to say a couple of things. First, Susan is right, and principles need to be pursued for their intrinsic value if we believe in them. Phil has a good point about political realities, too. But the important perspective is the patient. We know, professionally, that getting the patient out of the hospital into the community serves therapeutic ends. I have observed the difference in affect, spontaneity, social functioning, and so forth. It's far better with the patients in the community.

DIRECTOR: I want you to know that I've not made up my mind. This is an open meeting and we are going to arrive at a decision together. I need to say this, though. Phil is right, we have to modify, at least to some extent, what we're doing. We'll consider all factors, but we have to do something.

ASSISTANT DIRECTOR: Harriet, since you are in social services, let me ask you a question. Be honest. Has the community pressure and hostility toward the patients had adverse effects from a therapeutic perspective?

CHIEF OF SOCIAL SERVICES: I am in favor of continuing and even increasing the program, and I hope what I say doesn't influence us in the wrong direction, but, yes, there have been adverse effects. The tensions generated by community opposition have decreased the value of the therapeutic milieu.

There was an incident last week in which one of the patients was on the street acting quite well. Anyway, he met a child, a few words were exchanged, and the child ran home upset. The reaction of the family was to come to the community residence and bitterly complain. I don't blame them, but the effect on the patient was very bad—and tensions have increased because of that incident alone.

ASSISTANT DIRECTOR: So, from the perspective of service, the political pressures are causing a problem?

CHIEF OF SOCIAL SERVICES: Yes, I think it's true.

ASSISTANT DIRECTOR: Well, that's my point. Those are the political realities.

BOARD MEMBER: It's not a perfect program. But it's right and it works. And as Harriet said, the patients are far better in the community—that's the main point.

DIRECTOR: It's not easy for me to urge any change in policy—I've always believed very much in the concept, and I believe that it works—but we're going to lose the whole thing, if we don't act. Incidents like the one Harriet described will continue and will get worse. Now, I want to take all factors into consideration: what is therapeutic for the patients; what we believe in; and the political realities as well. Does anyone have a concrete suggestion?

ASSISTANT DIRECTOR: I think you have to make a statement in which you back off the position of unqualified, complete support of deinstitutionalization. I think that the public perspective at this point is that we're just going whole hog on this; that we really don't have a plan in mind and we're going to push it as far as it'll go. You've got to make a public statement that gives the impression that we're really more interested in consolidating what we already have, and go about it in a more pragmatic way.

CHIEF OF SOCIAL SERVICES: What do you mean by "gives the impression that we're really more interested in consolidating what we already have"? From a service point of view, consolidating what we have for a while might be a very beneficial approach. Upgrading the patients already in the community from medium to high-quality residences might be best, service-wise, from an interim point of view. But this "give the impression" approach sounds like we're interested

Analyzing the Organization

only in public relations and we're really not going to consolidate and upgrade.

BOARD MEMBER: Phil, what are you saying? That you want to improve the quality of what we have and then continue with placing more patients, or are you interested in public relations points?

ASSISTANT DIRECTOR: Well, I really hadn't thought it through. From a political point of view, we have to make that statement. And I do see your point that we actually could take the resources and improve the quality of current service. Then maybe over time, we could increase the number of patients.

DIRECTOR: In other words, we could buy time, and still increase the quality of care. All right. But, Phil, let me ask you this. There are costs that need to be considered. First, the state will get angry with us, because they want to get as many patients out as is possible.

ASSISTANT DIRECTOR: Look, that's the point. You've put distance between the county department and the state. *You've* become more pragmatic; *they're* overpushing it. That'll help us do what we need to do. It'll focus the political pressure on the state. At least we'll draw the distinction in the public's mind. And also with the county legislature.

DIRECTOR: O.K. What about inside the department? I think a lot of the clinical staff will not be happy with that kind of public statement. They're going to think that we have abandoned the principle. So, we need to be clear that we're not just giving the impression of an upgrading of the quality of care; but we will have a plan to improve the service that accompanies any other statement I make.

CHIEF OF SOCIAL SERVICES: You're right. People will be upset and as I said, I'm one of them. So a plan that shows, from a professional viewpoint, how service can be improved, needs to be developed. There's no question that service will gain, but the statement does contain risks.

DIRECTORS: O.K. Let me summarize what we've got so far. Phil is suggesting that I go on record with a statement saying that there is going to be a change in our policy of deinstitutionalization. Although we still believe in the idea and feel that it is helpful to patients, we need to reexamine carefully the way we're doing it—from the point of view of slowing down the number of patients placed in communities and upgrading the existing community residences. This will serve the overall policy far better than continuing the course we have taken. Also, that we in this room and in the department understand that we are not abandoning the policy, but will use resources to improve and consolidate for a while and then proceed back on the matter of increasing patient placements. Is that a fair summary?

ASSISTANT DIRECTOR: I'm satisfied.

BOARD MEMBER: I'm a little uncomfortable but at least I have the reassurance that we're not abandoning the basic policy —I'll be watching!

CHIEF OF SOCIAL SERVICES: I think all in all, it's a good overall plan. And maybe we'll end up saving the program. I am afraid we might lose everything if we don't do something. We do have to carefully plan and monitor the consolidation part of the plan to ensure the upgrading.

DIRECTOR: O.K. Thank you all for your time.

Analysis

In the dialogue, the positions have been somewhat polarized in order to illustrate the concepts. Clearly, the assistant director represented the political elements in the decision-making process, the chief of social services represented the capability elements, and the board member symbolized the value elements. The director seemed to integrate the three elements.[17] In an actual meeting situation, the elements would probably not be as clear-cut in presentation and more overlap would occur among the participants. In the dialogue, in its initial phase, the three elements are represented mutually exclusively, and accommodation evolves over time. Again, in an actual meeting, this process would consume far more time and would no doubt be characterized by more tension and conflict. In the dialogue, the assistant director eventually perceives and accepts the capability elements as an important part of the decision. At the same time, the chief of social services appears ready to accept the political perspective, as does the board member, although she appears more hesitant.

How congruent was the decision that was ultimately arrived at? It is difficult to be sure. If it is indeed true that the very existence of the program was at stake (a political judgment), then the decision seemed to maximize both the value elements (in pursuing a program in which everyone believed) and the capability elements in upgrading quality and in proceeding more cautiously into expansion. In this sense, the decision did display a high degree of congruence. If the danger to the program was less than the participants thought, it might have been possible to continue a full public endorsement of the program, expand the program, and upgrade it as well. Much rests on the accuracy of the assessment of the pressure. If the external political situation was aggravated, then the decision was highly noncongruent and destructive to the service product of the organization. If upgrading was indeed achieved, and the program ultimately continued and expanded, the accommodation of elements was sound and the decision was highly congruent. In either case, the framework provides a way of monitoring and understanding such decisions from the perspective of the utilization of service resources.

SUMMARY

This chapter addressed the use of decision making in human service organizations. The key question of the chapter was; How does decision making affect the utilization of service resources in human service organizations? In order to examine this question, decision making was viewed in terms of three major elements: value, capability, and political. The interrelationship of these three elements, both with regard to individual decisions and patterns of decision making over time, can have an enormous impact on the functioning of an organization. When the three elements are in congruence, that is, when their interaction serves capability outcomes, decisions maximize the service resources of the organization. When the elements are noncongruent, decisions achieve the least in utilizing the service resources.

Most decision making reveals different *degrees* of congruency. Hence a continuum best illustrates the use of the concept. A case illustration was also provided to help amplify the dynamics of decision making in human service organizations.

NOTES

1. For an excellent description of the conflict between the organization and professional norms, see Harry Wasserman, "The Professional Social Worker in a Bureaucracy," *Social Work*, vol. 16, no. 1, January 1971, pp. 89–95. Wasserman comments: "The social worker in such a bureaucracy is caught up in this brutal intersection of contradictory values. If he actually tries to help his clients and 'bucks' the organization, he often suffers from emotional and physical fatigue and becomes cynical and defeatist about the nature of social work. If he adapts to the bureaucracy, he at best experiences massive frustration. At worst, he becomes a 'mindless functionary.' " See also Weston E. Whatcott, "Bureaucratic Focus in Service Delivery," *Social Work*, vol. 19, no. 4, July 1974, pp. 432–447. Whatcott observes, "Social work has long been concerned with the time and energy a worker has left for actual service after he has made out extensive records, budgets, reports and so on. From the author's experience with various juvenile courts, he believes it can be estimated that workers spend less than thirty percent of their time in actual face to face contacts for rehabilitation. Most of their time is spent filling out reports, attending meetings and so on."

2. There may be other generic throughput variables as well but these and their interaction serve to categorize much of the organizational activity of a human service organization.

3. Herbert Simon in *Administrative Behavior*, 2d ed. (New York: Free Press, 1965), views organizations primarily as decision-making entities. See also Charles E. Lindblom, "The Science of Muddling Through," *Public Administration Review*, Spring 1959, pp. 214–229, for the classic presentation of decision making as an incremental process, and Amitai Etzioni, "Mixed Scanning: A 'Third' Approach to Decision-Making," *Public Administration Review*, vol. 27, no. 2, 1967, pp. 385–392.

4. For an analysis of the relationship of politics and technical considerations in budgetary decision making, see Aaron Wildavsky, *The Politics of the Budgetary Process*, 2d ed. (Boston: Little, Brown and Co., 1974).

5. Chris Argyris, "Interpersonal Barriers to Decision-Making," *Harvard Business Review*, vol. 44, March-April 1966, pp. 84–97.
6. J. Pfeffer, and G. R. Salavch, "Organizational Decision-Making as a Political Process: The Case of a University Budget," *Administrative Science Quarterly*, vol. 19, no. 2, pp. 135–151, 1974.
7. I am very much indebted to the work of Herbert Simon. His de- delineation of decision making into propositions of fact and of value (op. cit., pp. 1–18, 45–60) provided the basis for this conceptualization of decison making in human service organizations.
8. In the medical profession this is represented by the Hippocratic Oath. Psychologists have a code of ethics established by the American Psychological Association; nursing and social work have similar official statements.
9. Bert Gummer, "A Power Politics Approach to Social Welfare Organizations," *Social Service Review*, vol. 52, no. 3, September 1978, pp. 349–361.
10. For two books which perceive organizations as if they were jungles where nearly all activity is survival and victory, see Robert J. Ringer, *Winning Through Intimidation*, 2d Ed. (Los Angeles: Los Angeles Book Publishing Co., 1974) and Mark Monsky, *Looking Out For No. 1* (New York: Simon and Schuster, 1975).
11. Howard Polsky, "From Cliques to Factions: Subgroups in Organizations," *Social Work*, vol. 23, no. 2, March 1978, p. 93.
12. Marc Miringoff, "O.E.O.: The Formulation of Poverty Policy: A Study of the Relationship between Social Analysis and Social Planning," (Ph.D. dissertation, University of Chicago, School of Social Service Administration, September 1972).
13. Daniel P. Moynihan, *Maximum Feasible Misunderstanding* (New York: Free Press, 1969). See also Richard Cloward and Frances Fox Piven, Regulating *The Poor* (New York: Vintage Press, 1972).
14. Miringoff, op. cit., p. 56.
15. Ibid., p. 72.
16. For illustration, see S. M. Drezner, "The Emerging Art of Decision-Making," *Social Casework*, vol. 54, no. 1, June 1973, pp. 3–12 and A. Spindler, "On Decision-Making and the Social and Rehabilitation Programs," *Public Welfare*, vol. 29, no. 2, Fall 1971, pp. 307–315.
17. It is possible, from a theoretical perspective that a balanced representation of the three elements is a necessity for a workable, congruent decision. This requires empirical verification.

Chapter FOUR

THE THROUGHPUT:
How the Organization Utilizes
Its Service Resources: Goals

The next factor to be considered is the purposes and ends toward which an organization functions: the organizational goals. The specific question of this chapter is: *How do organizational goals affect the utilization of service resources in human service organizations?*

OFFICIAL AND OPERATIVE GOALS

Much has been written in the literature of organizational theory and analysis about the concept of organizational goals. One useful conceptualization breaks the concept of goals into two types: official and operative.[1]

The official goals of an organization are its stated goals, which are the designated, chartered, and manifest intents of an organization. These goals represent what the organization is designed to accomplish, its reason for being, and its objectives for society and for the population or clientele it serves. Most organizations possess such statements of purpose that specify their official goals. The official goals of a state mental institution, for example, might state:

> The purpose of the state mental hospital is to care for the mentally ill. It provides the patient with services which are needed to help restore him to normal functioning, so that he may assume his place as a productive and healthy member of society.

A similar statement describing the official goals of a public welfare system might read:

> The purpose of public welfare is to provide both financial and other social services for those citizens who are in need. These services are designed to alleviate the conditions of poverty suffered by this segment of our population, and help to enhance their functioning as productive members of society. Through these services, those in need of assistance will, in time, be able to sustain and support themselves.

The official goals of a human service organization generally reflect the public perception of that organization's place and purpose in the social welfare institution as a whole. The official goals express society's sanction of the ultimate purposes of that organization. In this way, official goals are statements that link each human service organization to the social welfare institution. Official goals, then, represent a profound influence in which forces outside the organization significantly affect internal organizational processes. The human service organization's reason for being is created initially by its environment.

The second type of organizational goals are operative goals, which indicate what the organization actually is doing or attempting to do on a day-to-day basis. These goals are generally not formally stated. As Perrow notes: "Operative goals designate the ends sought through the actual operating policies of the organization. They tell us what the organization is actually trying to do."[2]

As in the case of the juxtaposition of the three elements of decision making, the relationship of official and operative goals in a human service organization is of critical importance. Official goals, due to the level of generality at which they are typically stated, require intermediate steps in order to be achieved. Operative goals can serve as a series of means, or interim goals, in the achievement of an organization's overall aims. When operative goals are so ordered as to lead the organization's daily activities toward the attainment of official goals, a highly functional organizational situation exists. A situation of this type would serve to enhance the utilization of the organization's service resources and, therefore, the quality of its service outcome. Obviously, this cannot be the case at all times, and may, in fact, be true only rarely. When operative goals do not serve as means to official goal achievement the process is called *goal displacement*.

Goal Displacement

When operative goals that were designed as a means to achieving official goals become ends in themselves, the process is known as *goal displacement*.[3] This phenomenon was well observed by Robert Merton:

> This very emphasis leads to a transference of the statements from the aims of the organization onto the particular details of behavior required by the rules. Adherence to the rules originally conceived as the means becomes transformed to an end in itself; there occurs the familiar process of displacement of goals, whereby an instrumental value becomes a terminal end.[4]

Few organizations will indicate publicly that "the purpose of this organization is to survive, obtain as much grant money and other funds as possible, keep its employees in line, establish and maintain the proper political contacts, and dominate the community in our service area." These goals may, however, constitute the ends the organization is actually pursuing, ends that, in themselves, do not constitute official goal achievement.

Let us consider an example. A research institute is planned as part of a state government. The official goals of the institute, as reflected in its initiating charter, are to provide research and data on social problems and human service programs so that the state government can plan human services on a more rational and effective basis. Over time, however, different signals begin to emanate from the office of the governor. Instead of neutral analysis, the governor wants something else: not data to shed light on policy making in human services, but information that can justify selected policies that make him look good in a political sense. Eventually, the day-by-day activities of the institute leave the realm of objective social problem and policy assessment and begin to assume the function of providing the "right" information. The official goal remains the stated purpose of the organization, but the operative goal has changed.[5]

Other organizations can offer similar examples. In many prisons, the official goal of services is rehabilitation, to move the inmates from deviant to constructive behavior that can be sanctioned by the society. On a day-to-day basis, however, in many cases the operative goals of the correctional facility are either punitive or custodial, with little emphasis on rehabilitation activity. In some cases the outcome is actually in opposition to the official goals, the perpetuation and augmentation of criminal behavior.[6]

The dynamics of a state mental hospital are also illustrative. The official goals are treatment or therapy. They are designed to restore the mental health of individuals to a level of functioning accepted as "normal" by society and then to return these individuals to the community. This, in theory, is to be achieved through a series of service programs. However, what do the day-by-day activities of the state mental hospital actually achieve? Erving Goffman provides a description of what he has termed the *total institution* drawn from a study of a state mental institution:

> First, all aspects of life are conducted in the same place and under the same single authority. Second, each phase of the member's activity is carried on in the immediate company of a large batch of others, all of whom are treated alike and required to do the same thing together. Third, all phases of the day's activities are tightly scheduled with one activity leading at a prearranged time into the next, the whole sequence of activities being imposed from above by a system of explicit formal rulings and a body of officials. Finally, the various enforced activities are brought together into a single rational plan, purportedly designed to fulfill the official aims of the institution.[7]

As Goffman and others[8] have observed, however, these and other activities in a state mental hospital are often designed to achieve custodial rather than therapeutic goals. Hence to a large degree, the operative goals of custody supplant the official treatment goals.[9] Clearly, organizational dynamics are present that create operative goals differing substantially from official goals. In further analyzing the organizational functions of the state hospital, several of these differences become apparent. In many state hospitals the physician in charge of each patient must provide the hospital with a periodic written report of a patient's condition. This is sometimes called a "progress note" and, in principle, is designed to indicate the condition of a patient, how he or she is responding to treatment, and any alteration in condition over time. It should constitute, then, an indication as to how well an organization is meeting its official goals. In one hospital observed by the author, the "progress note" had assumed a very different function; it had become "bureaucratized." Because the physician was required to complete notes on his large case load in order to satisfy organizational needs, the procedure often consisted of gathering information on the patient, often from other staff members, and sometimes from an interview with the patient lasting only several minutes. The ultimate result was that the new note was barely distinguishable in substance from the preceding one. Clearly, the preparation of progress notes, in this example, is primarily designed to achieve goals that are quite different from the official goals of the hospitals. The procedure was aimed at bureaucratic goals, and the result in terms of substance *did not reflect the technology of mental health but rather the needs of the mental health organization.* The original aims were subverted by the functioning of the organization.[10]

The concept of goal displacement is a continuous rather than a discrete concept. In the sum total of the organization's function and activities, official goals can rarely be followed every day by every staff member nor can operative goals ever completely replace official goals to the extent that no vestige of the official goals remain.[11] The process is one of degree, and it can be very slow and subtle. Operative goals sometimes come to dominate without organizational members being fully conscious of the process. Over time, staff members may adopt certain procedures that are counterproductive to effective service. Immersion in these activities can subvert or even replace the service activities that are the true means to the official goals. In public assistance, for example, many income maintenance workers are more concerned, on a daily basis, with fitting clients into the categories and descriptions of the regulations than in meeting the financial needs of the clients. This is not necessarily the fault of the individual worker, but rather, it is the "force," or the "drift" of the organization which creates the necessity for that kind of functioning. It is a rare individual, indeed, who does not succumb eventually to that operative goal.

We have all heard, too, of situations in which a patient enters the emergency room of a hospital in obvious pain. An interview takes place with the person responsible for admissions. Forms need to be filled out, the details of the patient's life need to be provided, and insurance coverage needs to be checked. Certainly, the patient is experiencing pain, perhaps even additional harm due to the delay. Yet the goal of this activity is not medical but organizational. It is clearly a case of goal displacement, especially if the patient fails to survive the ordeal, in which case goal displacement is complete!

The balance between organizational goals is thus a continuous concept that can be viewed in the following terms:

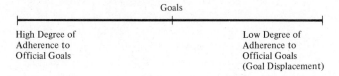

Goals

| High Degree of Adherence to Official Goals | Low Degree of Adherence to Official Goals (Goal Displacement) |

The presence and variation of goals as depicted by this figure indicate much about how the very goals of the organization affect its utilization of service resources. Clearly, as was the case with noncongruent decision making, *if there is a low degree of adherence to official goals, then service resources and their utilization become less significant.* Organizational activities that reflect goal displacement do not require service resources for their completion. It is only when the official goals of the organization are being pursued that there is a need to utilize service resources and consider the application of human service technology.

An obvious relationship can be drawn here between the input and the subject of goals. The higher the availability of service resources, the more likely that official goal adherence will be pursued. By the same token, with few service resources, goal displacement will tend to characterize organizational activities. A series of propositions in Chapter Six will specify the relationships between elements of the framework. Suffice it to say that the framework needs to be viewed from the perspective of the way in which its elements interrelate to form dynamics.

The more goal displacement exists in human service organizations, the weaker the social welfare institution becomes, and the more vulnerable to criticism. The issue of goal adherence is therefore vital to management. As in decision making, the dynamics of goal adherence and goal displacement need to be clearly understood. Management must view organizational activities not merely in terms of the personnel involved, the magnitude of expenditure, or the degree of efficiency, but whether the activity contributes in some way to official goal achievement.

CASE ILLUSTRATION: GOALS

The Situation

For this example we return to the situation utilized to illustrate the concept of decision making in Chapter Three. The time is two months after the director of the county department of mental health has made public the decision to "back off" the full endorsement of the policy of deinstitutionalization of mental patients. Since the meeting described in Chapter Three, there has been an increase in public and political opposition to the deinstitutionalization. In essence, the director's statement has failed to defuse the opposition; in fact, it appeared to promote the contrary effect, because those in opposition to deinstitutionalization felt they had gained an initial victory and attacked the program with new intensity. A county-wide organization against deinstitutional and community residences has been formed, and the chairman of the county legislature, an important figure, particularly with regard to appropriations for the county department of mental health, has joined with the group. A meeting is called by this legislator in his office. Present are the head of the citizens group (Fred) and three members of the county department who were present at the last meeting; the director, the assistant director, and the chief of social services.

LEGISLATOR: You all know why we're here. We have to discuss the department's policy. Fred, here, is the chairman of the citizens' organization, a county-wide group, which is opposed to the deinstitutionalization policy. And we are here because Fred's group has had a lot of contact with the legislature, and there's a lot of support; and citizen input into departments like yours is part of our job at the legislature. And I'm talking about real input. So, Fred, do you want to say what's on your mind?

CHAIRPERSON OF CITIZENS' GROUP: Thank you, Bill. I want to say, first of all, that we have sympathy for the mentally ill. There's nothing against them personally. I think you people from the department should understand that we sympathize with the problem. But, you have to see our situation, too. I live in a neighborhood where there are two community residences. One is two doors away from my home. Do you think I can sell my house now, we want to move, we want a better house. I can't sell. As soon as any potential buyer sees those patients, forget it! I worked hard for that house, nobody gave it to me. Now it's not worth much. O.K. That's the first problem. And it's not even the worst problem. The other thing is this: those people can be dangerous. I know they're being treated, and I'm not saying that something happens every day. But a lot does happen. They scare the kids. I found one of them on the back porch, and last week one broke into the house. Now, that's a big problem and the neighborhood is mad. And neighborhoods all over the county are mad. People don't want them in the neighborhoods, and they don't want new ones. There's a lot of tension caused by this. We want them out, and we don't want any more of it. If you can't protect your home and family, what can you protect?

DIRECTOR: We realize the problem. And that's why I made the statement and took the position I did. Because we want you to know that we're not going about this whole hog. We're being very careful. Selecting communities very carefully and, in fact, we've slowed down the process considerably.

CHIEF OF SOCIAL SERVICES: Let me say this. There is another side to the problem, and it needs to be mentioned. These patients have had a very difficult time in their lives. Most of them have suffered through horrible depressions and other mental illness. Now, they're at the point of getting out in the community. It's an important time for them. Now, nothing of a really terrible nature has happened as yet. I think Fred's case is overstated. Being in the community and interacting with people in the neighborhood is of enormous benefit to those patients. I think you need to consider this before making the kinds of judgments you've clearly made.

CHAIRPERSON OF CITIZENS' GROUP: The only thing that bothers me is that "nothing horrible has happened *yet.*" What are we supposed to do, wait until that happens before something is done?

ASSISTANT DIRECTOR: O.K., Fred, the point is well taken. Let's not get pushed too far here. What, exactly, is the actual level of opposition against this? How many meetings have you actually had?

CHAIRPERSON OF CITIZENS' GROUP: To tell you the truth, we've met every week, for the last two months. I have a copy of documentation of incidents which have occurred with patients around the whole county, and I mean recently. I tell you, there's one or two major problems in every community residence in the county. In our organization, there is at least one member from every township in the county, and a lot of legislators from different parts of the county.

CHIEF OF SOCIAL SERVICES: You realize that if we were able to upgrade the current community facilities, make them more pleasant and more efficient, even change them, then I think that the situation could be improved. There would be less tension, because the facilities would look better to the neighborhood and the property value would suffer far less. I think you ought to take this into consideration.

LEGISLATOR: No, I don't think so. I think that the basic problem here is the people themselves. You can have good facilities or bad facilities, the important point is that the patients are still in the neighborhoods. I don't think upgrading, making it fancier, putting a bucket of paint on it, or even moving them from one house to another is going to make any difference at all. I think you folks from the department have got to hear what these people from the committee are saying.

DIRECTOR: We do hear what you're saying; we're very concerned about it. You need to understand the department's position. Our job is the health and care of the mentally ill. And, on the other hand, our job as public officials is to be responsive to the public. You do pay our salaries, so it's a problem. We've got to try and see if we can balance it.

ASSISTANT DIRECTOR: I'll say this. I think that the whole idea of deinstitutionalization—where patients can be integrated into a community and neighborhood—is an excellent one. But I have to wonder at this point, and I hate to say this, whether the communities are in that kind of shape in terms of hostility and tension, whether we're going to have a real commitment and whether this is going to do any good anyway.

LEGISLATOR: I think he's got a point there, I really do. But I think we're just spinning wheels here. I think there's some disagreement and some agreement, but I don't see the point of continuing. What I'm going to do is to get in touch with the county executive and set up a meeting with just the director—maybe you can come along as well, Phil—the county executive and myself, and see where we should go from here. There's no question that something needs to be done. Now, Fred has a list of recommendations that I think we need to consider very carefully. You want to read them, Fred?

CHAIRPERSON OF CITIZENS' GROUP: Well, first, we're going to recommend to the legislature that the department be directed not to use any funds to upgrade any facilities, because that'll just lead to more of the same. Second, we're going to ask for a resolution of the county legislature that no new community facilities be established in any part of the county. Third, that we give consideration to removing a good many of the houses that now exist. Many of the patients are old, maybe we could have a policy where they could phase out because of attrition.

DIRECTOR: I think we can pursue this further. What do you think the county executive will say?

LEGISLATOR: Well, he's an old friend of mine, as you know. We're from the same party. I think he's going to go for this. I think these proposals are sound. Of course, we have to work out the details, so I'll set that meeting up.

DIRECTOR: Before you all leave, I just want to say this. That I am willing, and so is my staff, to go to the different townships; meet with anybody, anywhere, including members of the citizens' organization from different areas so we can talk about this. Besides this county executive meeting, I would like to meet all the members of the citizens' organization, and I will commit staff time for that purpose as well.

LEGISLATOR: Well, I think you can do that, though I'm not sure what it will accomplish; but do it. It's always a good idea for staff of a particular department to get out there. Anyway, I want to thank everybody for this meeting; and I'll be back to you. (The legislator and the citizens' chairman leave.)

CHIEF OF SOCIAL SERVICES: I was very upset with this. I had great reservations about the decision we made two months ago, and the whole thing is getting worse. Now, we're going to end up spending a good deal of our time, putting out political fires, instead of treating patients. And we're going to end up without community care.

DIRECTOR: I hope you're wrong!

Analysis

In the case example presented in Chapter Three, the congruence of the decision depended on the eventual outcome. If the department was indeed able to improve current services and "buy time" to continue the basic policy of deinstitutionalization, a strong case for congruent decision making could be made, as could the case for official goal adherence. As it turned out, this outcome was not achieved, and clearly the basic policy itself is in jeopardy.

If we consider the actual activities of the department with regard to deinstitutionalization, it is obvious that the continuum is moving toward goal displacement.

The decision to retreat from the full endorsement of deinstitutionalization clearly had the opposite effect to that intended. Originally designed to "buy time" for official goal achievement, the decision gave encouragement to opponents of the policy, who further organized and intensified the pressure against the policy. The result was to initiate a process by which the department and its staff would be drawn into committing time and resources not *in service of clients* but in political *activities designed to reduce* opposition. It is clear from the outcome of the meeting just described that activities relating to deinstitutionalization on the part of both management and direct service workers in the department will be utilized in meetings with county officials, citizen groups, and the general public, all of which will probably lead, as the social worker noted at the end of the dialogue, to a very significant decrease in this aspect of community mental health. In the last analysis, then, much energy will be utilized in political activities and in actual dismantling of a service concept that the department had once deemed an important mechanism for official goal achievement. The operative goals, the day-to-day activities, at least in this area of community mental health, will not lead to any official goal achievement, but will be aimed almost solely at the achievement of ends that are not directly beneficial to the actual care of the mentally ill. This is clearly a case of a high degree of goal displacement.[12]

The example demonstrates the use of the goal continuum as a dynamic rather than as a static concept. In the case of deinstitutionalization, the county department, as a result of external pressures and decisions, drifted into a situation where more and more activity was siphoned from official goal adherence to operative goals that reflected patient needs far less. The process reflected a pattern that evolved over time, and in all probability would intensify as the organization increased its contact with the local political structure and with the sector of the population opposing the policy.

The point of the case example is not to illustrate who is right, who is wrong, and how it could have been handled differently, but, rather, to illustrate the process by which a human service organization, with the best of intentions to achieve its official goals, can quite easily find itself involved in activities designed to achieve very different kinds of ends.

SUMMARY

This chapter concerned the second variable of the throughput, goals. In order to address the question of how goals affect a human service organization's use of its service resources, the concepts of official and operative goals were utilized. A continuum ranging from high adherence to official goals to goal displacement was presented. In a situation in which there is a high degree of official goal adherence, service resources are necessary in the achievement of these goals. When organizational activities are aimed at goals, such as individual advancement, which do not contribute to official goal achievement, the utilization of service resources becomes far less significant. In fact, service resources may be irrelevant in most situations of goal displacement. As in the case of decision making, the dynamics of goals and goal maintenance need to be understood by the human service manager. The case illustration at the end of the chapter illustrates the concepts of goals in a human service organizational situation.

NOTES

1. Charles Perrow, "An Analysis of Goals in Complex Organizations," *American Sociological Review*, vol. 26, no. 6, 1961, pp. 854–866.
2. Ibid., p. 855.
3. The pioneering study of this concept is Robert Michels, *Political Parties* (New York: Dover Press, 1959, reissue).
4. Robert Merton, *Social Theory and Social Structure* (New York: Free Press, 1968).
5. James Thompson and William McEwan, "Organizational Goals and Environment: Goal Setting as an Interactive Process," *American Sociological Review*, vol. 23, no. 1, February 1958, pp. 23–31.
6. Donald Cressey, "Achievement of an Unstated Organizational Goal," *Pacific Sociological Review*, vol. 1, no. 2, 1958, pp. 43–49.
7. Erving Goffman, *Asylums* (New York: Doubleday, 1961), p. 84.
8. William Rosengren, "Communication, Organization and Conduct in the 'therapeutic milieu'," *Administrative Science Quarterly*, 32(3) pp. 237–247.
9. Marc Miringoff, "Incomplete Technology and the Organizational Dynamics of a State Mental Hospital," *Administration in Mental Health*, vol. 3, no. 2, 1976.
10. Ibid., p. 143.
11. For a discussion of goal formulation, see Rino Patti and Herman Resnick, "Changing the Agency From Within," *Social Work*,

vol. 17, no. 4, July 1972, pp. 48–57. See also, David F. Gillespie, "Discovering and Describing Organizational Goal Conflict," *Administration in Social Work*, vol. 1, no. 4, Winter 1977, pp. 395–408.

12. Its cause lies primarily outside the organization. As we have seen in other examples, goal displacement can be caused internally as well.

Chapter FIVE

THE THROUGHPUT:
How the Organization Utilizes
Its Service Resources: Authority

The third important factor of the throughput is authority. Authority is exercised at all levels of an organization, both in the areas of management and in direct service. For the purposes of this analysis the kind of authority under consideration is that which is exercised between organizational members, between direct service workers and supervisors, among those performing administrative tasks, between policy planners, and so on. The key question regarding authority is the following: *How does authority affect the utilization of service resources in human service organizations?*

AUTHORITY DERIVED FROM PROFESSIONAL
ABILITY AND FROM HIERARCHICAL POSITION

One scholar who contributed much to the understanding of authority was Max Weber.[1] Weber's thesis was that in an ideally functioning organization, a person's position would be based solely on his or her possession of the technical knowledge that was relevant to that organization. Therefore, at least in principle, the authority of those higher in the organization is always exercised on the basis of knowledge superior to those in lower-level positions. Without the technical knowledge there can be no basis for authority.

Weber's concept must be considered as an ideal type or a

model (a standard by which to assess reality but not necessarily reflective of it). As almost anyone who has observed the functioning of organizations and its members can attest, authority can be based on factors other than professional ability.[2] This is certainly the case in human service organizations. Authority can, and often is, derived from the *position itself,* rather than from ability.[3] This can lead to the exercise of authority based merely on the superior's values, or his or her political needs vis-à-vis the organization. Hence, decisions and actions which do not utilize technology nor contribute to effective service may be imposed because the person is *in charge* rather than because he or she has made an accurate assessment of the situation.

In a state hospital, for example, physicians are usually in charge of the process of treatment. However, other treatment personnel may be overruled even when, in certain situations, they possess superior expertise. The physician usually cannot, for political reasons, relinquish authority; thus, treatment is based on "doctor's orders" but not necessarily on superior expertise.[4] Many other examples can be given, in which human service issues that affect service and service quality are resolved on the basis of superior organizational position and not on the basis of superior human service technology. This situation may constitute one of the most important problems experienced by those functioning within an organizational setting.[5]

When the authority exercised in an organization or organizational component becomes characterized to a significant degree by hierarchical position alone, then this may be considered a subversion of the kind of authority that fully utilizes service resources. Hence, where rank and hierarchy prevail, much of an organization's service resources become subordinate to the exercise of and compliance with authority: they are thus "lost" to an organization as a contribution to effective service.

The factor of authority like those of decision making and goals can be viewed as a continuous concept as follows:

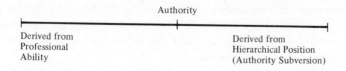

Authority

Derived from
Professional
Ability

Derived from
Hierarchical Position
(Authority Subversion)

Obviously, the degree of availability of service resources will affect the kind of authority relationships present in the organization. Where significant service resources exist, there is a basis for authority based on professional ability. Where there are minimal service resources the organization's authority will tend to be subverted.

The human service manager, then, must be aware of this factor of authority, how it varies, and how that variance affects the utilization of service resources. Such awareness is essential to understanding the dynamics of the organization's throughput functioning. The framework allows the manager, when viewing authority relationships in the organization, to consider not only the people involved and the roles which they may represent, but whether the authority-compliance interaction reflects professional ability or authority subversion. This perspective helps management to assess the effect of authority on service resource utilization and service outcome.

CASE ILLUSTRATION—AUTHORITY

The Situation

One way of illustrating the authority-compliance continuum is through an example involving the use of a consultant to a human service organization. Often, a person who is an expert in a specific field will be asked to consult with the staff of an organization, in order to improve the knowledge and skills of the staff.

Let us assume that a small agency (a local welfare department) is providing welfare recipients with counseling services. These services have been provided on a one-to-one basis, with the service provider helping the recipient with personal problems. The director of this small welfare department has come to believe that a family approach to counseling would provide better service. In short, rather than seeing the welfare recipient individually, family therapy would become the major emphasis of service. The director, therefore, brings in a family therapy consultant whose task is to provide the staff with knowledge and skills in family therapy.

The first meeting with the consultant takes place with the following participants: The agency director, the consultant, the chief of social services, and the social service staff members.

DIRECTOR: As you know, I feel that it would be a good idea, for the benefit of the clients, to change our orientation somewhat from one-on-one service to family therapy. Accordingly, I have brought in Ms. Diane Wheeler, who is a family therapist with a great deal of experience in agency consultation. Diane will, I think, be able to provide us with the essentials of the approach.

CONSULTANT: Thank you, Don. I must say that it is very gratifying for me to see a director of an agency support the family therapy concept so completely. Now, family therapy is very different from the one-to-one approach used by many.

CHIEF OF SOCIAL SERVICES: Before you continue I just want you to know that we are not totally sold on the idea of changing the concept of our basic service approach. We would like to believe that what we've done in the past has had some positive effects, and we really are a bit upset. I think we really have to work through whether this change is actually a necessity. I'm not sure it is.

STAFF MEMBER: I agree. I've been at this agency for 18 years, and I don't know if this kind of approach is valid. Now, Ms. Wheeler might be a very gifted family therapist, but I'm not sure she is sufficiently familiar with our clientele and with our agency policies to really be able to give us the kind of consultation we need in this regard.

DIRECTOR: I'm a little surprised at your attitude. I don't see any reason why we shouldn't allow an opportunity to have a person give us the benefit of her knowledge. I think that the organization needs some new ideas, and I don't see the objection.

CONSULTANT: I think that what Don has said here makes a lot of sense. We're not attempting to impose anything, but I think that one of the functions of a director of an agency is to try to improve staff performance; and that's all I'm trying to do and that's all that Don is saying.

STAFF MEMBER: What we're saying is that we're not convinced

that this is going to improve our performance. It's true that he's the director, and if he wants to do it, I'm not going to walk out of here, because—and I hate to say it—"he's the boss."

CONSULTANT: Well, what I have to say clearly has the endorsement of the director, and, really, you're quite right, he is the director; and I think we should get on with it.

CHIEF OF SOCIAL SERVICES: I'm not convinced.

CONSULTANT: Well, sometimes the director of an agency can see things—can see the whole picture—better than any individual staff person.

DIRECTOR: What the director does and thinks isn't the point. The point is that the staff needs to judge this consultant on the basis of what she has to offer—from a substantive, service point of view. If you like what she has to offer and can incorporate it, that's fine. My role as director and my own endorsement—so to speak—of her is not the point. I think what I'm going to do is take myself out of this and just leave you together to go over the substance of this matter. I do hope that it'll be helpful—but let's judge it on the merits. [He leaves]

CONSULTANT: Well, I'm sorry if there was a conflict, but now let me try to get on with what we're supposed to accomplish, and we'll see if we can achieve some communication. The idea of family therapy involves the interaction of systems of primary relationships. Instead of considering the individual and his or her relationship to the environment, you need to consider a group of individuals, their interchange, and how the environment affects the group.

CHIEF OF SOCIAL SERVICES: Actually, that's not much different from the therapy we do now, you're just adding a layer.

CONSULTANT: Right. You're just considering a more complex set of interactions. Now, maybe you can tell me a little about the techniques, procedures, and approaches that you use at this agency, and then we can integrate them with the family idea.

[As the discussion continues, the staff becomes involved in the concept of the family approach and begins to trade ideas, realizing that the idea is congruent with what is already being done. Slowly they begin to accept the consultant on a collegial basis.]

Analysis

This case illustration, because it is designed to demonstrate a single concept, oversimplifies reality. The key point, however, regarding authority is apparent. When the director was present, the authority of the consultant was very much derived from his hierarchical position. The consultant continuously refers to the director's hierarchical position in order to gain compliance from the staff. The compliance emerges, but it is clearly because "he's the boss." The staff endorses the consultant, but not because the service concepts are appealing. This kind of situation is obviously dysfunctional to enhancing the service outcome of the organization or actually developing the knowledge and skills of the staff.

The director understands the dynamics of the situation and explains to the staff, in essence, that they should comply not on the basis of his endorsement but rather on the substantive merits of the presentation. The director then allows this to become a reality, by taking himself out of the situation and leaving the meeting.[6] After that, the consultant is left with proving her expertise and value from a service point of view, and immediately takes a different approach, stressing substance as well as indicating that her approach is not vastly different from that which is already being utilized at the agency. The consultant also begins to ask the staff questions about agency procedures, thereby stimulating a sense of collegiality. In short, the consultant's authority moves away from the hierarchical position and toward a situation where her professional ability is more important. Although it appears perhaps obvious to note that this kind of authority relationship will generate far better results in terms of service, this kind of authority unfortunately is often not evident in the operation of many human service organizations. Such rationality often gives way to a variety of other factors involving personalities, political factors, and insecurities about role and task, and the result is the emergence of a reliance on hierarchical position.

The case example is a group dynamic example, indicating a specific incident. It is possible through the use of the authority continuum to understand *patterns* of authority between a director and his or her staff, a supervisor and subordinate, and even patterns of authority existing between a human service delivery organization and a human service planning organization that supersedes it in a service system.

THE THROUGHPUT AS A WHOLE: DECISION MAKING, GOALS, AND AUTHORITY

These three factors, then, decision making, goals, and authority constitute the major aspects of the throughput functioning of a human service organization. It is important to understand that the functioning of each is closely tied to that of the others. Changes in one factor will directly affect changes in the others. It is impossible, therefore, to identify any one factor as being the cause of the other two. The interrelationships are circular. This circularity can be depicted as follows:

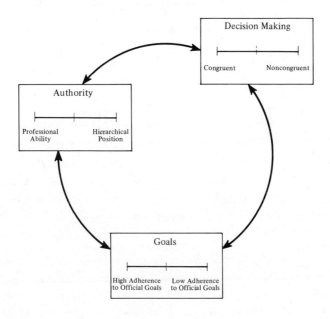

OPTIMIZATION AND CO-OPTATION

Let us now return to the question posed at the onset of Chapter Three as we began our consideration of the throughput: "Does the functioning of a given human service organization tend to co-opt or to optimize its service resources; does it, in fact, make full use of the human service technology available to it?" The three generic factors that we have discussed, decision making, goals, and authority compose the underlying dynamics through which the human service manager can examine this question, for these dynamics are fundamental to a variety of organizational activities such as budgeting, planning, and interpersonal relationships, which constitute the daily life of an organization. *Organizational optimization* is present when the service resources available to a given organization are utilized through functioning that is characterized by a high degree of congruence in decision making, official goal adherence, and authority based on professional ability.

Organizational Optimization

Goals
High Degree of
Adherence to
Official Goals

Decision Making
Congruent Mix

Authority
Derived from
Professional
Ability

FIGURE 5-2

Organizational co-optation is present when the service resources available to a given organization are diminished through functioning that is characterized by a high degree of noncongruence in decision making, goal displacement, and authority subversion (Figure 5-3).

Organizational Co-optation

Goals
Low Degree of
Adherence to
Official Goals

Decision Making
Noncongruent Mix

Authority
Derived from
Hierarchical
Position

FIGURE 5-3

Much as a clinician must assess his or her client or patient in terms of both strengths and weaknesses, the human service manager needs to assess an organization for signs of optimization and co-optation. As in the case of a client or patient, these states of organizational functioning are not static but change constantly, thereby compounding the difficulty of the managerial assessment. Given this condition of change, the potential for co-optation is significant. It is possible that with the appropriate combination of maintenance and service resources, and the right "mix" of personnel and organizational structure, optimization for a period of time can be a natural result. However (as we have seen), without effective managerial leadership based on an understanding of these dynamics, there is a strong likelihood of the occurrence of noncongruent decisions, goal displacement, and subverted authority that, feeding upon one another, can result in an extremely high degree of organizational co-optation. Such co-optation, it may be argued, is prevalent in many human service organizations, which often do not possess the appropriate service resources required to meet the social problems that they were created to confront.[7] This appears to be the case, for example, with many of the community-based antipoverty agencies first established in the 1960s, which often became characterized by extreme degrees of co-optation. In other cases where appropriate service resources may be available, the organization, through dysfunctional rules and regulations, cumbersome structure, and bureaucratic characteristics, may fail to make use of the resources that it does possess. Whatever the reason for such co-optation, its recognition and alleviation is a prime purpose of management in fulfilling the objective of enhancing effective service.

At the beginning of Chapter One, the basic question was posed to which Part I of this book is addressed: "What are the significant factors operating in the context of human service organizations that determine the ultimate quality of the service product?" At this point, we have discussed the input and throughput of that process which can be summarized:

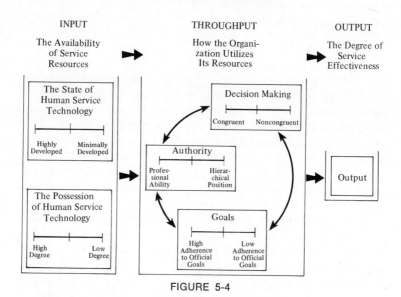

FIGURE 5-4

The next chapter considers the output, or the degree of service effectiveness.

SUMMARY

The third important variable of the throughput, authority, was examined in this chapter. In addressing the question of how authority influences the organization's use of its service resources,

Analyzing the Organization

authority was viewed as varying between that based on professional ability and that based upon hierarchical position.

A human service manager must not only understand the dynamics of each of these throughput variables but must also understand how they interrelate to form *patterns* of throughput functioning. Two contrasting patterns are evident. The first is *organizational optimization,* in which decision making is highly congruent, there is a high degree of adherence to official goals and authority is derived to a great extent from professional ability. The second is *organizational co-optation* in which decision making is noncongruent, there is a low degree of adherence to official goals, and authority is derived largely from hierarchical position. Obviously, the degree of optimization and co-optation can vary within a single organization over time and among its component parts.

This chapter ends our discussion of the throughput aspect of our framework. The next chapter considers the output, or the degree of service effectiveness that results from varying combinations of input and throughput.

NOTES

1. H. Gerth and C. W. Mills, *From Max Weber: Essays in Sociology* (New York: Columbia University Press, 1976).
2. See Amitai Etzioni, *Modern Organizations* (Englewood Cliffs, Prentice-Hall, 1964) and Peter Blau and W. Richard Scott, *Formal Organizations* (San Francisco: Chandler, 1962). Also, Amitai Etzioni, "Authority Structure and Organizational Effectiveness," *Administrative Science Quarterly,* vol. 4, 1949, pp. 43–67.
3. Mayer Zald, "Organizational Control Structures in Five Correctional Institutions," *American Journal of Sociology,* vol. 68, November, 1962, pp. 451–465.
4. Marc L. Miringoff, "Incomplete Technology and Organizational Dynamics of a State Mental Hospital," *Administration in Mental Health,* vol. 3, no. 2, Spring 1976.
5. Complicating the matter is the fact that professional norms generated outside the organization can mold the perception of organizational members regarding authority and its exercise.
6. For an interesting essay on this kind of situation and on leadership in general, see Abraham Zaleznik, "The Human Dilemmas

of Leadership," *Harvard Business Review*, July-August 1963, pp. 49–55.

7. Stephen M. Rose, *Betrayal of the Poor* (Cambridge, Mass.: Schenkman Publishing Co., 1972).

Chapter SIX

THE OUTPUT: The Degree of Service Effectiveness

In Chapter Two, we considered the input, or the availability of service resources to a human service organization. In Chapters Three, Four, and Five, the throughput, or how the organization utilizes these resources, was considered. The major concern of the human service manager is the quality of the output, the ultimate service product of a given organization. It is the quality of the output of the human service organization that constitutes the subject of this final chapter of Part I.

PATTERNS OF MOST EFFECTIVE AND LEAST EFFECTIVE SERVICE

The degree of availability of service resources, the input, and the degree to which the organization utilizes these resources (optimization or co-optation), the throughput, in combination, yields the *pattern* of effectiveness of service that an organization can provide to its population in need. These differing service patterns are depicted in Figures 6-1A and 6-1B (pages 78–79).[1]

It is important to understand that the equations illustrated in Figures 6-1A and 6-1B represent the most extreme cases, and like the other concepts that have been presented, *some degree* of availability of resources will be present and *some degree* of co-optation or optimization will be present in any organization.[2] Thus, another way to depict the framework is shown in Figure 6-2 (page 80).

Figure 6-2 portrays a dynamic, varying view of organizational functioning, showing the possible range of movement in

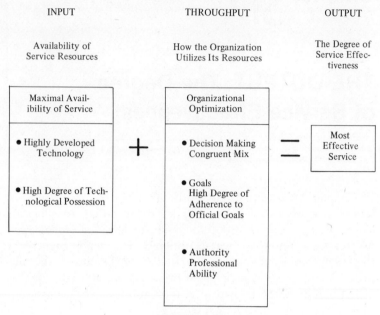

INPUT   THROUGHPUT   OUTPUT

Availability of
Service Resources

How the Organization
Utilizes Its Resources

The Degree of
Service Effec-
tiveness

Maximal Avail-
ibility of Service

• Highly Developed
Technology

• High Degree of Tech-
nological Possession

Organizational
Optimization

• Decision Making
Congruent Mix

• Goals
High Degree of
Adherence to
Official Goals

• Authority
Professional
Ability

Most
Effective
Service

FIGURE 6-1A

the input and throughput that culminates in moving the output
"toward" a pattern of most or least effective service. The effectiveness of service, then, is the result of an ongoing and change-
able interaction of the factors that compose the input and
throughput. For every organization, the actual "appearance" on
the continuum of *each* factor will be different, but the tendency
is for these factors to occur in discernible patterns leading to
either "polar" pattern—least or most effective service. The tendency toward most effective service is present when the components of the input and throughput vary toward the "positive"
alternative. Therefore, if the quality of the service resources is
high, and the throughput is characterized by a high degree of
optimization, the organization should produce a high level of
service effectiveness. There are, then, a series of specific relationships between the factors of the input and throughput that
need to be understood in order to assess organizational dynamics.
These can most easily be expressed in propositional form.

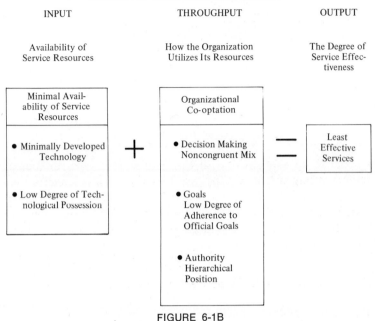

PATTERN OF LEAST EFFECTIVE SERVICE

INPUT — Availability of Service Resources

THROUGHPUT — How the Organization Utilizes Its Resources

OUTPUT — The Degree of Service Effectiveness

Minimal Availability of Service Resources
- Minimally Developed Technology
- Low Degree of Technological Possession

+

Organizational Co-optation
- Decision Making Noncongruent Mix
- Goals Low Degree of Adherence to Official Goals
- Authority Hierarchical Position

=

Least Effective Services

FIGURE 6-1B

Propositions of Most Effective Service

The following propositions indicate the specific relationships involved when a human service organization exhibits a pattern tending toward most effective service.

	Input and Throughput
Proposition I-A:	The higher the quality of the service resources, the more likely a human service organization will demonstrate a high degree of congruence in its decision-making process.
Proposition II-A:	The higher the quality of the service resources, the more likely a human service organization will demonstrate a high degree of adherence to its official goals.
Proposition III-A:	The higher the quality of the service resources, the more likely a human service organization will demonstrate a high degree of authority derived from professional ability.

	Throughput and Output
Proposition IV-A:	The more congruent the decision-making process, in a human service organization, the more likely service effectiveness will be maximized.
Proposition V-A:	The higher the degree of adherence to official goals, in a human service organization, the more likely service effectiveness will be maximized.
Proposition VI-A:	The more authority is derived from professional ability, in a human service organization, the more likely service effectiveness will be maximized.

To those concerned with the quality of service in human service organizations, the pattern leading to most effective service is obviously desirable. As has been noted, many human service organizations, however, are characterized by service patterns that are less than desirable. It is, therefore, equally important to recognize patterns of least effective service as well.

Propositions of Least Effective Service

The pattern of least effective service is present when the input, throughput, and output vary toward the "negative" or dysfunc-

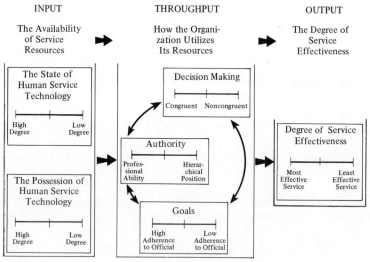

FIGURE 6-2

Analyzing the Organization

tional alternative. The following propositions summarize the relationships involved.

	Input and Throughput
Proposition I-B:	The lower the quality of the service resources, the more likely a human service organization will demonstrate a low degree of congruence in its decision-making process.
Proposition II-B:	The lower the quality of the service resources, the more likely a human service organization will demonstrate a low degree of adherence to its official goals.
Proposition III-B:	The lower the quality of the service resources, the more likely a human service organization will demonstrate a low degree of authority derived from professional ability.

	Throughput and Output
Proposition IV-B:	The less congruent the decision-making process, in a human service organization, the more likely service effectiveness will be minimized.
Proposition V-B:	The lower the degree of adherence to official goals in a human service organization, the more likely service effectiveness will be minimized.
Proposition VI-B:	The less authority is derived from professional ability in a human service organization, the more likely service effectiveness will be minimized.

The human service manager must be sensitive to the manifestation in an organization of those factors that characterize the pattern of least effective service. It is also particularly important that the manager understand that, as has been noted, the presence of one of these factors facilitates the appearance of others, which can combine to generate a pattern dysfunctional to service.

Patterns of least effective service, then, can be discerned in the interaction of the input and throughput. Many human service organizations throughout the social welfare institution appear plagued by such patterns. The important point for management is that an increase in organizational optimization can improve service effectiveness despite a low level of service resources in the input. For example, if it were possible to quantify the input, one could perceive a given human service organization as having a service resource level of four out of a possible ten.

However, due to organizational co-optation, this organization might be producing a two out of ten in its level of service effectiveness. With increased organizational optimization of the service resources available, the organization could approach a service effectiveness level of four.

In the final analysis, then, the contrasting patterns of most effective service and least effective service and their respective components can provide the human service manager with a tool for analysis and assessment. Let us now illustrate this framework in an organizational setting.

ILLUSTRATING THE FRAMEWORK

It is impossible within the confines of a single book to analyze many types of human service organizations, observe their patterns of functioning, and apply the concepts of the framework that we have described, in order to assess the process by which they derive their ultimate service product. Important aspects of the framework, however, can be manifested in the attitudes reflected in the statements that are made by organizational members regarding the functioning of their organization.[3]

Let us, therefore, consider the following sets of statements that, though hypothetical, may prove familiar to those with practical experience in human service organizations.

Organization A

1A I'm not sure where I fit in. I can't use my professional skills appropriately here.

2A My clients and case load are not relevant to the kinds of things I do well. I don't think what I know and can do make any difference here.

3A People are always doing things on the basis of what will benefit *them,* not the clients or the agency. It's very political.

4A I often disagree with others here about basic values—but there is no dialogue and nothing I can do. Even at formal meetings, this is never mentioned.

5A If they just cut the paperwork and the other hassles, I could do more service. I do not have a sense of satisfaction.

6A The atmosphere here is terrible. There seems to be little sense of overall purpose to the agency.

7A My supervisor has been here forever. His ways are set. There's no opportunity for input even if I'm right. It's hard to do it his way, just because he's the supervisor. What about the clients?

8A There's no sense of collegiality. We mostly relate in terms of our positions; and I make little attempt to modify the professional views of those above me; it's not worth it. So at staff meetings, I just keep quiet. Sometimes I worry about how that affects the clients.

Organization B

1B I think that conflict and other problems are minimized around here because most of us know what we're doing, and that competence is generally recognized by others.

2B Most of us bring in new information, studies, and research about treatment. This is always encouraged throughout the organization.

3B I have to say that there is less politicizing here than at other places I've been. People do seem to have the good of the agency and the client at heart. So when it comes down to making a decision, even a little one, people aren't bucking for something. People get their stature around here from achievement.

4B There's plenty of what I guess you could call politics, but politics are used to get things done; and that usually means for the good of the services and the clients.

5B There's usually a sense of what we're about around here. We don't always accomplish everything, but at least we know where we are going.

6B The things I do on a daily basis do seem to add something.

7B My supervisor does respect my professional viewpoint. If I make a judgment based on something I can't substantiate, it doesn't go, and rightly so. On the other hand, if I make a point in contradiction of his and I can back it up, it usually prevails. This way I don't have to play games. The result is beneficial for me, and a help for the clients, because we squeeze the last bit of expertise out of *both* of us.

8B At staff meetings there's a lot of give and take, especially about what benefits the clients. It's sometimes so collegial that you can forget who holds what position in the organization.

These statements, and others like them, can illustrate some underlying dynamics occurring in the organization. They reflect the relative satisfaction or dissatisfaction of the person making them, but also reveal much about the *functioning* of the organization with regard to its provision of effective service. It is clear that both of these sets of statements could be made about separate components of the *same* organization, but assuming that they are about different organizations, it is apparent that organization A is demonstrating significantly more organizational co-optation and probably an overall pattern tending toward least effective service than organization B.

Statements 1A, 1B, 2A, and 2B reveal the level of service resources that are available to the respective organizations. This may reflect both the state of development of the given technology and its degree of possession. In organization A, it is apparent that the person's possession of skills is not being applied to the client population in an adequate manner. It is not possible, in this kind of example, to determine whether the prime cause of the situation is the fact that the technology itself is not sufficiently developed, and as a result, the individual cannot perceive an appropriate role, or whether the individual does not possess an appropriately high degree of what has been developed. It is also possible that the organization is structured in such a manner that it does not allow the appropriate mix between the skills of a service provider and the problems of a service consumer. In any case, there is a distinct problem in the utilization of service resources in organization A that does not occur in organization B.

In organization B, the nature of the service resources is such that organizational members have confidence in their use of the appropriate knowledge, skills, and procedures of the given technology. Apparently this confidence is sufficiently widespread to elicit mutual respect, which, in turn, sets the stage for collegiality. The presence of a highly developed technology, elements of which are generally recognized and agreed upon, greatly facilitates this kind of process, and one would expect that human service organizations characterized by such a technology would function more like organization B than organization A (although this is by no means assured). Also facilitative are processes that are designed to *improve* service resources, by bringing to the organization innovations and improvements as illustrated by statement 2B.

Statements 3A, 4A, 3B, and 4B relate to decision making. Statement 3A indicates noncongruence in significant decisions, since political factors seem to predominate, which contributes significantly to co-optation. Service capability concerns appear to be minimized in this kind of climate, where decisions and payoffs from decisions are perceived in essentially political terms. Statement 4A indicates that basic values that need to be included in patterns of congruent decision making are apparently excluded from the decision-making process. As we have noted, decisions made *solely* on the basis of values can cause noncongruence, yet when values are omitted this can prove equally noncongruent and can aid in organizational co-optation. The decision-making process of organization B, however, seems to demonstrate more congruence and contributes to optimization. Statement 3B indicates such congruence in decision making and statement 4B reveals a situation in which politics are present but are utilized in the service of capability-related ends. Here again, optimization is enhanced.

Statements 5A, 6A, 5B, and 6B refer to goals. In statement 5A there is some goal displacement in that the organization appears to be displacing the service goals with extraneous tasks. This appears to be dysfunctional to the service changing the actual purpose of many activities so that the individual appears to be performing service activities that adhere less to official goals and more to some other kinds of goals that the organizational functioning requires. Statement 6A shows a sense of organizational purposelessness. This kind of statement indicates that a general awareness of official goals is not present. This lack can either cause or be the result of other factors of organizational functioning, such as noncongruency in decision making. In either case, the factors do tend to interrelate, and co-optation is the result. Statements 5B and 6B indicate the opposite. The individual's activities, although not always in achievement of official goals, appear *directed* at such a result. This aids in optimization of service resources that in turn is important to statement 6B, that what is done on "a daily basis" "adds something" and provides satisfaction.

Statements 7A and 8A indicate a situation of authority subversion. In statement 7A, the relationship with the supervisor reflects authority based on hierarchy, rather than on the technical skill of the supervisor. The individual involved perceives that because of the nature of the supervisor-subordinate relationship, he or she has little opportunity for input, even if that input is technologically sound. The same is true in statement 8A, in the context of a group, where there is a reluctance to participate because of the presence of superior authority. Since rank cannot always correlate entirely with superior expertise, this dynamic aids the process of co-optation. Statement 7B suggests that organization B is characterized by authority that optimizes service resources. The comment that "we squeeze the last bit of expertise out of *both* of us" clearly illustrates this optimization pattern. The same holds true in the case of statement 8B.

In perceiving organizations A and B as totalities, it is clear that what happens in one of the organizational processes, such as highly developed technology and decision making, can strongly affect other factors, such as goals and authority. If the tendency is adherence to official goals, for example, the tendency in decision making would be toward congruence and in authority toward professional expertise as the basis of interrelationships. If there is a great deal of goal displacement, then expertise becomes less important in authority because official goals are not being pursued. The same would be true in decision making where noncongruence might predominate because of patterns that lead an organization to co-optation or optimization. Maximal or minimal service effectiveness tend to be circular and self-perpetuating. It is important that this point be understood lest an organizational assessment become too sharply focused on an isolated factor.

These statements by "members" of these two organizations merely illustrate examples of how the framework can be utilized in assessing the everyday functioning of an organization with regard to how that functioning affects the development of its service product. They are "clues" to what is occurring in the organization. Far more information and observation would be required in order to conduct a comprehensive analysis. Yet it is the manifestation in an organization of such examples that can reveal the dynamics that underlie the organization's functioning, and it is these dynamics to which the human service manager must be sensitive.

A framework such as the one presented in Part I of this book can be the basis of service management. It can aid the manager who is involved in the service aspects of management, in his or her analysis of how the functioning of the organization is effecting service quality. It provides a basis on which the manager can probe beyond the everyday activities of the organization and its staff—the roles, the tasks, the relationships, the meetings, the rules, regulations, and procedures which shape organizational functioning—to examine the underlying dynamics and how those dynamics combine to evolve patterns of service effectiveness. In the perspective of such analysis, the everyday activities gain a context, and management can become more than a day-to-day reaction to events and to crises. As noted in Chapter One, the human service organization is the "front line" of the social welfare institution. Policy and program either succeed or fail at the organizational level. Our framework attempts to indicate how well a program does in an organizational context and thus represents an analytical basis of what can be the beginnings of a human service *management* technology. The utilization of such an analytical perspective can help clarify the dynamics of service outcome, and, through service management, can help human service organizations to function more effectively. The second part of this book is concerned with the application of this analytical perspective. It will consider the process and functions of human service management and how they can be utilized in order to move a given organization toward patterns of more effective service.

SUMMARY

This chapter completes the framework by which a manager can analyze and assess the functioning of a human service organization. Such functioning of a given human service organization can be analyzed and assessed with respect to the pattern of its service effectiveness, through the use of a framework derived from a combination of available resources and how those resources are utilized. Two overall service patterns can be identified, one leading to most effective service, the other leading to least effective service. Understanding and identifying these patterns within an organization can provide the human service manager with the dimensions by which to pursue the task of enhancing the effectiveness of service and service delivery.

The first six chapters, or Part I, have contained the presentation of a framework by which to analyze the dynamics of a human service organization. The emphasis has centered upon those factors that act and interact to evolve the service product of the organization. The next chapter, which begins Part II, initiates the presentation of the functions, tasks, and purposes of human service management.

NOTES

1. It is important to note that it is clearly impossible for a human service organization to produce a level of service quality *beyond* the service resources available. Hence, the terms "most" or "least effective service" refer to the highest and lowest level of service effectiveness which can be provided by a *given* agency and not by a whole field of human service.
2. Unfortunately, a given organization can conceivably possess almost no service resources. This would be most likely in the case where an agency is established to combat a social problem which is far beyond its capabilities. This sometimes occurs, particularly at the community level, where a social problem, due to its scope

Analyzing the Organization

and complexity, may render impossible any genuine alleviation (by a sole agency). In this case, few service resources are available to the organization and hence nearly total co-optation may become the inexorable result and an outcome approaching least effective service, the ultimate conclusion.

3. We are not implying that comprehensive conclusions can be drawn from one or two statements. These examples are meant to be illustrative of underlying attitudes which would require far more evidence to discern accurately.

PART II

Managing the Organization: Initiating and Maintaining More Effective Service

Utilizing the framework provided in Part I, Part II is concerned with the process of management. It contains a presentation of the functions, purposes, and strategies of management in both human service organizations that deliver a direct service and human service planning organizations that guide, coordinate, and fund the direct service organizations. The relationship of service management and maintenance management is addressed, and in the final chapter, human service management is considered in the context of the social welfare institution.

Chapter SEVEN

The Process of Management in Human Service Organizations

Any individual performing clinical tasks in human services, such as a social caseworker, a psychiatrist, or a counselor, approaches his or her client or patient with some kind of framework in mind. The clinician's framework contains a number of indicants and variables that reveal certain dynamics, providing the clinician with an analysis of a given situation. This framework is the basis on which a clinician understands client problems and recognizes certain behavioral patterns or syndromes concerning individual functioning; it represents the foundation on which the clinician devises appropriate interventions leading to an alleviation of the problem. Some concept of optimal functioning, as well as an organized notion of the variety of possible interventions, is therefore necessary. The clinician is conscious of this framework, or key aspects of it, as he or she engages in clinical tasks. A new or inexperienced clinician may apply the framework in a relatively structured and mechanistic manner, but with experience, the use of such a framework typically becomes more "natural" and more easily applied.

The preceding chapters presented a similar kind of framework for the human service manager. This framework provides indicants and variables that the practitioner must observe, understand, and assess. The framework indicates how these factors merge to form dynamics that are both functional and dysfunctional to service effectiveness. Like the clinician, the manager uses the framework to shape his or her thinking about an organization, assess certain patterns of functioning that either enhance or detract from service delivery, and evoke appropriate interventions. It is the nature of those interventions that is the subject of the following chapters.

In a human service organization, as in all organizations, there are individuals who function in staff or line positions. Their primary task in a human service organization consists of activities other than providing direct service to clients or patients. The activities of these individuals, as noted in Chapter One, may be viewed as comprising the process of management. The number of organizational members engaged in these processes varies greatly with the human service organization in question. In a small agency, the executive director, a few immediate staff, and a small number of supervisors may perform all the functions of management. In a large organization, such as a state hospital, the people performing these functions may number several hundred.

In this chapter, we consider the process of management. First, we define service and maintenance management and address their relationship. We then examine the strategies of management and conclude with a discussion of managerial style. This serves as a context for the four chapters that follow, in which four specific functions of human service management—budgeting, program evaluation, staff development, and community relations—are considered.

DEFINITIONS OF MANAGEMENT: SERVICE MANAGEMENT AND MAINTENANCE MANAGEMENT

Following the framework of Part I, it is important to differentiate service management from maintenance management; to distinguish between managerial activities that actually help to enhance service to clients, from those activities which serve to maintain the organization and help ensure its survival.[1] It is service management and maintenance management which combine to form the managerial process in human service organizations. This process can be termed human service management.

Service Management

As noted in Chapter One, service management is directly concerned with the issues and substance of the human service delivered by a given organization, and with the procurement, development, and application of service resources. In leading a human service organization to a pattern of most effective service, management is concerned with the highest possible quality of service resources as input, and optimization of these resources in the throughput. In general, this requires the recruitment and development of human service technology and technological ability, the pursuit of congruent decision making, adherence to official goals, and authority based on professional ability in the internal functioning of an organization. It means, as well, the careful guiding of factors external to an organization that influence service outcome, as well as procedures internal to the organization that may influence the patterns of service effectiveness. In short, service management represents a series of tasks in a human service organization that carry the responsibility for the *overall quality* of the organization's service product.[2] Service management needs to be based on a careful analysis of *how organizational functioning affects the quality of service provided by the organization.* In this way, service management can ensure increased effectiveness in human service organizations leading to the strengthening of the social welfare institution.[3]

Maintenance Management

Although, as noted in Chapter Two, service resources distinguish human service organizations from other formal organizations, these resources are not the sole input. All organizations require maintenance resources in order to function, such as equipment, materials for upkeep, a physical plant, support staff, funding, and so on. Maintenance management is primarily concerned with the procuring, processing, and allocating of maintenance resources and material, and with the operation of the organization in terms of the efficient integration of its components, which includes the reduction of organizational conflict and the achievement of organizational equilibrium and consensus. Maintenance management is concerned then with producing a "well-run" organization. It is concerned with such tasks as the standardization, coordination, and general execution of the rules, regulations, and procedures of an organization. Therefore, maintenance management is directed toward *efficiency in the use of resources and with survival* rather than *with the effectiveness of service*. Of course, a smoothly operating organization, which is fiscally responsible and accountable, and whose components adhere to procedures, conserve resources, and demonstrate consensus may be a well-run organization from a maintenance perspective, but may still deliver a vastly inferior service product. By the same token, however, the importance of successful performance of maintenance management in human service organizations cannot be overemphasized. This is particularly true in an era characterized by the need, on the part of human service organizations, to demonstrate efficiency and accountability. The cry of "mismanagement" has been a constant one and has often been made with some justification. Both human service organizations and the overall social welfare institution are very much dependent on the successful execution of maintenance management; without it, the service product of the organization will ultimately suffer.[4]

THE RELATIONSHIP BETWEEN SERVICE AND MAINTENANCE MANAGEMENT

A major problem of balance can often lie *between* maintenance and service management. This relationship can affect the functioning of the organization and its service product. As previously mentioned, the successful execution of maintenance can serve as a protection for service. Efficiency and accountability in the procurement and utilization of resources is vital for the survival of human service organizations. Without these activities, the very basis of the organization and its service is threatened. This relationship, in which maintenance supports service, is optimal for the quality of service outcome. However, overly emphasized maintenance management can have serious implications for the human service organization.

Within the management process, there is, in a sense, a "natural" conflict between service and maintenance due to the norms that each maintains and the objectives that each pursues.[5] Service, particularly human service, is not the most efficient endeavor, nor the most tangible or easily objectified. Yet it is objectification and tangibility that are the foundations of maintenance management. As a result, some conflict is possible and even probable. How this conflict is manifested in a given organization depends upon the persons involved and how the maintenance and service tasks are organized and divided. An imbalance toward maintenance can and often does threaten organizational optimization. Consider organizational decision making, for example. We have indicated that congruence should exist if service outcome is to be enhanced, and that other considerations, such as value elements, though present and important, should not predominate as the *basis* of decision making. If the values present are the values that support the given profession and the optimal application of its technology, there is little basis for conflict. However, the pursuit of maintenance objectives may be contradictory to professional values and capability considerations. Such a clash may lead to the appearance of political elements as well. Consider an agency that is under pressure from a major funding source to treat more patients in its outpatient clinic. The agency's current policy is to treat not only the principal individual patient, but to have ongoing collateral contacts with the individual's family. The agency's staff maintains that it is impossible to treat the patient effectively without seeing the family members as well; the funding source maintains that more primary clients could be treated if these secondary contacts were to be reduced.

In this situation, there is a clash between maintenance and service perspectives. The resolution should be decided on the merits of the issue from a service capability perspective, but clearly that is not always possible. A balance must be maintained. If this and several issues like it are *decided solely on the basis of efficiency, the organization will begin to co-opt its own service effectiveness.* Therefore, the managerial structure in a human service organization must evolve a balance in order to mediate service and maintenance management.

Another example further illustrates the point. Consider the maintenance tasks involved in resource procurement, which require a particular kind of reportage and persuasion that may tax the value and capability elements of an organization, and which may result in many dilemmas. Funds may be available, for example, to a given human service organization, only if it undertakes a new type of service that it is not capable of providing effectively. From a capability perspective, then, acquiring the grant will probably not produce effective service and may even detract from the organization's current service delivery. Yet the money may be considerable and receiving it promises expansion of the organization's domain. The decision might be reduced to: "Go for the money now, and we'll worry about the capability later" as opposed to "let's reject the money because we really can't deliver the service." Most human service organizations would indeed pursue the grant, and many agencies have been built on such pursuit. Co-optation, then, can be the result of such an imbalance between maintenance and service management. This is further aggravated by the fragmentation between management and service practitioners caused by the dominance of maintenance management. To the extent that management views itself as primarily involved with maintenance and removed from service—in short, a generic perspective of management—the overall patterns of service in a given organization remain unattended and unplanned, opening the possibility for the emergence of the kinds of dysfunctional patterns suggested by the framework of Part I. In such cases, the organization's effectiveness is diminished, its very reason for being is threatened, its contribution to the alleviation of social problems decreased, and its role in the strengthening of the social welfare institution rendered inert. The concept of management, viewed solely or to a large extent as maintenance, is not sufficient to lead the human service organization to optimization and patterns of most effective service. A finely conceived and aggressively pursued service management, balanced carefully with maintenance management, can contribute to the optimization of a human service organization and help that organization achieve some degree of effectiveness leading it to outcomes that actually work.

To strengthen the social welfare institution and make the programs and policies more effective in the organization in which they are implemented, the development and application of service management and its integration with maintenance management is a necessity. The next four chapters consider four central functions of human service management: budgeting, program evaluation, staff development, and community relations. Before presenting these four functions, it is necessary first to consider a dynamic central to all management—the trade-off mechanism.

THE STRATEGY OF MANAGEMENT: THE TRADE-OFF MECHANISM

Thus far we have dealt with the necessity, on the part of management, to be aware of the structures and processes of a human service organization. Much of the actual execution of management requires interaction with people. It is important before considering the functional areas of management to consider the strategies that human service management must pursue in order to carry out those functions.

In the course of performing the functions of management, those in managerial positions will need to pursue strategies and propose certain actions, plans, and policies. Each managerial "move" will utilize some combination of organizational components and will require the cooperation of members who are a part of these components. On what basis can the manager determine which "moves" are appropriate, in terms of their effect on the organization and its members, and how the organization will respond? No law or principle governing each possible situation faced by human service management can be given, but a general approach can be derived from the concept of *the trade-off mechanism.*[6]

PROFITS, REWARDS, AND COSTS

George C. Homans has provided considerable insight into the actions and interactions of individuals and groups.[7] Homans' work has been characterized as exchange theory. The basis of exchange theory is the following equation:

$$profit = reward - cost$$

On the surface, this equation appears as a simple explanation of the basic economics of a business; profit equals rewards, or income, minus costs, or what the business must invest. But Homans extends this prospective to social phenomena, that is, to interactions among individuals and groups, and suggests that such interaction can be analyzed through an application of this formula. Consider, by way of illustration, the _exchange_ between a small store and its customers. If the store sells a particular item at a certain price, that price (the store's reward) minus the cost at which the store initially obtained the item, must produce a reasonable profit for the store. This "trade-off mechanism" between reward and cost and profit must be continuously assessed in order that it be judged "worth it." The customer has his or her own trade-off mechanism. The customer must pay a cost (the store's reward) in order to gain a reward (possession of the item), and must determine whether the profit (the difference between the reward and the cost) is worth it: is the item worth the cost? Homans maintains that relationships among individuals and groups function in much the same manner in that both parties have a notion of their own trade-off mechanisms and the _exchange_ between them is based on an interaction that is profitable to both. Homans argues that "no exchange continues unless both parties are making a profit."[8]

In human interaction, the trade-off mechanisms and exchange are more difficult to calculate than in the case of money. What is rewarding and ultimately profitable to one person or group may not be so to others, and the same is true of cost. Rewards for some individuals may lie in the political realm; for others in upholding values or in technological achievement. One organizational member might compromise his or her values in order to gain politically; for others, the cost with peers and colleagues of such a political gain might prove too high. The pursuit of one's values might also eventually prove too costly and this realization might cause an individual to alter his or her behavior.

This is not meant to imply that people consciously behave in this calculative manner at all times. Trade-offs may not be apparent, and individuals and groups may unconsciously participate in unprofitable exchanges which are not in their self-interest. Much political functioning in an organization, for example, is based on the assumption that the "opponent" does not understand the true cost of a given exchange, and when he or she does realize it, it will be too late for him or her to act—the costs will be higher than anticipated. This is the essence of "one-upmanship."[9] Homans believes that given a rational process, exchanges can be understood and their course predicted on the basis of understanding the trade-offs involved. It is impossible, in Homans' view, to understand the dynamics of interrelationships without understanding these trade-offs and exchanges.

For example, in a graduate school of social work or any graduate school program, a number of students each year appear for the first day of classes. Each student has gone through some calculation and has arrived at some trade-off regarding his or her attendance. Obviously, the rewards, costs, and profits are different in each case, but the process is similar, and each student anticipates a profitable balance. The reward may be learning, it may be advancement in a job, it may be entering a profession in which one can pursue one's values, or a combination of these and other rewards. The cost may involve money, time, family responsibilities, aversion to school, or not doing something else that is positive and rewarding. In all cases, however, the profit (the difference between the rewards and the costs) has been judged to be "worth it." As their exchange with the school unfolds, the students assess the rewards, cost, and profits. Some may ultimately decide that the profits are too small and leave, perhaps expressing the decision in Homansian terms: "I'm not getting enough out of it." In each case a new trade-off has been perceived, which affects the basic exchange. The same dynamic holds for smaller decisions, such as which course to take. Each student has a trade-off worked out for course selection, in which the possible rewards might range from the instructor's reputation for knowledge, to the fact that he or she assigns only a few pages of reading for the semester and no paper! It does seem clear that alterations of such course requirements will change the prospective trade-offs of the students.

Similar calculations of trade-offs can also be applied to other kinds of endeavors. In applying a technology, a physician requires an exacting knowledge of trade-offs, but most medications or surgical procedures carry some risk of side effects, that is, costs for the patient. The reward in this case is an improvement in the patient's health. The difference between the reward and cost must represent a significant profit for the patient in order for the procedure to be undertaken. In some cases, the rewards and costs of a given procedure may be extremely close, but the cost of *not* undertaking it may be the determining factor.

The concept of the trade-off is by no means limited to discrete, individual interactions, but can also apply to patterns of interaction extending over time. The following three propositions from Homans illustrate this point:

> For all actions taken by persons, the more often a particular action of a person is rewarded, the more likely he is to perform that action (the success proposition).

> The more valuable to a person is the result of this action, the more likely he is to perform the action (the value proposition).

> The more often in the recent past a person has received a particular reward, the less valuable any further unit of that reward becomes for him (deprivation-satiation proposition).[10]

We will return to these propositions later in the chapter in the discussion of their application to managerial strategies.

Trade-off and exchange, then, can accumulate over time and come to represent an ongoing process, the dynamics of which can be both complex and subtle. Understanding and utilizing these concepts can prove extremely useful in devising the strategies necessary to carry out the functions described in the following chapters.

Trade-offs and the Functions of Human Service Management

In a human service organizational context, trade-offs and exchanges occur continually between individuals, groups, and organizations. As those with managerial responsibility perform the functions described in the following chapters, they must *maintain a thorough understanding of the nature of trade-offs and exchanges that operate between different organizational members and different organizational and interorganizational components.* These individuals need to understand the costs, rewards, and profits of all these elements as they interrelate and as they are viewed not only from the management perspective but also *from other viewpoints* as well. The manager needs to be able to discern shifts in exchanges and trade-offs in order to trace the response and implications of various managerial policies, programs, and initiatives. *In short, each significant managerial initiative brings changes to trade-offs and exchanges and without a clear understanding of these, it is nearly impossible to plan and effectively manage in human service organizations.*

Given an understanding of the currents of trade-offs in a human service organizational setting, and the knowledge that any managerial initiative will alter these trade-offs, the overall strategy for management is: *to govern these currents in such a way as to make the trade-offs and exchanges functional to organizational optimization and the service effectiveness of the organization.*

Trade-offs and exchanges are present in a human service organization as the staff acts and interacts. The issue is not *whether* they are present, but rather what is the substance of the trade-offs, the content of the profits, rewards, and costs. The objective of management is to ensure that the content of the trade-offs enhances service effectiveness. This is a subtle process in which mistakes can be costly. If the trade-offs or exchanges of a particular managerial move are assessed incorrectly, the results could be highly dysfunctional in terms of service.[11] Yet to stimulate and maintain meaningful change in the organization, which has a lasting effect on the service product, this process must be executed with a high degree of proficiency.

To further illustrate the concept of the trade-off mechanism, let us briefly consider this mechanism in the context of the elements of throughput described in Part I. As noted, various patterns of throughput functioning can bring about organizational co-optation. A significant factor contributing to this co-optation, as we have seen, is insufficient service resources. In addition, co-optation is maintained through patterns of exchange and trade-offs internal to the organization that lead functioning away from optimization.

In decision making, for example, capability elements that would contribute most directly to service outcome as the basis of decisions can give way to political elements that are pursued for their own end. One type of service component may be preferable to another in terms of overall organizational capability, but another service may be chosen for the expansion of staff because this component has yielded on some point in the past, and it is now "their turn" to receive a reward. Such trade-offs often detract from optimization, but they are common.[12]

Goal displacement itself may also be fueled by trade-off considerations. Certain operative goals may be maintained because they are to the advantage of individuals or groups in the organization, as in the previous example of the mental hospital where custodial goals have come to displace therapeutic goals. As noted, the hospital, as an accountable subunit of a larger system, requires some form of assessment mechanism and that mechanism may be based on custodial accomplishments. Therefore, the director in charge of a particular ward or building may see to it that custodial activities and functions are successfully carried out, because the director's rewards and profits in the context of the organization's assessment will be derived from custodial results. His or her costs, alternatively, will derive from unsuccessful custodial functioning. Thus, a series of major patient disturbances may cost the director more than will patients' failure to get well. Hence the strict pursuit of operative goals is the most profitable course, because the organization is conducted that way. This is not to imply that this particular director is necessarily an extremely insensitive person, but rather that in the normal course of events most people will pursue the course most profitable to them.

The same formula holds true for the exercise of authority. If a superior perceives that his or her most profitable course lies in exercising authority based on position rather than ability, that person may do so. A supervisor may find that allowing his or her subordinates to contribute as equals is too threatening and too costly. People in authority positions often conclude that the rewards of initiating collegial relationships do not outweigh the cost of relinquishing some of their authority in the process. From a service perspective, it is in fields with minimally developed technologies that a collegial perspective is probably most desirable, since clear-cut gradations in professional ability are difficult to discern. Yet, it is in just this situation that the superior is *less* likely to give up authority and initiate a collegial relationship because he or she may feel most threatened by his or her lack of sound professional ability. This is a great dilemma in human service organizations and very costly in terms of service, because the potential for a ritualized authority based on position is great. Innovative or alternative technological approaches may be suppressed or go unrewarded because of an inflexible authority structure. "Standing on rank" may become very common and technological activities may be rigidly controlled by superiors.

In these and other throughput processes, management must guide the reward system of the organization in order to influence behavior in the direction of optimization and effective service. Here maintenance management and service management can be closely integrated. Maintenance resources constitute a major source of reward that can be drawn upon by management. It is important that the internal dispersal (rewarding) of these resources be based on capability and not merely political trade-offs. To the extent possible, advancement in the organization, not only in terms of position but also recognition of various kinds, must be based on contribution to the organization's official goals and its service outcome rather than on the ability of members to successfully engage in purely political operations. The costs of not contributing technologically must be high and the rewards for doing so must also be high, so that the organizational dynamics will move toward optimization. In short, advancement of individuals in the organization must be closely tied to their technological achievement. Obviously, ongoing activities that are designed to achieve this vary with many organizational factors, one of the most important being size. In larger organizations, more formal means, such as policy and program initiative, will have the most impact, whereas in smaller organizations the process is characterized to a greater degree by interpersonal contact.

Consider the three elaborations of the exchange theory, previously mentioned: the success, the value, and the deprivation-satiation propositions. The success proposition, which suggests that a person is more likely to perform an act the more he or she is rewarded for it, illustrates a number of points. The rewards need to be based on the person's contribution to service effectiveness. But, in order to maximize this dynamic, a *system* of rewards is necessary, and not merely an undisciplined, occasional reward. Organizational mechanisms should be designed which *contin-*

ually reward members for positive contributions.[13] This might be a part of staff evaluations, a variety of ad hoc and ongoing tasks that are important to the organization, or the satisfaction that is gained when a person's participation and input become part of organizational policy. Although this may appear evident, it is an infrequent practice, particularly on a systematic basis, in most human service organizations. The task of devising strategies that include ongoing rewards based on service effectiveness is difficult but vital, and must be part of a management perspective. The trade-offs as perceived by organizational members need to be "tilted" in favor of contributing to service effectiveness in order to ensure that members gain rewards from positive contribution and not from dysfunctional organizational behavior.

The value proposition, stating that the more valuable an action to a person, the more likely he or she is to perform it, is also relevant and is related to the success proposition. What constitutes value (or reward) for the members of a human service organization is an important question, for it is, as we have noted, the basis of an individual's trade-off mechanism. The manager of a human service organization must set the value tone so that the pursuit of service effectiveness will be perceived as valuable or rewarding at all levels of an organization. This, of course, is not totally attainable, but it must be continually sought. A human service profession should socialize the practitioner to service and to the importance of effective, quality care. However, as has been indicated previously, when a practitioner functions in the context of an organization, it is possible for socialization to work in a negative direction. Where that individual once valued service, he or she may now come to place greater value on behavior ranging from ventilating hostility against the organization to learning the ropes in order to get ahead. Management must attempt to minimize such behavior by utilizing the reward system to enhance the influence of professional values and norms dedicated to service effectiveness.

The deprivation-satiation proposition illustrates how difficult these tasks are to accomplish. This proposition posits that the more often a person receives a given reward, the less valuable it is to him or her. The repetition of the same unit of a given reward, even if it is accomplishing the purpose of increasing the service effectiveness of the organization, will not yield a consistent result over time. Different kinds of rewards will be needed in order to perpetuate an appropriately oriented reward system. Therefore, in human service management, the strategy must continually be altered in order to ensure maximal result. It is this need to alter strategy that makes human service management so demanding an endeavor.

What has been presented is an overview of the use of trade-off mechanisms in the enhancement of service effectiveness. The ongoing assessment of trade-offs and the ability to utilize the appropriate initiative to elicit the desired response in terms of service effectiveness is a skill which is often perceived and developed by those who are successful in management as an intuitive process. The skill is utilized not only in planning but also in both formal and informal interaction. The need to function in this calculative manner is an important aspect of management. Whereas the inability to function politically may not be essential to the clinician in performing treatment tasks, it is a necessity to those who perform management functions in a human service setting. Being able to analyze the human service organization—the subject of the first six chapters—or to understand the functioning of management, as presented in this chapter, is not sufficient. Operationalization of the analysis and execution of the functions and strategies are required, and this necessitates strategic functioning, such as timing, what to trade, how far to go, whom to utilize, and so forth.

It is vital that an important point not be overlooked. These activities must be considered as a means to improving services and should not become ends in themselves. The tendency to do so can be a serious problem in management. The strategies presented in this chapter should be pursued only as they contribute to the functions described in the next four chapters, and not for the self-interest of the manager or others in the organization. In a clinical role the clinician must serve the client's needs and not his or her own. This is true of the manager as well. The client's needs and the organizational activities that affect those needs must be the goal which is served. In addition, the means must be integrated with that goal. This constitutes the ethics of human service management.

MANAGERIAL STYLES: INSTRUMENTAL AND EXPRESSIVE

We have considered the functions of human service management and the basis on which management must plan strategies in order to carry out these functions. The final subject area in this chapter concerns the style of the manager and the patterns of behavior that he or she exhibits in executing these functions and carrying out the strategies. There are two general kinds of style models, both of which are important in carrying out the objectives of management presented in this book. The first is the expressive, and the second is the instrumental. The expressive style emphasizes affect, human relationships, and interaction: the treatment of organizational members as fellow humans rather than as instruments designed to execute particular tasks. The instrumental style focuses on task accomplishment.[14] The emphasis is on what the organizational member can do in the pursuit of the organization's formal activity. Both of these styles are important and necessary in the functioning of human service organizations. Who in management plays each, at which time, and to what extent depends on organizational position, personality, and on other factors. One common pattern is an "inside person" and an "outside person." An "outside person" is often the head of the organization who generally performs the expressive role. A political candidate is a good example of this. The handshaking, the smile, the backslapping, and the attempt at being well liked are all part of an expressive-oriented style. Yet, the candidate must have an "inside person," a "nuts-and-bolts" person, who tends to the "hard" aspects of the campaign. This person need not have an effusive personality, because he or she deals with administrative matters and the style is instrumental. Obviously one person can assume both roles, but the conventional approach is that, at least in public, the "number two person" is more instrumental and the head person is more expressive.

The distinction between expressive and instrumental management styles has grown with the development of management theories. At the turn of the century, Frederick Taylor founded what he called "scientific management."[15] This was a highly instrumental concept that viewed organizational members as cogs in a machine designed to be as efficient as possible. "Time and

Motion Studies" originated from this approach and were designed to answer the question, "What physical movements on the part of the workers are most efficient in production?" Scientific management dealt with such ideas as the optimal span of control of a manager and the proper distribution of task. The whole notion was geared toward manufacturing plants of the era. The Human Relations School developed in response to this approach beginning with the Hawthorne study, conducted during 1929–32 at a Western General Electric plant to investigate the process of work.[16] The basic finding of this study was that other factors, informal in nature, can contribute much to productivity and to efficiency. Group norms, personality factors, loyalty, and so forth, affect workers as much or more than some of the structured measures and considerations of the scientific management school.[17] Today, much of management theory, in essence, has become a blend of the two with a stress on both structural approaches and the more intangible, but equally important, expressive aspects as part of job satisfaction and productivity.

Both the expressive and the instrumental style are important to management in human service organizations. From the point of view of exchanges, the cost to management of going too far toward either the expressive or the instrumental can be great. Many in human service management make the mistake of being too instrumental, too formal, too task oriented, or of performing management too much "by the book." This can often bring about a ritualistic and superficial compliance on the part of staff that is highly dysfunctional when management is attempting to move the organization toward more effective service and to make progress in the delicate areas which that task entails. The careful attempt to govern the reward structure and to alter the trade-offs of the organization will not yield the desired results if management's assumed role posture is almost exclusively instrumental. Members of the organization will tend to view management as crass and manipulative. Setting the value tone will be highly difficult, and conflict is the likely result. On the other hand, an overly expressive style, although perhaps more pleasant, can also be ineffective. "He's a nice guy, but he's no leader," or "She's very understanding, but we don't accomplish much" can be the likely attitude. This approach can be even more dysfunctional than an overly instrumental style. Ideally, management should seek a balance between instrumental and expressive styles. The goals of the organization must be clear, and the responsibility of each member for his or her part in goal achievement must be fully understood. But the camaraderie, satisfaction, and loyalty that can be the result of the expressive style is a necessity as well. The right balance is the goal of management. Knowing when to assume each style, to what degree, and with whom is part of successful management.

This discussion of style is designed to help sort out managerial behavior. Effective leadership in an organization is often a careful blending of instrumental and expressive style. There is a need to distinguish between the two styles and to utilize them when appropriate. It is impossible to further specify their application because so much depends on the nature of the organization and the people involved. As in the case of other concepts presented, the parameters of behaviors and the specifics used must fit the individual case.

SUMMARY

This chapter has been concerned with the process of management. Management tasks can be viewed as being divided between maintenance and service. Maintenance management constitutes those activities that are designed to ensure the survival of the organization. It is concerned with efficiency, coordination, standardization, and with the organization's maintenance resources. Service management is concerned with the quality of the organization's service product. As such, service management functions both inside and outside an organization to bring about organizational optimization and patterns of most effective service. The relationship between maintenance and service management is an important element in the functioning of a human service organization. If maintenance management tends to predominate in the organization, organizational co-optation can be the result. The relative absence of service management can lead directly to the kind of dysfunctions described in Part I. A balance needs to exist between maintenance and service management such that the former serves, and does not displace, the goals of the latter.

The process of management includes the strategy of management as well. The basis of managerial strategy is an understanding and utilization of what can be called the trade-off mechanism, the essence of which is contained in the formula:

$$\text{Profit} = \text{Reward} - \text{Cost}$$

Behavior in human service organizations is characterized by trade-offs between members. These exchanges can be beneficial to optimization and service effectiveness. They may, however, also contribute to organizational co-optation. Those in management must understand and assess the currents of trade-offs and exchange in the organization and guide them in the direction of optimization and service effectiveness. This applies to the performance of all the task areas presented in the preceding chapter. This calculative kind of behavior is a necessity in effective management, although the purpose inherent in enhancing the quality of care must be kept firmly as the motivation, lest such behavior be carried on for its own sake and not for the enhancement of the organization's service.

Regarding managerial style, there are two characteristic patterns of managerial behavior, the expressive and the instrumental. In executing the functions and carrying forth the strategies, combinations of these two styles should be utilized. Discovering the appropriate mix of these styles to fit the given situation is critical to achieving managerial effectiveness. The next four chapters consider four specific functions of management and how they can be utilized to improve service.

NOTES

1. For a similar distinction which is not applied directly to management, see Daniel Katz and Robert Kahn, "The Social Psychology of Organizations" (New York: Wiley, 1966); also, Arthur L. Stinchcombe, "Bureaucrats and Craft Administration of Production: A Comparative Study," *Administrative Science Quarterly*, vol. 4, September 1965, pp. 167–187.

2. Brager and Holloway argue that this activity can best be achieved by practitioners themselves. See George A. Brager and Steven Holloway, *Changing Human Service Organizations: Politics and Practice* (New York: Free Press, 1978).

3. For differing discussions on "management" or "administration" in the human services, see Harleigh B. Trecker, *Social Work Administration: Principles and Practices* (New York: Association Press, 1971); Joyce Warham, *An Introduction to Administration for Social Workers,* rev. ed. (Atlantic Highlands, N.J.: Humanities Press, 1975); Robert Hawkes, "The Role of the Psychiatric Administrator" in Hazenfeld, op. cit.; Robert Morris and A. Binstock, *Feasible Planning for Social Change* (New York: Columbia University Press, 1966). Works on the subjects of social planning and program evaluation can also be relevant to this concept of service management.

4. For particularly informative work on the general subject of management which can be related to the human services, see Peter Drucker, *Management: Tasks, Responsibilities, Practices* (New York: Harper & Row, 1974); Chris Argyris, *Integrating the Individual and the Organization* (New York: John Wiley and Sons, 1962); Peter Blau and Richard Scott, *Formal Organizations* (San Francisco: Chandler Publishing Co., 1962), ch. 7; Fremont Kast and James Rosenzweig, *Organization and Management: A Systems Approach* (New York: McGraw-Hill, 1969).

5. This is related theoretically to the differential made by Talcott Parsons between the "managerial" and "technical" as subsystems of organizations. The concept of service management is related to the "technical" subsystem and maintenance management to the "managerial." See Talcott Parsons, *Structure and Process in Modern Societies* (New York: Free Press, 1953), pp. 16–96.

6. This concept embodying the notion of managing the reward system of an organization is familiar in management theory. See Argyris, op. cit., ch. 11. Also the concept has been often tested empirically. See, for example, James C. Worthy, "Organizational Structure and Employee Morale," *American Sociological Review,* vol. 15, no. 2, 1950, p. 78 and Dimock, *Administrative Vitality* (New York: Harper & Row, 1959), pp. 189–191.

7. George Homans, *Social Behavior: Its Elementary Forms,* rev. ed. (New York: Harcourt Brace Janovich, Inc., 1974).

8. Homans, op. cit., p. 30.

9. For the consummate practitioner of this art, see Michael Maccoby, *The Gamesmen, the New Corporate Leaders* (New York: Simon and Schuster, 1977). See also Eric Berne, M.D., *Games*

People Play; The Psychology of Human Relationships (New York: Grove Press, 1964), and M. Shubik, ed., *Readings in Game Theory and Political Behavior* (New York: Doubleday, 1954).

10. Homans, op. cit., p. 28.
11. This applies outside the organization as well as shown in the case illustration of Chapter 4.
12. This is illustrated in our discussion of traditional budgeting in the following chapter.
13. For work in this area, see F. K. Gibson and C. E. Teasley, "The Humanistic Model of Organizational Motivation: A Review of Research Support," *Public Administration Review*, vol. 33, 1973, pp. 89–96; and A. R. Martin, "Morale and Productivity: A Review of the Literature," *Public Personnel Review*, vol. 30, no. 1, 1969, pp. 42–45.
14. Talcott Parsons and Robert F. Bales, *Family Socialization* (Free Press: New York, 1955).
15. Frederick W. Taylor, *Scientific Management* (New York: Harper & Row, 1947).
16. Elton Mayo, *The Human Problems of Industrial Civilization* (New York: Macmillan, 1933).

Chapter EIGHT

The Budgetary Process In Human Service Organizations

Having considered the process of human service management, the next four chapters will address four of its central functions: budgeting, program evaluation, staff development and community relations. These functions are generic to human service organizations and contain aspects of both service and maintenance management. Each contains the possibility or even likelihood of predominance by maintenance management and each requires the balance of maintenance and service management.

The budget in a human service organization is a summary of organizational process, policy, and program. It is a statement of goals, values, priorities, political trade-offs, decisions, authority structures, and, as such, is probably the single most revealing document about how an organization functions.[1] The budgetary process represents the point at which the interrelationships between maintenance and service management are most keenly manifested. For those who perform maintenance functions, budget preparation represents the opportunity for the efficient dispersal of resources throughout an organization, whereas the prime concern of service management centers upon how these resources are converted to an effective service product. Although, as noted, these concerns are not necessarily complementary and often in conflict, it is extremely beneficial to the organization that a balance between them be attained in the budgetary process. The major question regarding budgeting therefore becomes: How can the resources of a human service organization be dispersed in such a manner as to be both efficient and to maximize the organization's service capability and service effectiveness?

The budgetary process represents a significant opportunity for management to contribute to organizational optimization.[2] By the same token, the preparation of a budget is an organizational task that is highly vulnerable to co-optation. This chapter focuses on how to achieve the former while minimizing the latter.

ORGANIZATIONAL CO-OPTATION AND OPTIMIZATION IN THE BUDGETARY PROCESS

By supporting those programs, components, and staff that bring about effective results, the budgetary process of an organization can do much to optimize that organization's service resources. This process may also co-opt these resources by distributing funds in a manner that is not supportive of effective results. The direction that the process eventually takes depends on a series of decisions. The budgetary process should be viewed primarily as a decision-making process—probably the most important on-going decision-making process undertaken by a human service organization.[3] As in all decision making, the budgetary process involves the relationship of political, value, and capability elements. The very question, "What should we be spending the organization's money on?" reflects value choices that may range from "We should spend it on programs for the poor because they are most in need" to "We should spend money on programs that are most efficient." When a decision is made to concentrate financial support on the most effective programs, an assessment of capability elements becomes a necessity. Throughout the budgetary process, the manager must also continually consider how to balance the competing political interests in the organization, which are often at their keenest in the context of budgetary support.[4]

In the discussion of the political elements of decision making in Chapter Three, the emphasis was upon an assessment of gain and loss, advantage and disadvantage. One of the most important gains or advantages to a program component is the amount of the budget it can command. This is one of the major ways that status and prestige between components can be measured. The decisions leading to "who gets what" are therefore of singular political importance. Often, capability and value elements are severely diminished when such questions are considered. It is a rare occurrence, indeed, for a staff member of one program to say "Why don't you cut our program and give more to them?" It is conceivable in probability terms, with no other information present, that 50 percent of the time the other program is superior. Nevertheless, it is almost a political imperative that representatives of any program would not make such a suggestion.

It is important to note that "who gets what" this year is often strongly influenced by "who got what" last year. The budgeting process is rarely conducted in a vacuum; probably the most significant factor in preparing this year's budget is the composition of last year's budget. In a sense the previous year's budget represents the first draft of the current year's budget and it carries great significance from a political perspective. Clearly, in the previous year, some kind of political equilibrium was established between representatives of competing political interests, or the budget could not have been finalized. Sufficient compromise had been reached and the trade-offs involved had been sufficiently appropriate to achieve consensus.[5] This consensus might very well have contained the implicit promises of future budgetary rewards to those who perceived that their position had been diminished, and their compliance was in a sense "bought" by a future, more beneficial (from their perspective) trade-off.

The Traditional Approach to the Budget

Given this trend toward the status quo, the overwhelming temptation for management is to take last year's budget, include in it any promises that might have been made, and with few alterations present this modification as this year's budget. This approach, the *traditional approach* in budgeting, is of least cost to management from a *political perspective*, and one that promotes the least amount of organizational conflict. The following example is more appropriate to the times: Assume that an organization is being compelled to absorb a 5 percent cut in funding. The traditional budget approach calls for an equal or proportional cut from each component of the budget until an overall 5 percent reduction is attained. On the surface, this appears to be a fair solution, which would probably not bring much protest from inside the organization. A very different approach, however, would be to operate under the assumption that some programs are better than others and should be maintained at present levels or even enhanced, and that most, or all, of the cuts should be absorbed by other programs that are not as good. This approach would upset past political equilibria and lead to conflict and to a more stressful budgetary process. A major consensus could probably not be attained easily and the organization would tend to be divided among those who stood to gain from the proposed new budget and those who did not. This kind of conflictual situation, disturbing to organizational consensus, would probably be avoided in most instances.

How, then, does the traditional approach, in which proportional allocations change little from year to year, affect optimization and co-optation of service resources? This approach will, over time, lead to co-optation. Unless, through an unforeseen natural process, the organization is functioning at an optimal level and expenditures are actually going to those components of the organization that maximize capability and service resources, optimization is probably not being served. Implicit in the traditional approach is the notion that the comparative effectiveness of programs is constant and hence funding should be unchanging—a condition that appears unlikely.

This traditional approach to budget preparation is utilized in most human service organizations. With the potentially politically charged factors minimized, the budgetary process assumes a maintenance-oriented character with the emphasis on mechanistic and technical considerations such as uniformity and standardization of fiscal reporting and accountability, and efficient processing of organizational funds.[6] All of these are necessary to achieve a tightly run organization from a fiscal perspective. The problem with the maintenance-dominated process is that little attention is given to considerations important in the fulfillment of service functions such as official goal achievement; in short, there is little concern with considerations of service outcome, and the budgetary process rarely reflects an assessment of the organization's effectiveness in reducing human need.

The traditional approach to budget preparation, then, represents a further example of how the drift of organizational dynamics can upset the balance between maintenance and service management. Here, as in the other examples, the task of matching financial resources to optimal service capability is achieved at the probable expense of organizational consensus. The utilization of the budgetary process to fulfill the objectives of service management cannot be achieved without disturbing the current patterns of organizational trade-offs, and some resulting conflict. Maintenance management is the easier path. This is the case because choices are made in the context of a "zero sum game" when someone's gain is somebody else's loss. However, if the budgetary process is to serve organizational optimization and improved service output, management intervention is necessary.

TOWARD OPTIMIZATION IN THE BUDGETARY PROCESS

A number of techniques have been developed in recent years that can help move an organization toward optimization. Many of these techniques relate directly to the budgetary process. They include zero-base budgeting, program planning budgeting systems, management by objectives, and cost benefit analysis. These techniques are _result-_, or _performance_-oriented rather than _activity_-oriented. They concentrate on assessing organizations and determining those components that best achieve the organization's goals rather than on merely funding the various ongoing activities in which the organization is engaged.[7] In this way, each of these techniques represents an attempt to depart from the traditional budget approach.[8] Each technique has its proponents and its detractors; none is a panacea.

A close scrutiny of the four budgeting techniques will reveal that they are not mutually exclusive; some overlap exists both in concept and in technique. Their major contribution lies in presenting new ways of thinking about budgeting which augment our concept of service management rather than in their specific technical application.

Zero-Base Budgeting

The essence of zero-base budgeting is conveyed by its name. The concept is that each component of a program or organization must begin each year with a "zero" budget allocation. This departs dramatically from the traditional approach where the "base" is the previous year's allocation.[9] By beginning with zero as a base, representatives of program components must justify their *entire* allocation for the current budget. This justification presumably is based on an agreed-upon set of program goals. This concept accomplishes several objectives. First, it removes the budgetary process from a ritualistic, mechanistic mode and encourages annual discussion and debate about program goals and capabilities, allowing for the consideration of what we have termed service management. Second, this approach forces organizations to choose between programs, requiring some level of ranking and some form of agreement on priorities. Third, it can lead to the consideration of programs and proposals on the basis of the service resources actually present and their contribution to the achievement of official goals. Each of these possible results of zero-base budgeting can aid management in helping the organization optimize its service resources. However, the mere presence of a zero-base approach will not ensure optimization. There is no guarantee that the process through which a program component moves from zero to the funding it ultimately obtains will be marked by a congruent series of decisions.[10] The process may remain essentially a political one. In all likelihood, the political atmosphere will intensify under conditions that annually reconsider the very basis of the organization's functioning. Secondly, zero-base budgeting lessens the organization's capacity for long-range planning. If each year is to actually be zero-based, long-term programs are not practical. If, on the other hand, long-term programming is desirable, this would tend to mitigate against a zero base each year. Finally, an actual zero base is virtually impossible under the manner in which most human service organizations are funded. Many costs, such as salaries, equipment, and space are fixed, so that some of the traditional approach seems likely.[11]

PPBS, first established at the Department of Defense in the early 1960s, has been viewed by some writers as the conceptual antecedent of zero-base budgeting. PPBS, as the name implies, is a technique designed to construct a system that uses the budget as an instrument to integrate long-range planning and specific program utilization.[12] Such an approach was utilized by the Office of Economic Opportunity and the Department of Health, Education, and Welfare, and numerous other attempts have been made to apply PPBS to human service programs.[13]

Essentially, the budgeting concept in PPBS is that no item in the budget should stand alone. For example, an item such as:

$$\text{Psychologist} = \$25,000$$

cannot be justified on its own merit. It must be an aspect or component of a program that carries duly stated objectives so that the expenditure for the psychologist must be justified only in terms of *how the activities to be performed contribute to that objective.* This is called an item in a *program budget.* Each item is analyzed on the basis of cost-benefit analysis (a term explored in greater detail later in the chapter). The budget then is constructed in terms of program and program component rather than line items as in the traditional approach. PPBS is perhaps better illustrated when the focus is upon entire program components and how they fit in terms of cost benefit, into an overall, long-range plan. Nevertheless, the concept is equally applicable in the case of a single human service practitioner such as the psychologist, who would be viewed in budgetary terms as part of a larger team of practitioners, and be judged on the basis of how he or she contributed to that team's achievement of its goals.

An important benefit of the PPBS approach is that, like zero-base budgets, it provides the organization with the opportunities to examine its goals, priorities, and capabilities. Unlike zero-base budgeting, however, it links expenditures around program objectives. This tends to radically alter the budgetary process because the competing interests are program interests. It is not the social service staff, or the occupational therapy unit that is putting in a budget request, but rather the antidrug *program* or the outpatient treatment *program.* Hence the process becomes centered far more on capability and outcome. With the use of PPBS there is also an opportunity for long-range planning, not possible in the case of zero-base budgeting.

PPBS can be of significant help to management in bringing about organizational optimization. It can lead to an analysis of whether an organization is achieving service goals and of the relative costs and benefits of each component's contribution toward that goal. There are many levels of sophistication at which a program budget and an integrated planning system can be implemented, ranging from a highly quantified series of cost-benefit choices to a more loosely formalized structure. Much of the success in applying PPBS to a human service organization will depend on the funding patterns of the organization's different programs and whether they allow a sufficient amount of freedom for comparative assessment and integration. Also, and perhaps more importantly, the state of the human service technology is a vital factor. It must be of a sufficient level of development to permit the kind of critical and useful assessment needed to render a PPBS appropriate. Despite these potential problems, the general approach inherent in PPBS can provide management with the opportunity for organizational optimization.[14]

Cost Effectiveness and Cost-Benefit Analysis

Cost effective analysis (CEA), as implied in the discussion of PPBS, is a technique for the quantitative evaluation of program alternatives.[15] Essentially, CEA asks: "What are the costs of a given program approach and what are its benefits?" The answer to the question, if such quantification is possible, will provide a "cost-benefit ratio"—the cost over the benefit. This ratio can be compared with the cost-benefit ratio calculated for another program—such that a quantitative comparison becomes possible. In the human services such quantification is rare, but it is possible. For example, a cost-benefit or effectiveness ratio could be derived by comparing two programs providing alcoholism counseling. If "success" could be defined as keeping the patient without alcohol for six months, two variables, the number of "success units" and the relative costs of the programs, could provide comparative ratios. The result could indicate a measure of which program was more cost-effective.[16]

Cost-benefit or effectiveness analysis is most relevant in the context of the application of other techniques such as PPBS. It also can be an important aspect of program evaluation, the subject of the next chapter. Suffice it to say at this point that in the human services, it is far easier to measure precisely the cost (in dollars) of a service than it is to measure the benefits, and it is almost impossible to measure another important benefit, the cost to society of *not* providing human services.

Management by Objectives (MBO)

MBO is a system in which management attempts to aim all significant activities in an organization toward the achievement of specified, agreed-upon objectives. MBO is designed to promote goal attainment, organizational clarity of action, and increased satisfaction on the part of organizational members who benefit in an environment of achievement.[17] Although it is fairly standardized in the literature as to its general parameters, the point is often made that the application of MBO varies with the characteristics of the organization involved.[18]

Essentially MBO is summarized by the following characteristics:

1. Makes objectives explicit; recognizes multi-objective situations.
2. Identifies conflicting objectives; provides for participation management.
3. Ensures a control mechanism providing for feedback and measurement of accomplishment.
4. Fosters managerial acceptance of responsibility and evaluation of managers by results.
5. Encompasses little formal administrative machinery.[19]

Such listings are common in defining the tasks of MBO. As in the case of PPBS, budgeting under MBO does not apply expenditure to activities, personnel, and the like, as in traditional budgets.[20] Rather, objectives are the basis of budgeting and contributions to those objectives determine the priorities for spending.[21] When such objectives are integrated, systematized, and long-range, the difference between PPBS and MBO becomes blurred.

Each of these techniques, zero-base budgeting, PPBS, CEA, and MBO, is designed to provide management with tools that can be utilized in the budgeting process to bring expenditures more in line with organizational goals and objectives. The techniques are outcome or result oriented rather than activity oriented. The emphasis is on minimizing organizational co-optation through the budgetary process. Obviously, in business where these techniques were first developed, the goal of the organization is profit, which is easily measured in quantifiable terms. The application of these techniques is more difficult in a human service organization where the outcome is a proposed change in the lives of a recipient population. In a human service organization, what determines whether and to what extent techniques like PPBS can be applied is the level of service resource the organization possesses. If the quality of the input is not sufficiently high, it is unlikely that the actual basis for the use of PPBS is present. With little technology and capability, it is difficult to reach a realistic consensus on program objectives and goals that are attainable. What then occurs, in all probability, are goals and objectives arrived at through noncongruent decision making, with the resulting budgetary process based on values and politics and not on capability.

This creates a serious dilemma for management in a human service organization. If management is to make choices between programs, set some priorities, reduce organizational co-optation, and utilize budgeting expenditures to obtain organizational objectives, then a firm and rational basis for choice must be present. Evidence of where in the organization the service capability is located and where most effective results can be achieved are needed by management. Making choices between programs and staff on the basis of their relative quality, and appropriately increasing or decreasing their expenditures is in keeping with the trade-off strategy described in the previous chapter. Without a firm objective basis for assessment, the outcome is likely to intensify the political atmosphere in an environment of a "zero sum game," with an optimization of service resources achieved only by chance.

The major way in which management can attain a firm and objective assessment on which to base a budgetary process that optimizes service resources and effective outcome is through some form of program evaluation. Program evaluation can provide evidence through which decisions about expenditures can be based on actual capability, thus paving the way for the application of the techniques described in this chapter to the human service organization. The next chapter explores the state of the art of program evaluation.

SUMMARY

In this chapter we explored the subject of the budgetary process in human service organizations. The budgetary process is one of the most important, ongoing series of decisions that the human service manager will confront. The major question surrounding the budgetary process is how can the resources be dispersed in such a manner as to be both efficient and to maximize the organization's service capability and service effectiveness? The traditional approach to budgeting, although minimizing organizational conflict, tends to move the organization toward co-optation of its resources and away from the fulfillment of the objectives of service management. Several approaches for reversing this trend were considered: Zero-Base Budgeting, PPBS, Cost-Benefit and Cost Effectiveness Analysis, and Management By Objectives. Each of these techniques represents a departure from the traditional approach and can serve to aid management in organizational optimization. Although the specific application of these approaches may vary with the characteristics of a given organization, their applicability should be carefully explored by management.

A departure from traditional budgeting is a difficult task for management for the maintenance of the organization is served through its perpetuation. However, the quality of care may depend on alternative patterns of fiscal distribution. The concept of service management cannot be realized unless this process is undertaken. Through this process, individual human service organizations can improve their service and social welfare as a whole can benefit.

NOTES

1. H. Glennester, *Social Service Budgets and Social Policy: British and American Experience* (New York: Barnes and Noble, 1976).
2. Alan Walter Steiss, *Public Budgeting and Management* (New York: D. C. Heath and Co., 1972).
3. Aaron Wildavsky, *The Politics of the Budgetary Process* (Boston: Brown, 1964).
4. Leonard Merewitz and Steven H. Sosnic, *The Budget's New Clothes* (Chicago: Rand McNally College Publishing, 1971).
5. This is an illustration of "incrementalism" or "muddling through." See Charles E. Lindblom, "The Science of Muddling Through," *Public Administration Review,* Spring 1959, pp. 214–229.
6. Saul Feldman, "Budgeting and Behavior in the Administration of Mental Health Services" (ed. Saul Feldman), (Springfield, Illinois: Charles C. Thomas, 1973).
7. For an informative presentation of this kind of budgetary reform see Allen Schick, "The Road to PPB: Stages of Budget Reform," *Public Administration Review,* vol. 26, no. 4, December 1966, pp. 243–258.
8. For a discussion of the difficulties of such an endeavor see Allen Schick, *Budget Innovation in the States* (Washington, D.C.: Brookings Institute, 1971), chap. 7, pp. 192–218.
9. See Logan Cheek, *Zero-Base Budgeting Comes of Age* (New York: American Management Association, 1977). Also, Peter A. Pyhrr, *Zero Base Budgeting* (New York: John Wiley, 1973).
10. Also much of the funding in human service organizations is often earmarked for specific purposes, making a true "zero base" impossible.
11. For a description of a zero base budget developed by a graduate school of social work as part of its annual budget request see Shirley M. Buttrick and Vernon Miller, "An Approach to Zero-Base Budgeting," *Administration in Social Work,* vol. 2, no. 1, Spring 1978.
12. For an excellent anthology on the concepts and application of PPBS see Fremont Lyden and E. Miller, eds., *Planning, Programming and Budgeting: A Systems Approach to Management* (Chicago: Markham, 1968).
13. Virginia Held, "PPBS Comes to Washington," *Public Interest,* vol. 22, no. 4, Summer 1966, pp. 102–115.
14. For an appraisal of PPBS see Leonard Merewitz et. al, op. cit.
15. For an anthology of the subject of cost benefit and effectiveness analysis which utilizes human service examples see M. G. Ken-

dall, ed., *Cost Benefit Analysis* (New York: American Elsevier Publishing Co., 1971); see also Leonard Merewitz et. al, op. cit.

16. For other examples see John A. Morris, Jr., and Martha N. Ozawa, "Benefit-Cost Analysis and the Social Service Agency: A Model for Decision-Making," *Administration in Social Work*, vol. 2, no. 3, Fall 1978, pp. 271–282; David W. Young and Brant Allen, "Benefit Cost Analysis in the Social Services—The Example of Adoption Reimbursement," *Social Service Review*, vol. 51, no. 2, pp. 249–264.

17. For standard works on MBO see Stephen Carroll and Henry Tosi, Jr., *Management by Objectives* (New York: MacMillan, 1973); George Morrissey, *Management by Objectives and Results* (Reading, Mass.: Addison-Wesley, 1970); George Odiorne, *Management by Objectives—A System of Managerial Leadership* (New York: Pitman, 1965).

18. Jong S. Jun, "A Symposium on Management by Objectives in the Public Sector," *Public Administration Review*, vol. 36, no. 2, 1976, p. 3.

19. Bruce H. DeWoolfson, Jr., "Public Sector MBO and PPBS: Cross Fertilization in Management Systems," *Public Administration Review*, vol. 35, no. 3, 1975, p. 391.

20. For an application to human service management see M. C. Raider, "A Social Service Model of Management by Objectives," *Social Casework*, October 1976, pp. 523–528.

21. For critiques of MBO see Harry Levison, "Management By Whose Objectives?" *Harvard Business Review*, vol. 31, no. 2, July-August 1970, pp. 125–134; Raider, M. E., "An Evaluation of Management by Objectives," *Social Casework*, vol. 56, no. 2, 1975, pp. 79–83.

Chapter NINE

Program Evaluation and Reporting in Human Service Organizations

Program Evaluation, unlike budgeting, is not often conducted as a regular task in human service organizations.[1] Some organizations, in fact, make no attempt to formally evaluate service. Most human service organizations, however, do maintain reporting systems that gather program data, but do not assess outcome.

Reporting systems exist because of the organization's external environment. Organizations are nearly always required to account for their funding to outside sources such as political bodies, private funding, and government offices. As a result of these external relationships, formal systems of reporting are devised. Sometimes elaborate schemes of accounting for program effort (to be distinguished from outcome) are conducted.[2] The number of client visits and the number of staff hours spent are calculated as are the number of miles driven, phone calls made, therapy hours conducted, and so forth. Client characteristics of various kinds are often assembled and analyzed. For example, demographic characteristics such as sex, age, race, geographical dispersal, marital status, and so on can often be gleaned from case records. Sophisticated analysis of this kind of data can often lead to such activities as comparing the frequency of certain demographic characteristics in the general population with those clients whom an agency is serving. It has been suggested that if those two measures are comparable, then an organization is successful in serving the population. For instance, if 20 percent of the population of a county is black, then it is felt that the agency should have about the same percentage of blacks in its clientele.

All of these activities do not evaluate outcome, and they

do not assess effectiveness. They do measure program effort or client characteristics, but they tell little about whether the organization is fulfilling need or reducing the incidence of a social problem. Yet it is outcome evaluation that can help management to bring about organizational optimization and prepare a budget effectively. Although reporting systems may be of benefit, they often tell about how *money* is spent, but not how *service* resources are utilized. Again, as in the traditional approach in budgeting, reporting systems serve the maintenance aspect of management rather than the service aspect.

In addition to the pressures on the organization to evolve reporting systems rather than evaluative systems, there are problems with the concept of program evaluation itself, which limit the frequency with which it is utilized in human service organizations.[3] One problem lies in the internal functioning of an organization. A program evaluation mechanism that truly assesses the quality of outcome would tend to disturb the organization's equilibrium as would a departure from the traditional budgetary approach. The organization's system of trade-offs is altered when the results of evaluation lead to the drawing of qualitative differences between program components and staff. If, for example, two programs are in a state of parity in terms of their standing in the organization, and a program evaluation demonstrates one of the programs superior in its achievement, political ramifications are inevitable. Therefore, like any significant innovation, the prospect of proper evaluation can constitute a threat, and, as a result, there is a certain resistance to the idea. From a political perspective, this reaction is very natural for both management personnel and clinical practitioners. From the managerial perspective, there is the ever-present need to protect the organization from the criticism of external groups, such as the general public, present and future clientele, political figures, funding sources, and so on. There is much to lose, then, from a program evaluation that reveals negative results. Of what benefit is it to the organization to allow the risk of negative results to cause external pressure, perhaps leading to problems such as a reduction in funding? A strong case can be made that a negative result can hamper the performance of the organization. It is a great political cost for the representative of a human service organization to acknowledge *externally* that anything less than official goal achievement is occurring *internally*.

Clinical practitioners can be resistant to program evaluation as well, because of what they view as a violation of professional autonomy, an intrusion into clinical relationships, and because, politically the individual practitioner stands to lose much from a negative evaluation.[4] From both the management and practitioner perspective, it would appear that a greater investment would lie in a positive evaluation or the avoidance of a negative evaluation, rather than an objective analysis, which would reveal precisely the quality of the organizational service product.

This probable resistance on the part of organizational members constitutes the greatest dilemma confronting program evaluation.[5] If the organization is characterized by the patterns of least effective service described in Part I, program evaluation is less likely to be welcomed than if the organization's pattern of functions tends toward an outcome of most effective service. If the quality of input is low, and if there is a high degree of goal displacement, decision making is noncongruent, and there is a high degree of authority subversion, program evaluation that assesses outcome is then unlikely to be accepted. Under conditions where a fairly high degree of optimization exists in the throughput, program evaluation poses less of a threat. It appears logical to surmise that, in general, those human service organizations that need program evaluation the most are the least likely to accept it, and organizations needing it the least are probably most likely to accept it.

For our purposes a distinction is drawn between evaluation and reporting systems. Reporting systems, as noted, usually describe aspects of a human service program or clientele in statistical or numerical terms. Although important for accountability and administrative purposes, reporting systems in themselves do not generally aid in organizational optimization and the enhancement of program quality. They serve to maintain the organization, not to improve the quality of service. Program evaluation is limited to *evaluation,* an objective assessment of outcome, coupled with some manner in which information can be utilized in the improvement of service delivery. Both are important to human service management and they can be used in concert to aid in the optimization of service resources. Reporting systems are far more involved with maintenance management than with service management. Let us first consider reporting systems.

REPORTING SYSTEMS

Both reporting systems and program-evaluation systems are designed to answer specific kinds of questions through a number of particular techniques. As noted, reporting systems are generally confined to a description of program components, clients, or organizational efforts, and are often needed to justify its funding to external services. Three important examples are accountability audits, administrative audits, and time and motion studies.

Accountability Audits

Accountability audits, according to Tripodi et al. are "used to review the consistency, dependability, and accuracy of records pertaining to program expenditures, allocations of resources, and processing of program beneficiaries, for the purpose of program accountability."[6] There are two kinds of accountability audits, which can be termed *general* and *social*. A *general accountability* audit is specifically concerned with the accuracy and efficiency of procedures and records that chart an organization's financial transactions. It is generally conducted by an accountant not only from the perspective of verification but also from that of improvement. Since financial accountability is basic to the survival of any organization, this is clearly a vital function. More human service programs have run into trouble because of inaccuracies in financial accountability than for low quality of outcome. Although this activity is within the purview of maintenance functions, it is the sine qua non of the successful achievement of management. A *social accountability* audit deals with the organization's relationship to its clientele, and constitutes a review of how the agency keeps records on the recipients of its service. It "involves an appraisal of the existence, reliability and accuracy of the program's procedures for reporting on those persons who have been processed through the program—from recruiting and program contact efforts to follow-up."[7] In short, this constitutes a review of the organization's data processing system. Such a system, if it is comprehensive and accurate, should yield a vast quantity of data on client numbers and characteristics. This data, though indicating nothing about service effectiveness, has a role in informing the management process in the pursuit of organizational optimization. Any management innovation that is designed to improve service, be it in the budgetary process, the authority structure, in organizational goals, or any other area, requires documentation and support. It is from the data system that some aspects of this documentation must come. Hence social auditing that assesses this client data system is an important organizational task.

Administrative Audits

A second example of a reporting system is what is termed the *administrative audit*. This audit assesses organizational aspects such as personnel practices, division of duties and responsibilities, kinds of activities in which people are engaged, patterns of work, and program procedures and policies, all of which are measured against some outside standard. This standard may be bureaucratic as in the case when certain funding guidelines must be followed. For example, a program for alcoholism that involves a halfway house may require a building of a specified size and particular personnel who must perform specified tasks. Such external standards do not, unfortunately, call for outcome measures. Obtaining information for administrative audits is more difficult than it is for accountability audits. Policy and procedure manuals, personnel handbooks, minutes of meetings, and organizational charts, combined with staff interviews, can sometimes provide an accurate picture. Again, this does not indicate the effectiveness of the outcome, but rather the existence of activities.

Time and Motion Studies

A final example of a reporting system is the time and motion study, which, as noted previously, derives from the Frederick Taylor Machine School of Management of the early part of the century. The original concept was that by measuring the individual motions invested by workers in each step of a project, management could discern the most efficient way to perform each activity and establish procedures of work based on this information. Today, the term refers to a measurement of the time devoted to each activity on the part of organizational members. This can provide an overall breakdown of the effort invested in a program and indicate precisely which activities have priority and which do not, based on the actual time invested. The organization's operative goals can be ascertained in this way.

Each of these reporting systems, accountability audit, both general and social, administrative audit, and time and motion describe *what* the organization is doing.[8] They describe effort in the area of an organization's financial transactions; records of clients; overall plans of procedures, functioning, and activities; and the amount of time devoted to these activities. All of these approaches and techniques are important in human service organizations. For the most part, they relate to the maintenance function in that they concern external funding and accountability or internal efficiency. They can, however, provide the basis for actual program evaluation that can lead most directly to a pursuit of organizational optimization.

PROGRAM EVALUATION

Program evaluation can be defined as follows:

> Evaluation (1) assesses the *effectiveness* of an ongoing program in achieving its objectives; (2) relies on the principles of research design to distinguish a program's effects from those of other forces working in the community; and (3) aims at program improvement through a modification of current operational practices.[9]

The literature of program evaluation is by no means uniform in defining evaluation, or in describing its functions. Aspects of reporting are sometimes included within the rubric of evaluation. For example, Paul[10] proposes three major categories for evaluation; assessment of effort, assessment of effect, and assessment of process. Assessment of effort is obtained from reporting; it describes what activities are being performed. Assessment of effect focuses on the results that those activities are designed to achieve. Assessment of process is concerned with how the results are achieved. Clearly, the latter is important if program improvement is to occur. A further categorization has been proposed by Suchman who indicates five categories of evaluation: effort, performance, adequacy of performance, efficiency, and process. Effort in this case has the same meaning as in Paul's definition. Performance constitutes an analysis of the results of effort and, as Suchman points out, requires a clear statement of the objectives that the effort or activities are designed to achieve. Adequacy of performance measures the performance against the incidence of the specific social problem that a program is attempting to alleviate. As Suchman notes, "a program of intensive psychotherapy for a small group of mentally ill individuals may show highly effective results, but as a public health measure prove thoroughly inadequate to meet the problem of mental illness in an entire community." Efficiency is defined as an analysis of alternative ways of achieving the same level of performance. This would involve cost-benefit analysis as described in the previous chapter. Here maintenance and service functions are integrated, as the pursuit of efficiency does not hinder the quality of program outcome. Finally, process is again an assessment of what factors in the organization account for the particular level of outcome that is attained. Other definitions and concepts stress different aspects of evaluation, some of which include more components of reporting systems than others.[11] Others have the additional step of evaluating the process of evaluation mostly with pessimistic results:

> The record is hardly spectacular when one takes a cold clear look at just how useful and how cost effective program evaluation has been for improving service programs and delivery sys-

tems. Just as most of those responsible for human service programs have been unable to demonstrate success in improving the lot of clients, most of the researchers who evaluate programs can show little impact on program quality.[12]

In general, the tasks of evaluation are far more difficult than those of reporting. The kind of opposition, as has been noted, can be far more severe. One important factor stressed by many authors is the need for concern about the organizational context on the part of evaluators. Although techniques exist for precise measurement, it is important to apply these techniques with the necessary attention to fit the organizational situation. Such factors as organizational size, kind of staff, nature of the goals and techniques, organizational history, stage of development of its programs, and other factors play an important role in determining the method of evaluation. The following evaluation approaches need to be considered in this context.

Experimental Designs

Most of the techniques for program evaluation have been adopted from the methodologies of social science. The most traditional approach to evaluation is a classic experimental design. A group of clients who are recipients of service are measured against a control group, who share important characteristics demographically and in terms of the relevant social problem, but who are not service recipients. Questioning, and/or itemizing interviews can be utilized in order to determine the differences between the groups. Quantitative analysis, particularly tests of significance, can indicate whether differences between the groups are significant and, at least in theory, if the samples are valid and the variables isolated and controlled, these differences can be attributed to the intervention of the service. There are many drawbacks to the use of experimental designs, the most important of which involve ethical considerations. Most practitioners in the human services would probably be opposed to denying services to a control group for the sake of an experimental design and justifiably so.

Modification of experimental designs are possible and useful. Tripodi et al. suggest two:

1. A group that is similar to the experimental group on many relevant variables is selected after the experimental group has received program intervention.
2. A group which is similar to the experimental group but receives less frequent program efforts rather than no program efforts.[13]

The experimental design can produce the most reliable data to aid management in performing its major functions. The establishment and implementation of a true experiment is highly difficult, however, in most human service organizational situations.

Before-After Studies

A second approach to program evaluation is a before-and-after study. This approach requires no control group. A questionnaire or other appropriate instrument can be administered at the point where service is initiated and also at periodic points throughout the duration of service. In this way, programs can be measured. The appropriate time interval and the nature of the instrument are flexible and dependent to a great extent on the nature of the program and the clientele. Before-and-after studies are easier to initiate than experimental studies and can prove nearly as beneficial in terms of the data obtained.

Surveys

The survey technique involves selecting a sample of a given population and administering a questionnaire in order to learn certain characteristics, attitudes, and similar data. A survey of a community to evaluate the results of a public education program might indicate the change in attitude or knowledge about a given social problem or service, and a survey of a recipient population before, during, and after a specific program is implemented would indicate the success of that program.[14] Surveys can be expensive, but they can be extremely useful in specific instances. Often a quick telephone random sample can reveal feedback to the organization that can be of use in planning or other endeavors.

Techniques for evaluation, such as experimental designs, before-and-after studies, surveys, and the like are research oriented approaches designed to achieve the most reliable data from a quantifiable and scientific perspective. Other evaluative activities, such as supervision, promotion, and other personnel matters, often contain evaluation of performance as well as outcome, although sometimes this can assume an almost intuitive form.[15] Any kind of evaluation is greatly facilitated when technology is more highly developed, and when the goals and outcome are tangible. Evaluation, for example, of a therapeutic mental health process is more difficult than alcoholism treatment in which criteria can be established, such as no drinking for a specified amount of time, or in manpower training services, when a criterion of success can be a full-time job at or above the minimum wage within six months of service completion.

On-Going Evaluation: Some General Guidelines

Often, in the context of a given human service organization, it is impossible to conduct any formalized evaluation. There may be a lack of funds, interest, or support. Management, however, needs to continue to evaluate and monitor the activities of a human service organization with regard to how its functioning affects the patterns of its service provision. Management must be on guard against the emergence of the patterns dysfunctional to service achievement described in Part I.

Consider decision making, for example. The ability to evaluate patterns of organizational decision making is an organizational skill. It requires the ability to identify the elements of decision making, understand their interaction, and help guide them toward congruence. Decisions, then, need to be monitored and evaluated by the following criteria.

1. Does the decision actually serve the capability of the organization? Does it help maximize the application of technology?
2. Does the decision ultimately conform to a set of guiding values or philosophies on which there is common agreement?
3. Are the appropriate political elements calculated to ensure the success or effectiveness of the decision? In short, do the political elements serve as a means to the achievement of service capability?

Consideration of these questions is often overlooked in organizational decision making and an almost ritualistic process of decision making may prevail in very important areas that affect the quality of service. The ongoing application of these and similar questions to specific decisions will help the organization to guard against non-congruence between political, value, and capability elements that can contribute to organizational co-optation. The manner and mechanism in which these questions are raised will vary with the level and style of management; what is vital is that the substance of the questions be included, as they often are not, in the process by which the organization's decisions are made, particularly when they affect the quality of service.

In addition to monitoring decisions in specific limited domains, some in management have executive-level responsibility in which the organization as a whole represents their focal domain. In this case, the organization's overall *patterns* of decision making become a major concern. Congruence in decision-making patterns *over time* is a vital objective for executive management. In addition to the previous criteria, then, other questions gain importance.

1. Does noncongruence in decision making emanate equally from all organizational components? Or is noncongruence likely to come from a specific component of an organization? Are there any discernible patterns regarding specified kinds of issues to reflect particular patterns of noncongruency or congruency?
2. Do specific personnel, such as professionals, tend consis-

tently to represent or advocate one element of decision making (value, political) more than the others? Does this advocacy relate to the hierarchy of the organization, with those nearer the "top," for example, advocating political, and those lower in the hierarchy advocating value or capability?

3. What changes of procedures involving the organizational structure can aid in achieving a higher degree of congruence in organizational decision making?

The pursuit of this evaluative function should involve coordination between all levels of management, be it executive, supervisory, middle management, line, or staff. Congruent decisions at the supervisory level, for example, clearly relate to the attempt at the executive level to enhance overall patterns of congruence. This is no easy task, but the pursuit of congruence in decision making can have a profound and lasting effect on helping the organization optimize its service capability.

Management must also continuously assess organizational goals. As in the case of the decision-making task, most organizational members with managerial responsibility, both staff and line, will perform in a limited organizational domain. Within this domain, a variety of activities will be performed by a variety of people on a day-to-day basis. Each of these activities ultimately serves to accomplish a particular end. This end is either irrelevant to the organization's official goals, helps in their achievement, or is counterproductive. These activities need to be monitored to determine the ultimate objective and purpose that they serve. This can prove a complex endeavor since in an organizational context a series of means may serve one end, or ends, and means may link to form chains of activity where a means serves a particular end that in turn, becomes a means to another end, and so on. Despite these complexities, this function is a necessity if organizational optimization is to be enhanced.

Each activity, therefore, needs to be assessed and monitored by means of the following:

1. Can an operative goal be discerned for each activity?
2. What is the nature of the operative goal which the activity is designed to achieve; or is, in fact, achieving?

3. Does the activity, to any degree, help to realize any significant aspect of the organization's official goals?

Executive-level management must be concerned with individual activities as well, but must also consider the patterns that the goals assume for the organization as a whole. In addition to the foregoing criteria, other questions thus gain importance:

1. Do official goals permeate the organization and its internal communication? Is there an effort, or policy, on the part of key members of the organization to communicate and convey these official goals?
2. Are official goals measured in a systematic way? Is organizational feedback and assessment based on official goal achievement?
3. How does goal displacement occur? Is it strongly related to decision making? To authority? Is it to the advantage of a particular segment of the organization to maintain goal displacement? Can goal displacement be linked consistently with a specific organizational component? A specific kind of personnel, such as professionals, or administration? Can it be linked with relative position in the hierarchy?

The monitoring of both individual activities and overall activities in the context of the ultimate goals they serve needs to be systematically pursued. As in the case of decision making, the execution of this evaluative function must be coordinated between all levels of management. A decrease in goal displacement in one component of the organization will affect the pursuit of goals in others. Because this function is difficult, it is often ignored in human service organizations. The result is a high degree of co-optation, and a decrease in service quality.

The exercise of authority and the gaining of compliance occurs at all levels of an organization; this exercise can be very obvious and overt, or it can be subtle and informal. Therefore, the nature of authority relationships are often difficult to ascertain, yet they are vital to the evolution of the organization's product and can contribute significantly to optimization or co-optation.

In each organizational component, where such managerial responsibility is present, a great deal of authority interaction occurs on a daily basis. In order to execute this management task the nature of authority needs to be continuously analyzed and assessed on the basis of how its exercise affects service outcome. The following criteria are important:

1. Can the act of authority and the particular authority-compliance relationship be clearly discerned on the basis of hierarchical position and professional ability? Do the formal rules and regulations of the organization with respect to position and authority cause movement in a specific direction?
2. Does hierarchical position or professional expertise dominate? How does this affect task performance?
3. Does the exercise of authority enhance or hinder the application of technology? Is technological input encouraged on the part of subordinates?
4. What can be done to maximize ability as the basis for authority?

For management at the executive level, overall patterns of organizational structures of authority are the focus. In addition to the foregoing criteria, other considerations include:

1. Is the relationship of position and expertise different at different levels of the organization?
2. Do different kinds of personnel exhibit different patterns of authority?
3. Does the manner in which executive-level management utilizes authority set a tone for the organization as a whole? If so, what is the nature of that tone?

The assessment of authority on this basis and the facilitation of movement toward professional ability can contribute significantly to optimization. This may ultimately involve staff changes and changes in rules and regulations governing authority. Obviously, the process is a demanding one, because authority is often jealously guarded. Yet, like noncongruence in decision making, and goal displacement, authority subversion can be very detrimental to the general interaction between staff in an organization. This affects both the atmosphere that surrounds the rendering of human service, and the outcome of that service.

Whatever the service involved and the kind of evaluation utilized, management must initiate any program evaluation mechanism with great caution. The following principles should be remembered.

1. *Evaluation cannot be imposed by management.* As has been noted, evaluation can be a potentially threatening prospect to the staff of a human service organization.[16] Therefore, any plan to utilize program evaluation must involve the full participation of key members of staff who represent all affected components of the organization. Staff need to play a role in all decisions about the evaluation including what aspect of the program will be evaluated on what criteria, how the evaluation will be administered, how will the outcome be utilized, and so forth.[17] Without such participation, the natural resistance to evaluation will most likely neutralize any improvement in organizational optimization on the part of management.

2. *Evaluation should be initiated on a limited basis.* In a human service organization that has had little or no history of actual evaluation, the evaluative mechanism should begin by concentrating on one limited component of the organization. This might involve one or many programs, a ward, a service unit, a service team, or any other component that is appropriate to the size and status of the organization.[18] The implications of choosing a single component within an organization are highly significant, and the choice needs to be made with care. But a more comprehensive, inclusive approach will, in most instances, cause far too much disturbance in an organization, and the results will be of less value.

3. *Evaluation should be presented in the context of official goal achievement.* Because of the potentially divisive nature of program evaluation, management should present it in the context of official goal achievement and optimization. Any potentially divisive or threatening aspects need to be minimized, and values and objectives about service that are, or hopefully are,

held by organizational members need to be stressed. Management should not assume that evaluation speaks for itself in terms of its importance for service improvement and, as such, will gain ready acceptance.

4. *Evaluation should be attempted with full cognizance of the trade-offs involved.* If program evaluation is established in the context of too great a cost for certain factions of an organization, severe problems can result. There must be a possible payoff or else the results of the evaluation may prove harmful rather than helpful because political equilibrium will be upset. The initiation and implementation must be conducted with this in mind.

One important way in which the results of evaluation can be utilized in optimizing the service resources of the organization is through staff development. If program evaluation mechanisms are developed and implemented with staff participation, staff development is an important by-product. Yet more formalized staff development needs to be an outgrowth of evaluation as well. This subject is considered in the next chapter.

SUMMARY

Program evaluation is the key to organizational optimization and to its achievement through such activities as budgeting. Without some kind of objective assessment of outcome, optimization becomes an almost impossible task. There are many obstacles to the successful application of program evaluation, including the fear of external political costs that might be the result of negative evaluation, and resistance from members of the organization. As a result, reporting systems that describe and measure program effort are far more prevalent in human service organizations than program evaluation which assesses outcome, illustrating another imbalance between maintenance and service management.

Examples of reporting systems include accountability audits, administrative audits, and time and motion studies. Examples of evaluative techniques include experimental designs, before and after studies, and surveys. An ongoing assessment by management of patterns of decision making, goals, and authority can also be utilized as an evaluative mechanism. Whatever evaluative approach is adopted, several factors should be kept in mind: evaluation cannot be imposed by management; evaluation should be initiated on a limited basis; evaluation should be presented in the context of official goal achievement; and evaluation should be attempted with full cognizance of the trade-offs involved.

Service management can have only very limited impact without some kind of program evaluation. The improvement of the quality of care requires ongoing assessment. If such quality is to be improved, program evaluation cannot be confused with reporting systems, and a better balance must be struck between evaluation and reporting.

NOTES

1. See, for example, Carol Weiss, "Overview," in Carol Weiss, ed., *Evaluating Action Programs* (Boston: Allyn and Bacon, 1972), pp. 1–29.
2. See, for example, H. R. Catherwood, "A Management Information System for Social Services," *Public Welfare*, vol. 32, no. 3, 1974, pp. 54–61.
3. Tony Tripodi et. al, *Differential Social Program Evaluation* (Hasca, Illinois: F. E. Peacock Publishers, Inc., 1978), pp. 1–3.
4. Morris Fritz Mayer, "Program Evaluation as part of Clinical Practice: An Administrator's Position," *Child Welfare*, vol. 54, no. 6, p. 381.
5. Murray B. Meld, "The Politics of Evaluation of Social Programs," *Social Work*, vol. 19, no. 4, July 1974, pp. 448–456.
6. Tony Tripodi, Phillip Fellin, and Irwin Epstein, *Social Program Evaluation Guidelines for Health, Education, and Welfare Administrators* (Itasca, Illinois: F. E. Peacock Publishers, Inc., 1971), p. 63.
7. Ibid., p. 65.
8. For a more detailed discussion see Tony Tripodi et al., *Differential Social Program Evaluation*, chapter 4.
9. Joseph Wholey et al., *Federal Evaluation Policy* (Urban Institute: Washington, D.C., 1969), p. 24.
10. Edward Suchman, *Evaluation Research: Principles and Practice in Public Service and Social Action Programs* (New York: Russell Sage, 1967), chapter 3.
11. Marilyn A. Biggerstaff, "The Administrator and Social Agency

Evaluation," *Administration in Social Work,* vol. 3, no. 2, pp. 71–78; Melvin N. Brenner, "The Quest for Viable Research in Social Services: Development of the Ministudy," *Social Service Review,* Sept. 1976, pp. 462–444; Francis G. Caro, ed., *Readings in Evaluation Research* (New York: Russell Sage Foundation, 1971); Robert D. Coursey et al., *Program Evaluation for Mental Health: Methods, Strategies, and Participants* (New York: Grune and Stratton, 1977); I. Epstein and Tony Tripodi, *Research Techniques for Program Planning, Monitoring, and Evaluation* (New York: Columbia University Press, 1977): J. L. Franklin and J. H. Thrasher, *An Introduction to Program Evaluation* (New York: John Wiley and Sons, 1976); Perry Levinson, "Evaluation of Social Welfare Programs: Two Research Models," *Welfare in Review,* vol. 4, no. 10, 1966, pp. 5–12; Peter H. Rossi and Walter Williams, eds., *Evaluating Social Programs: Theory, Practice, and Politics* (New York: Seminar Press, 1972); Carol H. Weiss, "Alternative Models of Program Evaluation," *Social Work,* vol. 19, no. 6, 1974, pp. 675–681.

12. Carol H. Weiss, "Alternative Models of Program Evaluation," *Social Work,* vol. 19, no. 6, 1974, pp. 675–681.

13. Tony Tripodi, *Social Program Evaluation Guidelines,* p. 87.

14. Eaton, Joseph, "Symbolic and Substantive Evaluation Research," *Administrative Science Quarterly,* vol. 6, no. 2, 1967, pp. 427–442.

15. This will be considered in more detail in the following chapter.

16. Norman Blonney and Lawrence A. Streicher, "Time-Cost Data in Agency Administration Efficiency Controls in Family and Children's Service," *Social Work,* vol. 15, no. 3, October 1970, pp. 23–31.

17. Ultimately, clinical staff should be conducting evaluation as part of practice. See Walter Hudson, "Elementary Techniques for Assessing Single-Client/Single-Worker Interventions," *Social Service Review,* vol. 51, no. 2, June 1978, pp. 315–326; M. F. Mayer, "Program Evaluation," pp. 379–394.

18. J. David Hawkins and Donald Sloma, "Recognizing the Organizational Context: A Strategy for Evaluation Research," *Administration in Social Work,* vol. 2, no. 3, Fall 1978, pp. 283–294.

Chapter TEN

Staff Development in Human Service Organizations

Unlike the subject of program evaluation, there is little literature on staff development in the field of human services in which clear-cut, formalized techniques have been developed.[1] Like evaluation, however, staff development is rarely pursued on an organized and purposive basis in most human service organizations.[2] Staff development can be defined as those purposive activities that are designed to increase the knowledge and skill of those who are directly responsible for the provision of an organization's service product. Hence, the goal of staff development is to increase the service resources through increasing the possession of technology of service practitioners. Staff development can encompass a wide variety of activities including performance appraisal, continuing education, lectures, conferences, seminars, supervisory relationships, and numerous interorganizational relationships, which allow staff to enhance their possession of human service technology and skills.

SERVICE AND MAINTENANCE MANAGEMENT IN STAFF DEVELOPMENT

As with the other functions of management, the tasks of maintenance may obscure the service benefits to be derived from staff development. The manner in which the desirable opportunities in staff development are distributed may have little to do with correcting organizational co-optation. For example, the opportunity to participate in continuing education (a further degree, a series of courses, and the like) may be granted on the basis of political trade-offs. The staff member who desires continuing education (and the leave of absence that may go with it) may be owed something, may be on good terms with those who are making decisions, or perhaps has "something coming" because he or she may never have participated in anything similar or has been at the agency longer than anyone else. In short, staff development opportunities may be "spread around" so that everyone gets something, similar in concept to the traditional budget approach that was discussed in Chapter Eight. In other instances, politics may play a smaller role and staff development may be distributed over time merely to those who uncover an opportunity for themselves, or "who ask first." In this way, management often fails to make full use of staff development as a tool to help bring about organizational optimization.

Staff development entails more than increasing the capacities of current staff, but is concerned, as well, with recruiting new staff who possess appropriate capabilities that are important to the success of the organization. The tasks of maintenance management involve filling vacancies, which is necessary for the survival of the organization.[3] Sometimes the process of attracting, interviewing, and evaluating candidates results in a decision that enhances the organization's capabilities, and sometimes the process can be a more ritualistic one: a slot that requires specific qualifications needs to be filled. Someone knows someone who "fits" the slot and that person is hired. Politics, can also play a role and can render irrelevant the opportunity for technological improvement: someone must be hired because a favor is owed as a result of a previous trade-off. Or consider the following possibility: a candidate may be under consideration to fill a vacant position. When he or she is interviewed by the staff, it becomes apparent that he or she possesses a level of technological knowledge and skill that surpasses many of those currently on the staff. From a service perspective, the person clearly would add to the organization's effectiveness. Will this candidate be hired? To answer this question, the trade-offs of the staff members involved would have to be assessed. Would bringing a person with superior credentials into the organization cost anyone too much in terms of his or her own position? Would the rewards and the profits be greater if a person of lower caliber were hired? If this were true, some organizational members might discover a reason for finding fault with the candidate without revealing their true motivation. As in traditional budgeting and reporting systems, maintenance considerations can cause an imbalance in the important area of staff development. This pitfall must be avoided if staff development can provide an important opportunity for management to contribute significantly to service effectiveness.

STAFF DEVELOPMENT AND ORGANIZATIONAL OPTIMIZATION

In the last analysis, staff development from the perspective of service management deals with the quality of an organization's service resources. Management then can deal directly with the input component of the framework provided in Part I. As the propositions of Chapter Six indicate, the whole pattern of service effectiveness rests on the quality of the input. The greater the quality of the service resources, the less likely is the occurrence of goal displacement, authority subversion, and noncongruent decision making. Staff development, then, can provide service management with a significant opportunity to improve the organization's overall pattern of service.

The pitfalls mentioned that can surround staff development can be eliminated through a purposive, goal-directed staff development system, which is aimed at the weaknesses of the organization and is designed to alleviate these weaknesses. *Staff development is inextricably linked to overall program evaluation,* and should not be viewed in isolation by management.[4] In essence, *staff development should be designed to ameliorate those weaknesses in the organization that are uncovered by program evaluation.* If the program evaluation mechanism merely evaluates the effectiveness of service, but does not demonstrate those aspects of the program that require improvement, it is of limited use. Any staff development program needs to focus on specific areas in which individual effort combined with group effort can serve to improve a program component. In this way, staff development can play a major role in increasing the effectiveness of the service product. It can achieve this in both the input and in the throughput. In a very real sense, purposive staff development can increase the service resources available to the organization. Under normal conditions the *state* of the human service technology will not be altered, but possession of such technology on the part of practitioners will be increased if staff development is successful. Therefore, the quality of the input is enhanced, and this has specific kinds of effects in the throughput.

In the absence of a system of program evaluation that can detect weakness in the organization's patterns of service, staff development needs to be pursued as systematically as possible. It must not be episodic but should reflect pursuit of official goals. Management must therefore understand the nature of the technology utilized in an organization and how that technology interrelates with the organizational structure and personnel. The questions concerning the possession of technology, which were presented in Chapter 2 are relevant here as well.

1. Is there a profession involved in the technology? Do the formal educational credentials relate to a significant degree to the actual carrying out of tasks? Does the profession have different gradation levels and do these levels relate significantly to the possession of ability?
2. Can the degree to which the technology is possessed be determined and evaluated? Are standards of assessment part of the profession? Is an assessment on the level of training and the nature of the professional background available?
3. To what extent does the technology lend itself to mutually exclusive division and specialization that can be appropriate to organizational tasks and roles? Does the given human service organization accurately reflect the true technological divisions and specializations?[5]

In order to utilize staff development to bring about organizational optimization, the human service manager must be aware of the manner in which technology is being utilized in the organization in terms of how tasks are distributed, roles assumed, and activities carried out. Some kind of performance appraisal is necessary, then, for staff development to be effective. As noted in the previous chapter, performance appraisal of staff is a very difficult activity for management to initiate because of the implicit threat that is present,[6] and often program evaluation is limited to an assessment of overall programs or components rather than of individual staff. Yet in the final analysis, the actual program effectiveness does evolve from what occurs between client and worker, and hence the individual performance of staff is of vital importance. Traditionally, such individual staff appraisal is an aspect of the supervisory function.[7] In most human service organizations, a certain number of staff are assigned to a supervisor, usually a more experienced practitioner, whose task is to guide their clinical performance.[8] Often there is a periodic meeting in which cases are reviewed, suggestions for improvement made, and this becomes an ongoing situation. Yet as Turem notes, perhaps a bit sarcastically, "One rarely hears of the dismissal of a relatively nice person . . . who met the standards of dress, who was cooperative with colleagues, who was on the job when expected, but whose services did not seem to do anyone any good."[9] Sarcastic as this may appear, this situation often reflects reality, because any negative assessment of staff is generally viewed in the context of being punitive rather than as staff development. This norm is probably present in many human service organizations, because negative performance appraisals of staff are often perceived as being based on personality considerations, value choice, or political machinations, rather than upon previously agreed to, standardized, professional criteria. The opportunity for organizational optimization, through the supervisory structure, is often lost to the organization.

One possibility for improving technological possession and its application among staff is to revolve roles and tasks to the maximum extent that is possible in a given organization. This has two possible payoffs for the organization. First, the work of a practitioner who deals with only one kind of client and social problem can become ritualized; technological insight and creativity can become stifled. Working in other program areas can aid the investment and satisfaction of the practitioner in his or her work. Clearly, this would be voluntary on the part of practitioners. Second, such alteration of tasks can have a positive influence on the supervisory structure of an organization. A practitioner, therefore, could be supervised by one person when he or she is working with one kind of client and a different person with a different kind of client. The basis of supervision becomes centered more on the type of client than on the hierarchical relationship between the two staff members. They are relating not because one is supervisor and the other is subordinate but rather because the client has a particular kind of problem. This might tend to reduce organizational co-optation by placing authority relationships more on the basis of professional ability, thereby decreasing authority subversion. In short, the *technology* and its components and requirements should govern formal relationships between staff, and not hierarchical and ritualistic considerations. The more this can be accomplished by management, the more actual staff development can be achieved.

In addition to the alteration of staff internally in order to optimize resources and develop technology, another important area of staff development relates to the organization's need for an ongoing awareness of and response to technologically new developments in the relevant area of human service endeavor, and the application of these developments to the functioning of the organization. Several questions are relevant for management:

1. Where in the social welfare institution are technological developments occurring? What kind of formal and informal linkages can be established with these organizations?
2. Is the organization generally resistant or amenable to new technological input? What elements in the organization can be utilized in support of new input?

This task requires the translation of technological issues and developments in the field to a specific organizational context in order to enhance service capability. The activities involved are varied, ranging from the preparation of systems of organized knowledge about human service technology and the formal channeling of this knowledge to the relevant organizational components, to the utilization of such a system in staff recruiting and development. In short, it is the process by which the organization understands, assesses, and "keeps up with the field." In the first six chapters, great emphasis was placed on the state of the service resources and their relationship to every factor of the through-put and output. The contribution of service resources to the effectiveness of service received a great deal of attention. The state of technology, however, may increase and become more highly developed without the fruits of that development ever reaching a particular human service organization, and thereby aiding its capability.

This endeavor may appear to be a natural enterprise, but human service organizations often function as a "closed system" with little change in established ways of performing service tasks and where technological advancements and modifications, developed externally to the organization, do not find a formalized, legitimized, and organized channel into the functioning of the organization, but rather remain serendipitous and informal, at best. Therefore, knowledge and techniques that could improve the service product of an organization remain excluded from the organization's delivery of service.[10]

If the service effectiveness of a human service organization is to be enhanced, the organization must make optimal use of the technology that is available to it. In order to achieve this, the enhancement of service capability must not be limited to a few individual practitioners who may, on their own initiative, utilize new technological input, but should be structured as a formal input into the organization in such a way as to improve the overall service capability.[11] The opportunities for bringing new technological developments into the organization and the opportunities for staff to obtain new technology through education need to be distributed on the basis of how they can serve this end rather than upon the political trade-offs at the given time. What is needed in the fulfillment of this human service management function, then, is a thorough knowledge of the technology and its possession, its strength and limitations, where it can be more developed and where it remains uncertain, how it relates directly to the organizational structure in terms of service delivery, and where in this structure additional technology can best be maximized. Through the ongoing execution of this function, continuous input can help prevent the organization from functioning in a manner that is closed to technological modification and innovation. The ultimate effect of this is the improvement in the quality of service outcome.

An additional aspect to staff development, which involves something more intangible than what has been discussed thus far, must be considered. It relates to the atmosphere and the morale of a human service organization. In any organization, but particularly a human service organization, morale is important to the organization's product.[12] Because the results of the human services are often themselves intangible, a sense of purpose and achievement is often difficult to sustain. The underdevelopment of the technology and the often precarious nature of an agency's survival can contribute to such a feeling. This kind of morale problem can be devastating to organizational optimization. As discussed in Chapter Seven, management needs to convey and often reaffirm a sense of purpose through the communication of the value of official goal achievement. This can have a positive effect on staff development.

A low-level investment in the organization and a ritualistic compliance to its structure and procedure detracts from the development and use of technological capabilities.[13] The use and encouragement of expressive kinds of interaction can be of help in this process. Such expressive relationships between people who are working for a shared purpose are as important to staff development as in-service training, continuing education, and the like.[14] This is particularly true in human service organizations where technology is less developed. In these cases, the kinds of formal staff development programs to which we have referred carry less impact on organizational optimization, because there is less basic technology upon which to draw and to improve. In these cases particularly, intangibles such as morale, positive attitude and atmosphere can contribute to the effectiveness of service.

Staff development, then, encourages a wide variety of activities, all of which can contribute to increasing service effectiveness. Some of these activities occur as a matter of course in an organization such as hiring and firing, personnel appraisal, and supervisory relations. In the daily operation of the organization, these activities can often become dominated by maintenance, however, and the opportunities for staff development can be lost. Hiring and firing, personnel appraisal, and supervisory relationships will always occur, but will the outcome serve to enhance organizational optimization, or will it merely serve to maintain the organization or the status, position or advantage of some of its members? Other staff development opportunities involve the bringing of innovative technology into the organization, such as in-service training or continuing education. The degree to which this can be achieved will depend on the resources available. It is important that management closely monitor their implementation so as to ensure that the content of these programs closely matches specific opportunities for organizational optimization. With both kinds of activities, the efforts need to be carefully organized and coordinated, so that staff development becomes an integrated aspect of the organizational structure. It needs to be a *planned* function of the organization with carefully set goals. Since the enhancement of the actual service resources is the objective, staff development cannot be left to informality and chance.

SUMMARY

Staff development can provide management with the opportunities to improve the quality of service resources of a human service organization, thereby profoundly affecting its patterns of service effectiveness. A systematic program of staff development, based not upon maintaining political trade-offs but upon improving technological capability, is a task of service management. The manager must understand the nature of the human service technology and its relationship to the structure of the organization, its roles, and its norms. Staff development can be achieved in many ways: through internal restructuring, such as the revolving of tasks and supervisory structures, and by suffusing the organization with a variety of technological innovation and information drawn through formalized linkages to other organizations. In-service training, continuing education, and other kinds of opportunities are available. Finally, staff can be developed and technology can be maximized through the more intangible task of providing the organization with a sense of purpose and morale. Such expressive leadership can be a vital factor in staff development.

Staff development is an important function of human service management, because it can serve to enhance service resources—the input. If staff development in a human service organization is disorganized, or oriented toward maintenance, an important opportunity for management to improve optimization and the quality of service is lost. As in traditional budgeting and the lack of program evaluation, this is often the case. Our concept of service management indicates a perspective for staff development that can help alter this.

NOTES

1. For general works in the field see Armand Lauffer, *Doing Continuing Education and Staff Development* (New York: McGraw Hill, 1978); Carol H. Meyer, *Staff Development in Public Welfare Agencies* (New York: Columbia, 1966); Dolores B. Reid and Merle E. Springer, "The Formulation and Integration of a Staff Development Program in a Public Child Welfare Agency," *Public Welfare*, vol. 28, no. 3, 1970, pp. 291–296; S. Weber, "Goals for Staff Development," *Public Welfare*, vol. 29, no. 2, 1971, pp. 255–261; Carol H. Weiss, "Evaluation of Staff Training Programs," *Welfare in Review*, vol. 3, no. 3, March 1965, pp. 11–17.
2. E. Tropp, "Expectation, Performance and Accountability," *Social Work*, vol. 19, no. 2, 1974, pp. 139–145.
3. Aden Melzer and Marie Haug, "Staff Development and Differential Recruitment," *Social Work*, vol. 19, no. 2, 1974, pp. 467–476.
4. Carol H. Weiss, "Evaluation of Staff Training Programs." *Welfare in Review*, 3(3), March, 1965, 11–17.
5. Walter E. Beck, "Agency Structure Related to the Use of Staff," *Social Casework*, vol. 50, no. 3, June 1969, pp. 341–346.
6. Charles Levy, "The Ethics of Supervision," *Social Work*, vol. 18, no. 2, March 1973, pp. 14–21.
7. Kenneth W. Wetson, "Differential Supervision," *Social Work*, vol. 18, no. 6, pp. 80–88.
8. Alfred Kadushin, "Supervisor-Supervisee: A Survey," *Social Work*, vol. 19, no. 3, May 1974, pp. 288–297.
9. Jerry S. Turem, "The Call for a Management Stance," *Social Work*, vol. 19, no. 5, 1974, p. 622.
10. Robert Rothman and R. Perucci, "Organizational Careers and Professional Expertise," *Administrative Science Quarterly*, vol. 15, no. 2, 1970, pp. 282–294.
11. Gertrude Leyendecker, "A Comprehensive Staff Development

Program," *Social Casework,* vol. 52, no. 3, December 1965, pp. 607–613.

12. A. R. Martin, "Morale and Productivity: A Review of the Literature," *Public Personnel Review,* vol. 30, no. 1, pp. 42–45.

13. Alaya Pines and Ditsa Kaffrey, "Occupational Tedium in the Social Services," *Social Work,* vol. 23, no. 6, November 1978.

14. See Frederick Herzburg, *Work and the Nature of Man* (Cleveland: World Publishing, 1966), and Abraham Maslow, *Motivation and Personality* (New York: Harper & Row, 1954).

Chapter ELEVEN

Community Relations in Human Service Organizations

Every human service organization is surrounded by a community to which it must respond. The community may include a variety of publics, including potential clients, the general public, political bodies, other human service organizations, and other organizations and groups. The relationship of this community to the human service organization is an important one, and one that influences the functioning of the organization and the quality of its service.[1]

The management of a human service organization, then, involves community relations. Some of the tasks involve maintenance management, whereas others involve service management. As in the case of other functions of management, such as budgeting, program evaluation, and staff development, a balance must be struck between maintenance and service management in order that organizational optimization be served. As is also the case with the other functions, the service management aspects of community relations need clarification and development.

This chapter addresses two basic tasks in community relations: public relations and interorganizational relations.

PUBLIC RELATIONS

Many human service organizations do not engage in an organized program of public relations. Recently the notion has been growing that the human services need more and better public relations.[2] This notion may focus on the feeling that the public needs to know more about "what the organization is doing." It may also focus on merely "making us look good," whatever the quality of the actual service product may be. This kind of approach is the basis of much of the advertising that exists in American industry. The process of selling soap, toothpaste, or similar products needs to concentrate on the packaging and the image or impression of the product, such that the actual substance is often ignored. Public relations in the human services, designed merely to maintain the organization, and perhaps to enhance its image by making it "look good" in the eyes of significant elements in its community, can be detrimental to that organization's functioning. The goal of merely "selling" the agency in order to improve its image, increase its grants, give it political clout, or make it competitive with other agencies—in short maintain the organization—can supplant the service goal of public relations.

Let us view public relations from a service management perspective. Here the goal is organizational optimization designed to increase the organizational pattern of service effectiveness. Public relations can thus be viewed in terms of three major service tasks: education, outreach, and advocacy.

Education

Every human service organization deals with a social problem, be it alcoholism, mental retardation, drug abuse, unemployment, or a variety of others. It is a safe assumption that most of the public remains uninformed about the components, severity, and incidence of these problems in their community. Yet these problems exist and often affect large numbers of community residents. It is therefore an important task of a human service organization to educate the public about the social problem in which it is involved and the human service it provides. Consider a program dealing with alcoholism, for example. It is important that the public know what the disease of alcoholism is and what kind of harm it can cause for the alcoholic, his or her family, and the community as well. By successfully bringing such aspects of a social problem to the attention of a community, a human service organization can certainly improve its standing and its importance. A payoff for the organization then is possible through public education. Informing the public about a social problem and the technologies available to combat it can prove a small but significant contribution to the strength of the social welfare institution by underscoring its basic need and value to society. Obviously, for any significant impact, such public relations would need to be pursued in many communities throughout the country, and be concerned about many social problems. It is vital, then, that human service management acknowledge education as an important aspect of its functioning. Although the method utilized in this aspect of public relations is important, the social problems faced in this country are severe enough that exaggeration is not a necessity. Many techniques, such as brochures, newsletters, a variety of literature, speakers, conferences, the use of the media, the sponsoring of such activities as "mental retardation awareness week," and other kinds of programs can be beneficial.[3]

A program of education about social problems represents a direct way in which human service organizations can achieve some degree of official goal achievement. If effective, such education programs can lead to the prevention of some social problems before they reach the point at which treatment is necessary. The results of education programs are difficult to measure, but it is possible that the incidence of a given social problem could be reduced over time in a community if a carefully conceived and organized education plan were mounted, and feedback on its effects were included. A randomized survey could be utilized to evaluate the program. For example, public awareness of the problems of alcoholism could easily be measured through the use of a telephone survey. After one year, the survey could be repeated to assess the impact on changing attitudes about alcoholism. This kind of education is inexpensive and can produce accurate results if the sample is correctly selected.

In public relations for education, it is usually better to stress the human aspects of a social problem and its treatment, rather than descriptive statistics and program details. Stressing the latter is a tendency on the part of those who attempt public education in social welfare and usually elicits a less significant response. For example, a public presentation including the following is probably not compelling: "The problem of alcoholism is a dangerous one in our community. One out of four of our citizens drinks to excess, which could be termed a problem; 40 percent of all traffic fatalities in the community are due to driving while intoxicated." The recitation of such statistics, particularly in large quantity, can have less impact than: "As a social worker, I see many frightening things. One occurred recently. A family of four was driving up Elm Street when an oncoming car crossed over the line; a head-on collision occurred. The father was the only one who survived. I have been counseling him since the accident. When he asks 'Why?' it's difficult to answer him. But it's not difficult to answer this from another perspective: the driver of the other car was drunk." Obviously, statistics and problem descriptions are important, but a public portrayal of the problem in human terms, something which professionals often avoid, is necessary as well.

Outreach

It is generally the case with most social problems that far more people are in need of service than are receiving it from a given agency. It is a rare organization, indeed, which can make the claim that all potential recipients in a given community are receiving service. It is also the case that many clients who do seek service cannot be helped by a particular agency. Both of these trends can be alleviated through a well-organized outreach program.

Many of the techniques and approaches that apply to the educative task also apply to outreach. Outreach is a specific kind of educative task, which is education directed not to the general public but at potential clients. Many clients who could be successfully served by an agency are often not sufficiently informed about the organization's service capabilities to realize that their problem could be treated or alleviated. Many may feel that their problem is unique, or that they need to face their problem alone.

In outreach, the potential clients' anxieties about seeking service need to be addressed in realistic terms. In this task there should be less stress on the general social problem and more emphasis on the problem's individual manifestations and how they can be addressed by the specific capability of the organization. Matching the client problem with the organization's service capabilities is obviously vital to organizational optimization and patterns of effective service. If, at the onset, the appropriate clientele seeks agency service with realistic expectations, a positive effect is more likely. And successful outcome contributes to the organization's standing in the community, probably more than any other factor.

Advocacy

An important task of human service management in public relations is the role of advocate. Although related to the task of education, advocacy is designed to persuade, not merely to inform. In the educative task, a human service manager might describe the problem of aging in a given community to inform the public of its existence. In advocacy, the task is to persuade the community that something needs to be done. In the case of advocacy, the audience may be the general public, but it may be aimed at a more specific audience as well. Advocacy may be designed to convince those who have access to, or control of, resources that the organization requires in order to function.[4] Hence, a local legislature may need convincing that a particular program or organization is a worthwhile recipient of funding. This might require direct lobbying or the organization of community support.

The role of advocate has a long history of conceptual development in the literature of community organization practice in social work.[5] In recent years, community mental health has adopted it as a basic concept. Advocacy has rarely been perceived in the context of management. Yet advocating for the solution of a social problem, and for the organization that confronts that problem, is a vital part of any manager's role when he or she seeks public support. The acquisition of both maintenance and service resources can hinge on the effective pursuit of advocacy. The danger in any public relations effort is to "oversell," and this is particularly true in the case of advocacy. An approach to advocacy represents a series of organizational decisions, and these decisions need to be congruent. The actual technological capability of the organization must not be exaggerated for political reasons—payoffs for individuals or for the organization—or for considerations of value—the belief that a problem should be solved. This kind of noncongruence can lead to a kind of "promise without performance" that can weaken the social welfare institution of a community as well as ultimately, if pervasive, a society.

In all three public relations tasks, education, outreach, and advocacy, the objective needs to be in conformance to the organization's official goals of service.[6] Goal displacement in public relations occurs when the operative goal of image replaces the official goal of service. When this occurs the organization will not benefit in the long term. However, when management, working in conjunction with service practitioners, is involved with these tasks in the community, the fragmentation between management and other staff can be reduced, because the perception of management as being concerned solely with maintenance and not the issue and quality of service can be altered and greater cohesion between staff and management can be the result. A sense that there is a commitment to official goal achievement, which is being pursued outside the organization, can aid in the development of optimization.[7] The perception on the part of the organization's members that representatives of the organization are relating to the environment in terms of service can lead to a strengthening of norms of service inside the organization.

INTERORGANIZATIONAL RELATIONS

The second important area of management functioning is interorganizational relations. Most human service organizations are part of an interorganizational network of agencies that provides similar or closely related service products to the same or similar client populations. This network may be formal or informal with a highly integrated or loosely assembled structure. Whatever its character, this network constitutes a significant aspect of an organization's environment.[8]

Since that aspect of the social welfare institution in the United States that deals with service is highly decentralized, service delivery systems in many areas of the human service endeavor are often characterized by a high degree of fragmentation, overlap, and duplication. Similar services to one client population, for example, may be provided by a large number of different agencies and organizations, or a variety of different organizations may treat different aspects of the same social problem. This occurs on the community level as well as at the state and federal levels.[9] Besides being highly confusing and dysfunctional for clients, this situation can be the basis for competition and controversy between individual organizations over task and domain. Here again, maintenance and service management may collide and balance is necessary. Maintenance management may take the form of protecting one organization's domain against that of another. Such conflict over organizational domain can often politicize interorganizational relationships in the human services. The protection of the interests and boundaries of the organization that the manager represents is necessary, but it can create problems for service. The predominance of political considerations may serve to undermine the capability potential of interorganizational linkages, and the manager may thus begin to function at cross-purposes to the goal of enhancing effective service. "One-upmanship" and the gain of advantage may become the primary motivation behind interorganizational exchange. When this occurs, there is goal displacement in interorganizational relations.

The primary objective must be the enhancement of service resources and service outcome.[10] Service capability considerations, therefore, must play a significant role in determining the nature and basis of interorganizational relationships. Human service organizations may interrelate because there is a mutually perceived need to exchange capability components.[11] One organization may provide an important service that is needed by the clientele of a second organization, or representatives of two or more organizations may conclude that duplication between agencies can be alleviated by better coordination and further specialization of service delivery.

Service effectiveness often can be enhanced through formalized linkages between human service organizations that can replace more informal linkages.[12] For example, clients who visit a local community mental health service may also be receiving service from the local social service (public assistance) organization. If the exchange of information concerning specific clients depends on staff workers knowing each other, the linkages will be sporadic and undependable. A more formalized linkage may be desirable, in which the service capabilities of more than one agency may better serve the client population. This kind of interorganizational cooperation clearly serves to enhance service delivery. However, such capability exchange is not always possible and conflict over organizational domain often politicizes interorganizational relationships in the human services.[13]

Value may also be an important motivation for interorganizational relationships. Organizations may come together to jointly pursue a shared concern in a given community. Much of the practice theory of community organization is based on this kind of activity. Often the goal of such practice is to stimulate the development of a "community of shared interests or concern"[14] among agencies and people involved in a particular human service endeavor. The agencies in a local community involved in the service to the poor or in mental health or drug abuse services may organize to support a particular program or project, or to publicize a social condition deemed worthy of attention. A wide variety of possibilities for organized effort are present in most communities where voice can be given to shared values and concerns. This can represent significant public relations in the educative, advocacy, and even outreach areas.

In all of these interorganizational endeavors, the primary objective of management must remain the enhancement of service resources and service effectiveness. Most interorganizational linkages will contain implications for the internal effectiveness of service outcome, and this must be a prime consideration. The need, on the part of management, to ensure that interorganizational activities do not co-opt service effectiveness is overriding. Interorganizational endeavors must be weighed from the perspective of service capability and effectiveness. The pitfall of an overemphasis on political functioning or even joint participation in shared value activities must be avoided. The pattern of a human service organization's external relationships is the center of concern. Interorganizational relationships based on political or value considerations are both necessary and desirable; however, the major underlying consideration must be capability factors in order to maximize the service product. It is an important task of management to ensure that this is, in fact, the case.

In the preceding four chapters, we have considered four specific functions of management and the variety of activities which they encompass. In the case of budgeting, program evaluation and reporting, staff development and community relations, we have placed the emphasis on the activities of service management and argued that opportunities for enhancing service quality may be lost if these functions are viewed from the perspective of maintenance alone. It is in the successful performance of the service aspects of these four functions that organizational co-optation can be alleviated.

As noted in Chapter One, there needs to be a component in a human service organization responsible for the overall quality of care, the degree of service effectiveness. An organized pursuit of these four functions can constitute such an organizational component. In order to combat the patterns of least effective service described in Part I, the four functions need to be a formalized and coordinated aspect of the organizational structure. The manner in which the functions are organized and their relation to the maintenance functions will vary with different human service organizations. Under optimal conditions, each function should constitute an individual department or at least have full-time staff assigned to develop and execute the necessary tasks. For example, a director of program evaluation, with as much staff support as possible, is a vital position in a human service organization. The development, implementation, and cooordination of evaluative activities existing apart from reporting activities is necessary if service improvement is to be attained. With no *formalized* component responsible for such evaluation, there is no interest whose trade-offs depend on its successful achievement. Therefore, the incentive for program evaluation is drastically reduced. A director of program evaluation and a staff might undertake other tasks as well, but at the very least, program evaluation would occupy a formalized position in the organizational structure. The same holds true for budgeting. The programmatic and service aspects of the budget need to be organized in such a manner as to represent an interest which requires a reward in order to gain organizational status. This establishes a trade-off mechanism designed to ensure that such aspects are considered in the budgetary process in addition to the maintenance considerations. It is possible that the program evaluation staff could perform that function as well as the budgetary function. Certainly there would need to be close coordination, for as we have noted, optimization in budgeting needs to be based on some notion of program effectiveness. This is the case from the most informal program evaluation to the most sophisticated PPBS described in Chapter Nine. Staff development and community relations need to be part of the organization's formal structure as well. Most human service organizations engage in budgeting and at least reporting, but organized staff development and community relations programs are rare and can be overlooked by the organization. This makes their formalized inclusion into the organizational structure of great importance. Obviously, the staff development tasks of hiring and firing, supervision, and personnel appraisal are different from such tasks as in-service training and continuing education, yet they are connected because the goal is the enhancement of the quality and potential of the staff. Therefore, they need to be linked organizationally as well. There should be a department in the organization concerned with all staff development, the members of which receive rewards for the actual enhancement of overall technological possession. This component needs to be closely coordinated to budget and to program evaluation in order to have the greatest effect on organizational optimization. A "Department of Staff Development" is rare, but the propositions of Chapter Six indicate that a significant effect on organizational optimization and effective service can be achieved through the increase in technological input, and justifies such an organizational component.

As we have seen in the previous chapter, the organization's relationship to its community can have enormous impact on its functioning and service. Hence the public relations, education, outreach and advocacy task, as well as the interorganizational function need to be formalized and integrated as part of the organization's structure. In the case of sufficient resources, organized units of education, outreach, and advocacy could be established, to plan and coordinate the strategies and approach of those members of the organization's staff involved in these efforts. With goals clarified and roles developed, the pay-offs for both the organization and the social welfare of the local community could be greatly enhanced. A separate component established for the relationships to other organizations would be appropriate if resources permit. An organized, coordinated plan which formalized interorganizational relations, in activities ranging from coordinated referrals of cases, to funding opportunities, to opportunities for joint service efforts, would greatly aid the functioning and service of a given human service organization. Again, coordinating these activities with other aspects of service management would be desirable.

What is most important is that a *structure* must be established providing the mechanism for a human service organization to pursue the tasks of service management. Maintenance management is pursued of necessity, service is not, and therefore, such a mechanism is essential. It is vital because the patterns of organizational functioning which diminish the quality of care (described in Part I), can be alleviated only through a mechanism which generates organizational optimization. The organized pursuit of these four management functions can help enhance the service resources of the organization, can aid in official goal attainment, augment congruent decision making, reduce authority subversion and hence set in motion a chain of dynamics which can initiate and sustain an improved pattern of service effectiveness. Optimally, a human service organization might be structured to include a single component with substantial resources which could encompass all the tasks of service management. These would include the performance of as many of the tasks of service management as possible in the most highly coordinated manner. Such a component could help redirect the energies of the organization into service enhancing activities. Most human service organizations currently possess such energy in the talents and values of its staff; what is needed is the channelling of such energy into organized effort.

The manner in which these functions can be accommodated to organizational context will require creative effort on the part of those who manage human service organizations. The point remains that this concept of service management needs to be part of our human service organizations, if those organizations are to serve the clientele whose social problems they are designed to alleviate, and help strengthen the social welfare institution.

SUMMARY

An important task of management is relating the organization to its environment or community. Community relations can be designed to be primarily self-serving to a human service organization, with an emphasis on techniques that serve to make the organization "look good." Some service goals can be achieved through community relations. Several functions are involved in service management as it involves community relations, including public relations and interorganizational relations. Public relations involves education, outreach, and advocacy, all of which can play an important role in organizational optimization and in strengthening social welfare in a given community. Interorganizational relations are often surrounded by conflict over domain and other political considerations. Management must attempt to minimize such activity and maximize the improvements in service capability that interorganizational relationships can provide.

In its community relations, management must stress those activities which improve and promote service. In community relations, as in the case with the other functions, the pursuit of maintenance can become an end in itself and eclipse the service aspects of management. Management needs to become involved with the kind of tasks that have been stressed in order that this might be avoided.

NOTES

1. Shirley Terreberry, "The Evolution of Organizational Environments," *Administrative Science Quarterly*, vol. 12, March 1967, pp. 590–613.
2. Richard Steiner, *Managing the Human Service Organization* (Beverly Hills: Sage Publications, 1977), p. 156.
3. For other ideas and strategies see Huntington Harris, "Community of Interest: A Concept of Public Relations," *Quarterly Review of Public Relations*, vol. 6, Spring 1961, pp. 2–8; Scott Cutlip and Allen H. Center, *Effective Public Relations* (Englewood Cliffs, New Jersey: Prentice-Hall, 1971); Melvin Glaser, "Public Relations," in *Encyclopedia of Social Work* (New York: National Association of Social Workers, 1965), pp. 618–624.
4. See Irving Spergel, *Community Problem Solving* (Chicago: University of Chicago Press, 1969).

5. For discussions of the role of advocate and other community organization roles relevant to management and community relations, see Spergel, op. cit.; Jack Rothman, "Three Models of Community Organization Practice," *Social Work Practice* (New York: Columbia University Press, 1968), pp. 16–47; Arnold Gurin, *Community Organization and Social Planning* (New York: John Wiley and Sons, 1972); Charles F. Grosser, *New Directions in Community Organization: From Enabling to Advocacy* (New York: Praeger, 1973).

6. See Frances Schmidt and Harold N. Weiner, eds., *Public Relations in Health and Welfare* (New York: Columbia University Press, 1960).

7. See William Fisher, Jr., "Social Agencies: A New Challenge for Public Relations," *Public Relations Quarterly*, vol. 4, April 1959, pp. 14–21.

8. For theoretical works, see Roland L. Warren, "The Intraorganizational Field as a Focus for Investigation," *Administrative Science Quarterly*, vol. 12, no. 3, December 1967, pp. 396–419; Eugene Litwak and Henry J. Meyer, "A Balance Theory of Coordination between Bureaucratic Organizations and Community Primary Groups," *Administrative Science Quarterly*, vol. 11, June 1966, pp. 31–58; Evan William, "Toward a Theory of Inter-Organizational Relations," *Management Science*, vol. 11, August 1965, pp. 217–230.

9. This situation does not appear unique to American social welfare. See, for example, Leonard Schneiderman, "Collaboration between the Health and Social Services in England," *Social Work*, vol. 23, no. 3, May 1978; Linn Mo, "Coordination of Social and Medical Services: An Issue in Norway," *Social Service Review*, vol. 52, no. 4, December 1978.

10. George O'Brien, "Interorganizational Relations," in Saul Feldman, ed., *Mental Health Administration* (Illinois: Charles C. Thomas, 1973).

11. P. Fellin, "Issues in Making Decisions on a Merger of Agencies," *Child Welfare*, vol. 51, no. 5, 1972, pp. 280–286.

12. William Reid, "Interagency Coordination in Delinquency Prevention and Control," *Social Service Review*, vol. 38, December 1964, no. 4.

13. Norton E. Long, "The Local Community as an Ecology of Games," *American Journal of Sociology*, vol. 48, 1958, pp. 251–261.

14. Robert Perlman and Arnold Gurin, *Community Organization and Social Planning* (New York: John Wiley, 1972).

Chapter TWELVE

Management in the Human Service Planning Organization

The emphasis of this book has been upon the human service delivery organization. Yet the analytical framework and the concepts of management that have been presented in the preceding chapters can be applied to the human service planning organization as well. This chapter focuses on management at the level of the planning organization.

Although there is little uniformity in both name and organizational structure in the vast array of human service planning organizations,[1] there can be little question that these organizations maintain a great influence on the nature, quality, and direction of human services at the delivery level. How planning organizations perform the tasks involved in administering, funding, and generally overseeing human service delivery is crucial to the ultimate service product.

The ultimate objectives and processes of management remain the same at the planning level; the difference is a much enlarged domain of responsibility. In short, there is a change in what can be termed the *focal domain*. The focus thus changes from concern with individual organizational members and components to concern with the overall functioning within and between a number of organizational totalities. These domains vary in size with the organizational level (state, multistate, and so on). Since the overall perspective differs from that of the service delivery level, the focus of managerial attention may move toward greater emphasis on structural and systemic factors rather than upon the interpersonal elements that often characterize the functioning of smaller organizations. Nonetheless, the overall dynamics with regard to service outcome and the ultimate purposes of management remain the same as those on the service delivery level.

What, then, represents the official goals of a human service planning organization and what represents service effectiveness for such an organization and its focal domain? Consider a state department of mental health that has as its focal domain a number of state hospitals for the treatment of the mentally ill. If the official goals of the hospitals are to promote and enhance mental health in a given geographical area through direct service, then the official goal of the state-level planning organization is similar, with two modifications. First, no service is directly provided by the planning organization, so that the pursuit of the goal must be more indirect; and second, the domain of concern is larger in terms of both geographical area and numbers of potential consumers. The quality of the *collective service product, and the collective level of service effectiveness in the focal domain* are thus the concern and responsibility of management at the level of the human service planning organization. Instead of concern for the quality of service in an individual human service organization, it is the collective product of the seven state hospitals, the fourteen local units of a service for the aging, or the organizational units that service youth, which commands managerial attention. The ultimate purpose of management can thus be viewed from the same perspective as that at the human service delivery level, and both the framework of Part I and the management process of Part II applies. Let us consider some specific applications of this material to management at the planning level.

PUBLIC RELATIONS AND STAFF DEVELOPMENT

As in management at the delivery level, public relations and interorganizational relations are important tasks. Interorganizational relations at the level of the planning organization include *planning* organizations that function in *different* areas of the human services. As noted previously, a great many interrelationships between human service organizations at the delivery level do not ultimately enhance the quality of service. The same holds true for linkages between human service planning organizations. Although there are a great many linkages between focal domains, they are often based on past history, political structure, or even informal interrelationships between individuals and not necessarily on what will most enhance service effectiveness. What often results is an isolation of human service systems from one another. This isolation in organizational terms can lead to the politicization of relationships as different human service organizations vie for resources and influence and advantage vis-à-vis other political structures (a governor's office, a budget bureau). This can be the cause of dysfunctions *internal* to the domain as political pursuits become necessary at the expense of official goal achievement. This isolation of human service systems in terms of political interest can lead to fragmentation and duplication of services across human service areas, and confusion for both service provider and service consumer, not to mention wasted resources.[2] There is a need, therefore, for human service planning organizations to develop the kind of ongoing interorganizational processes that will enhance service effectiveness within respective focal domains.

In order for management to achieve this, the focus of interorganizational planning needs to be centered upon *the effect on service effectiveness generated by interorganizational relationships.* As is the case on the service delivery level, the relationship of political, value, and capability elements needs to reflect congruence to the greatest extent possible, when decisions are made about interorganizational relationships. The emphasis of this congruence needs to be based on the similarities that exist in different human service delivery systems: between the technologies utilized, the kind of social problems confronted, and the clientele served. There are many similarities, for example, in the technologies utilized in child protective services, family services, mental health services, and corrections services. Yet more often than not, these services are delivered in separate systems characterized by few linkages designed to enhance service effectiveness in either system. This constitutes a lack of the full utilization of the resources that may be present in the human service network of a state government, for example. A significant opportunity to strengthen the social welfare institution is lost as a result. Well-defined, carefully planned linkages that follow the logic of technology and service effectiveness in different service areas could greatly enhance the service product across different human service focal domains. This kind of interorganizational and intersystemic linkage needs to be pursued by management at all organizational levels of human services. Yet, it is at the level of the planning organization that the greatest impact can be achieved because linkages can have implications for entire domains rather than for a few organizations.

To state the need for interdomain linkages based on the elements of human service technology is not to ignore the enormous problems that exist in making them a reality. Politics, values, traditions, and resources can all prove very serious impediments.[3] One problem that certainly can be addressed, however, is that of managerial perception. Traditionally, a director and staff of a state program for drug abuse, for the aging, or for youth, for example, have generally perceived their role and function solely in terms of service to that group of clientele and to mobilize resources and support, develop programs, and policy for that group alone. Typically, the building of linkages *between* service domains has not been perceived as an important, ongoing managerial function, and it is often ignored as a basis for service improvement *within* a focal domain. Clearly, however, if the primary purpose of management, as we have contended, is to enhance the quality of service, this task needs to be viewed as an institutionalized function of management at the level of the human service planning organization. This area remains a very fertile one for creative managerial initiative.

As is the case at the service delivery level, the task of public relations needs to be an important component of management at the level of the planning organization. Public relations at the planning level can command a greater audience than at the delivery level and therefore can make a greater difference in aiding social welfare. The nature of the focal domain as a whole needs to be explained and communicated to the general public. The service capabilities need to be described and presented as does the nature of the social problem and the categories of people who can be helped by the service.

There are two underlying reasons for public relations. The first deals with maintenance and accountability. In times of resource limitation and increasing demand for accountability for

Managing the Organization

expenditures, the public relations function gains increasing importance in that there is a greater need to justify the expenditures made in a given human service area to both the public and to the pertinent political structure. An effective ongoing public presentation of the services offered and the benefits for the public that result can be of great assistance to the maintenance of a planning organization and the procurement of resources for its domain. Obviously, if a program is generally recognized as performing an important and needed service, resource procurement itself is facilitated. This is a good example of how maintenance and service management can interrelate.

The second reason lies solely with the content of what is being communicated to the public about a human service area. Public relations at the planning level should be viewed primarily as a service in itself, in terms of information, education, prevention, and outreach. In some human service areas, education about a specific social problem can be an important public service.

Staff development, viewed not from the perspective of a single delivery organization but from a focal domain, can be another task of management at the planning level. Like their counterparts in human service delivery organizations, managers in planning organizations are limited in their pursuit of official goal achievement and service effectiveness by the state of the technological development. Managers in an office for the aging, for example, can do no better in terms of the service product of their focal domains than the state of development of technology in working with the aging. Hence, the quality of the input is of vital consequence for the nature of the collective service product. Management at the planning level, then, needs to aid organizations throughout the focal domain in obtaining the benefit of pertinent technological development and innovation and in securing personnel who possess a high level of technological ability. Obviously, this needs to be done in concert with management at the delivery level.

The essential task is to construct planned linkages with pertinent systems outside the focal domain that are involved in technological development in the human service area of concern. These might involve human service programs conducted in other states, other regions of the country, or in the voluntary sector, in which similar kinds of clientele are being served in the pursuit of similar official goals. Universities, foundations, and other centers where pertinent technological development relevant to the implementation of the service product are taking place provide another possibility for formalized linkage. It has often been observed that innovative ideas and program approaches are being developed and attempted throughout the country with little cross-fertilization or even communication about the results to other programs involved in similar endeavors. Such linkages need to be formalized feedback systems, rather than merely occasional informal interactions. In many cases the planning organization has more opportunity to accomplish this than at the delivery level, because of the wider arena of contacts from which to draw.

PROGRAM EVALUATION AND BUDGETING

Because the functions of program evaluation and budgeting can be far removed from the actual delivery of service, their contributions to the effectiveness of that service are not easily achieved. Both in allocating funds for service and in evaluating the results of that service, planning organizations need to develop their capacities to relate to delivery organizations in the pursuit of optimization and official goal achievement. The following case illustration highlights some of the problems that can occur around the interrelationships of planning and delivery organizations as the former pursues the management function of program evaluation.

CASE ILLUSTRATION: MANAGEMENT IN THE HUMAN SERVICE PLANNING ORGANIZATION

This case illustration, which involves a state department of social services (public assistance), focuses upon the services rather than the income maintenance aspects of public welfare. This state department has jurisdiction over 41 county-level departments where the actual service is carried out. A decision has been made to attempt to measure the effectiveness of local services through a formal mechanism of program evaluation. The problem facing management at the planning level is how to initiate program evaluation without alienating the county-level operations. A meeting takes place to consider this problem. Present are the state commissioner of social services (Patricia), the newly appointed state director for program evaluation (Ernest), and a county commissioner (Arnold).

STATE COMMISSIONER: The reason we're having this meeting is that it's clear to us at the state that we need to do some outcome evaluation of local services. I'm open to ideas about how to do this. That's why I've asked Arnold to the meeting. The state has worked very closely with you in the past and we need the local perspective.

LOCAL COMMISSIONER: Well, first of all it is a threat to the local level. If you and I didn't go back a long way, I'd be threatened. It's very difficult from the local perspective to see what the benefit is if the state wants us to do program evaluation. You come in with your evaluation team; it's more forms for everybody to fill out, and the whole thing's an imposition. That's the way many will see it.

STATE COMMISSIONER: Well, there must be some way we can diffuse the threat and gain beneficial results.

DIRECTOR OF PROGRAM EVALUATION: Look, if the evaluation is going to yield valid and reliable results, it needs to be done correctly, and under proper conditions.

STATE COMMISSIONER: That's a technical problem. We need to get the cooperation first.

LOCAL COMMISSIONER: I think the major thing is that you can't force it. It's got to be evolved in a very nondirective way. It's got to be built slowly.

DIRECTOR OF PROGRAM EVALUATION: Let me ask you this, Arnold. Has there been any interest in or concern about program evaluation? Have you heard any discussion about evaluation among the commissioners or the staff?

LOCAL COMMISSIONER: Actually, it's very informal discussion. There are some people in different counties who are interested and talk about it occasionally; staff members of different program components, some commissioners, some middle-level people. It's diffuse; it's there, but it's not organized. It is, I think, something on which to build.

STATE COMMISSIONER: How about this? We send a memo to each local commissioner in the state inviting each local department to send one or more members of its organization who has any interest in program evaluation. The commissioner himself could come, or any member of his staff, the main thing is to get at the interest that people have. And we would have a conference in the capital solely on the subject of evaluation. We'll bring in outside experts to stimulate discussion and interchange, and we'll make every effort to apply the material to the local situation. I think this way we can get to meet and interact with those who are interested and begin to build a base of support for evaluation through different follow-up mechanisms that will spin off from the conference. At least this will start people thinking about program outcome and we'll have a link to each local department. I can't see how this would be at all threatening.

DIRECTOR OF PROGRAM EVALUATION: I don't see how we're going to get very far that way, because those people don't know much about program evaluation.

LOCAL COMMISSIONER: I think we can develop the expertise later. First, you need the interest and support. And I think this is the way to do it. We'll build a community of interest in the state, and develop a network of evaluation from that. If we just propose evaluation mechanisms without doing this first, it just isn't going to work.

[The conference is organized along the lines discussed. Most counties send representatives, a list of those interested is compiled, and an ongoing communication between the state office of program evaluation and the local levels is established. As a result of the conference, a number of local staff who are interested in beginning actual program evaluation and their local commissioners meet with the state commissioner and the director of program evaluation to discuss setting up the program.]

STATE COMMISSIONER: The reason we're here is to come up with some concrete ideas concerning program evaluation. We've

Managing the Organization

discussed it a good deal informally; now we need to do a little program design and planning. First, I'd like to talk a little about why we're doing program evaluation. The main reason, it seems to me, is one of values. We're interested in providing useful, beneficial, and compassionate service. It's our obligation, professionally. We don't talk much about this but it is the primary motivation. And I want you to know there's no hidden agenda. Our reason for being is service; if we can do it better in our programs, we ought to try. It should not be just an exercise in academic or bureaucratic futility. If it turns out that we can't do evaluation which helps improve the program, then we'll forget it. I want to say also, and I said this at our conference, evaluation can't be imposed, it must be evolved at the local level. We're going to do it together with the state office, providing assistance but not dictating programs.

LOCAL COMMISSIONER: I've really been convinced that we need program evaluation. The thing that bothers me is that program evaluation is a nebulous term. One thing that has emerged from the discussions is that there is really no agreed-upon, systematic methodology for evaluating human service programs. The term seems to mean different things to different people.

DIRECTOR OF PROGRAM EVALUATION: Well, I wouldn't go that far. I think there are a number of different methodologies that can be used, ranging from controlled, experimental design, to just collecting information.

LOCAL COMMISSIONER: Collecting information bothers me because that means more forms, and I don't want to see forms filled out for their own sake. If we're going to get into a lot of forms, it has to mean some kind of improvement in service, not forms for their own sake.

DIRECTOR OF PROGRAM EVALUATION: We don't want to just collect forms. I'd like to stress that experimental designs are far superior to any other methodology, and I think that is what we need if we're really going to be able to measure the effect of what we're doing. We need a control group situation.

LOCAL COMMISSIONER: I don't like the word *control*. Not control over clients, and not control over the local situation by the state. I'm not saying it would be purposive, but it is a potential problem. I think it's important that we do the best we can from a scientific point of view, but we need to be careful. I'm not sure we can set up an actual controlled condition.

STATE COMMISSIONER: Well, that's what I meant when I said before that we need to evolve the appropriate methodology.

LOCAL COMMISSIONER: O.K.! The thing that still bothers me is this: Are we saying that we need one kind of evaluation for every county? Or are we saying that each county should do its own? It seems to me that our problems in Duke County are far different than those in Brown County. I think maybe we need as many different kinds of evaluation mechanisms as there are counties.

STATE COMMISSIONER: It seems to me that looking at it from the county perspective, I understand your point. From the state perspective, what you just said is a problem. If we have 40 kinds of measures and program data coming in to us, it's going to be very difficult for us to look at evaluation from a statewide perspective. If I'm asked: "Are you achieving successful services in the state?" I'm not going to be able to respond clearly. It's going to be tough to answer if we have 40 different measures. So I think we're going to have to strive for at least some uniformity, if that's agreeable. Obviously, we need to consider local differences, but the whole thing won't make much sense without some uniformity.

LOCAL COMMISSIONER: Your point is very well taken, but it's a time problem. I can't afford the staff time to work with all the other commissioners to come up with one approach. We all have too much to do. The state will need to take the coordinating function on this.

STATE COMMISSIONER: We're prepared to do that. My proposal is this: we're agreed on the potential usefulness of evaluation. We need specifics. I sympathize with the fact that you're limited in time; so we'll do a draft—just a first cut, nothing written in stone. And we'll get your input along the way. Then we'll reconvene and take it apart. And see where we go from there. Nothing we do will bind anyone.

LOCAL COMMISSIONER: That sounds fine.

Analysis

In this case illustration, the state commissioner represents the role of manager at the planning level. At the first meeting, her major objective was to gain an understanding of the potential support for program evaluation around the state and also to determine the sources of probable opposition. Believing in the official goals and what program evaluation can provide toward their achievement, she also understands the need to calculate the trade-offs involved. This is obtained from the observations of a local commissioner with whom she has a working relationship. In an actual situation, this would probably be obtained from more than just one source. This is vital information because it is needed in order to integrate this political assessment of the local situation with the expertise as represented by the director of program evaluation. Clearly, the reward for the director lies in the establishment of a formalized program evaluation mechanism. More than likely, the local commissioner confirms what the state commissioner already believes to be the case: program evaluation, if it is to work, cannot be imposed by the state. The director, perceiving that the establishment of evaluation will be a slow and less than certain process, is not overly pleased. A strategy is conceived by the state commissioner that involves the establishment of conferences on the general subject of program evaluation. The emphasis then is on the idea and concept of evaluation rather than upon actual implementation. By inviting the local commissioners to attend or send a representative to the first conference, the state commissioner is introducing the subject of evaluation, but minimizing the cost that the locals have to pay in terms of any loss of autonomy. The conference poses no threat. Yet the strategy serves to support an interest in evaluation throughout the state. This establishes some linkage among the local-level organizations and between the local and the state levels. It also seems to have representatives of the delivery system as a whole begin to think about official goal achievement.

After the conference, a second meeting is held, which does concern implementation. Here the local commissioner (a different one from the first meeting) represents the probable response of the delivery organizations when the trade-offs begin to involve the actual establishment of the program. Again, the meeting begins with the state commissioner's reiteration of official goals and the merit of evaluation in their achievement. This receives little disagreement. Understanding the trade-offs involved, she raises the subject of local autonomy and indicates that there will be no imposition by the state. The local commissioner, has accepted the value of program evaluation from the conference, but is concerned with the lack of clarity regarding the concept. The local commissioner then raises the question of local autonomy by indicating the need for separate evaluative mechanisms tailored to each local county. This illustrates the point that the delivery organizations that make up the domain of a human service planning organization generally view themselves as unique and tend not to assume a network-wide perspective. When this view is put forth, the state commissioner understands that this is a threat to the project as a whole. Here she assumes a directive approach, rejecting the notion that each county should construct its own plan. She perceives that although the idea of evaluation has been generally accepted, it would probably be lost in implementation with so decentralized an approach. She presses the need for some uniformity on substantive grounds. The response is agreement, but an unwillingness to invest organizational energy and resources in the project. The task of conceiving a first draft at program conception thus falls to the state. In a real situation this probably would have been the ultimate calculation of the state commissioner.

As the case illustrates, the task of stimulating a human service network to give formalized attention to official goal achievement is difficult. In most delivery systems, given the organization of the social welfare institution and the presence of interest and domain, the development of a system of program evaluation would be a long-term developmental prospect. If official goal achievement is to be the objective, the task of human service management, at the planning level, is as demanding and difficult as that at the delivery level.

As noted, some small benefit has probably been achieved for the domain of this planning organization. Some formal discussion has occurred regarding program outcome and other similar subjects. The path leading from where this case is left to actual implementation is an arduous one, with constant care given to interorganizational interests. This case indicates what this kind of management process entails.

The problems inherent in this case illustration of program evaluation are similar to those encountered in attempting to aid organizational optimization through the budgetary process. The institution of zero-base budgeting, program budgeting, or some modification of these concepts would be a long-term, highly political, and extremely demanding process for management. Much would depend on the existing conditions that govern the budgetary interactions between a state-level planning organization and the delivery organization in its domain. As indicated at the onset of the chapter, there is a great variation in these relationships. In some cases, the planning organization would possess considerable leverage through the use of trade-offs involved in funding. In others, a very high degree of local autonomy exists where funds are virtually assessed. Much can be achieved by planning organizations, to the degree possible, in relating budgets and funding to service and service outcome. Since the planning organization is in the unique position of responsibility regarding the service outcome of an entire domain, it can achieve much in strengthening the social welfare institution by helping delivery organizations achieve programs that "work." The use of the budgetary process by management at the planning level to help evolve organizational optimization at the delivery level is a fertile field for managerial initiative.

MAINTENANCE AND SERVICE MANAGEMENT: AN IMBALANCE

In order to pursue its management tasks and contribute to the quality of the collective product throughout the focal domain, the planning organization must construct a carefully conceived system of management that is integrated with the service delivery organizations. The major obstacle to the effective pursuit of these functions lies with the nature of the linkages that *currently* exist within focal domains which, by definition, characterize the interorganizational relationships between planning and service organizations. *Much of the actual functioning of planning organizations in the human services constitutes a series of activities aimed at maintenance and not at the enhancement of the service product.* Owing to the nature of a decentralized social welfare institution in which revenues are handled at a variety of governmental and organizational levels, the fundamental goal of the planning organization often becomes closely involved with the procurement, processing, dispersal, and monitoring of resources, creating complicated administrative structures and procedural processes designed to perform maintenance tasks.[4] This goal strongly influences the interorganizational relationship between planning and delivery organizations, causing the essential linkage to be maintenance oriented rather than service oriented. "Management" is typically viewed almost synonymously with maintenance and not to any significant degree with actions designed to improve service.[5] Not only is the interorganizational linkage greatly affected but the tasks of management at the service level become, of necessity, intertwined with maintenance relationships as well. For example, much of the "top layer" in delivery-level management is often involved in maintenance tasks, many of which require relating to the state, regional, and federal level agencies in the fulfillment of administrative and procedural responsibilities. Many of these involve reporting systems as discussed in Chapter Nine. Maintenance functioning therefore becomes over time, the actual *content* of much that consumes the daily routine.

Maintenance functioning dominates the trade-off relationships within focal domains as well. Those in delivery-level management who are responsible for resource procurement have much to gain by establishing the reputation of being people who can "get money." Often, particularly in smaller human service organizations, this task is carried out by the director of the organization or an organizational component close to the director. Without a well-integrated relationship between available money and available technology and program concept, which is insisted upon by the resource-granting organization, resource procurement assumes a maintenance orientation. The process of obtaining funds tends to become an end in itself, an operative goal, with substantial pay-off for those involved in its successful achievement. This phenomenon tends to move management into the "let's get the money now and justify the program later" posture, and optimization of technology and the evolution of effective service eventually suffer. From the point of view of management operating in an environment containing few options, this dynamic does not reflect an irrational course, because the end product may be rewarding and profitable in terms of status, prestige, and growth of the organization as well as in terms of individual careers. Not only can funds be obtained in this manner but they can be sustained as well. There is often a lack of clearly defined, accountable effectiveness built into the program-funding process, and so the continuation of funds can be justified on the basis of other kinds of measures than the effectiveness of service. The problem lies in the lack of technologically oriented planning to underlie the concept of programs and the distribution of funds. And this very much influences the behavior of management and the functioning of human service organizations, both at the delivery and planning level.

The general imbalance between maintenance and service management obscures the incentive on the part of planning and service organizations to engage in management processes that can lead to a better quality service product. The highest priority needs to be given, therefore, to rectifying the imbalance and directing the emergence of service functions of management in planning organizations. As has been previously noted, efficient maintenance is vital but should be viewed in human service management as a means rather than as an end; maintenance needs to serve the goals of service, and not dominate organizational functioning.

As with the other areas of management discussed previously, the prospect of a well-developed concept of service management at the planning level contains great problems. Yet, the opportunity for a contribution to more effective service, through the pursuit of these service management functions, is considerable. A human service network in which management at the delivery level is working closely with management at the planning level in the pursuit of *service* objectives, could effect significant changes in service output and a change in the image of the human service that may be held by the public in a particular focal domain. The fact that planning organizations have not generally engaged in this type of managerial initiative does not prohibit their doing so. The development, then, of the concept of service management at the planning level requires the attention of both practitioners and students of human service management.

SUMMARY

Management at the level of the planning organization shares ultimate purpose, content, and approach with management at the service delivery level. The difference is one of perspective and scope. Where management in service delivery organizations is responsible for the product of a component of one organization, or the organization as a whole, management at the planning level is concerned with the collective product of a number of human service organizations operating in what has been termed a focal domain. As with the delivery-level management, management in planning organizations is grounded in technology and the pursuit of service effectiveness: "what actually works."

The problems and prospects characterizing functions of management at the delivery level are similar to those confronted by planning-level management. The development of service management in the areas of public and interorganizational relations, as well as staff development, program evaluation, and the budgetary process, is an important endeavor.

Linkages between human service planning organizations, as well as with those organizations engaged in the development of human service technology, can aid in organizational optimization. Public relations for education and advocacy can, as at the delivery level, help contribute to the strength of the social welfare institution when initiated from the planning level organization. Program evaluation and the budgetary process, which involve the direct relationships between planning and delivery organizations, hold great promise for the evolution of more effective service programs, although implementation contains many problems.

In the last analysis, the planning organization, which is the locale of responsibility for large systems of service delivery, can prove an important component in the survival and development of the social welfare institution. The concept of service management can serve to aid in this endeavor.

NOTES

1. *Public Welfare Directory 1978/79*, Washington, D.C.: American Public Welfare Association. This work (cited in Chapter 1) presents an overview of the organization of state and local human service delivery systems.
2. James Sundquist et al., *Centrally Planned Change: A Re-examination of Theories and Concepts* (Urbana, Illinois: University of Illinois Press, 1976), chapter 8.
3. Neil Wright, "The States and Intergovernmental Relations," *Publius*, vol. 1, Winter 1972, pp. 7–68.
4. Sophie Dales, "Federal Grants to State and Local Governments, 1970–71," *Social Security Bulletin*, vol. 35, no. 2, pp. 29–38.
5. For a discussion of the subject of federal funding and accountability, see Alice Rivlin, *Systematic Thinking for Social Action* (Washington, D.C.: Brookings Institution, 1971), pp. 122–144.

Chapter THIRTEEN

Human Service Management and Social Welfare

AN IDENTITY FOR MANAGEMENT IN THE HUMAN SERVICES

As one approaches a building that houses a drug abuse program, a mental health clinic, an education program for the retarded, a family counseling program, or a training program for unemployed teenagers, the intent of the service within that building should be evident. But the recurring questions of how much service is actually being provided, what is its quality, and what is its result, cannot be ignored. The general public, the clients, and public officials ask these questions, and so should those working in human service.

Other questions also arise: What else is happening under the roof and between the walls of this building? How much activity is there that is not service related? How much political activity is a struggle for advantage? How much ritualistic behavior is occurring that has no purpose? How many formal activities are sanctioned by the organization that are dysfunctional to service? In short, how much service potential is lost in the *functioning* of the organization?

These questions form the core of the approach to human service management that has been developed in this book. The primary objective of management is to maximize the service-providing capacity of the organization and to minimize those activities that are dysfunctional or irrelevant to the quality of service. Utilizing this perspective, this book has presented an approach to human service management. The framework has pre-

sented key factors which vary and combine to form the underlying dynamics of service effectiveness and service dysfunction,
with the aim of providing an insight into "what to look for." This
book has discussed the functions of management both internal
and external to the organization, the formulation of strategies
designed to accomplish these functions, and the managerial styles
needed in the performance of human service management.
Further, we have presented an approach for defining the role of
management in the human services, a role that is closely inter-
related with that of the provision of direct service.

One question that often arises when human service management is discussed is: What formal background and training
should the human service manager possess? Is it necessary that
he or she have formalized training in the organization's specific
field of human services? We have stressed throughout that although there are similarities, the process of management is quite
different from that of providing direct services; a competent
clinician might not necessarily be an effective manager. Clinical
human service training may not prove a necessity in order to
perform some of the functions of management; however, the
enhancement of service resources and service effectiveness, both
internal and external to the organization, does require specific
knowledge of the particular human service field concerned. Although the manager need not be a highly skilled clinician, he or
she must possess a thorough knowledge of the state of the technology and should have an extremely sound basis on which to
assess the staff's level of technological possession. The manager,
as has been noted, must pursue an active role in enhancing organizational optimization and ultimate service effectiveness. It
is difficult to imagine that this could be done without the manager's having a formal familiarity with the human service field,
unless the technology is at a very primitive state. The tasks of
public relations as we have defined them, for example, would be
difficult to perform effectively without the authority of expertise. And it is unlikely that a manager could accomplish the
internal management process if the staff saw that he or she possessed no knowledge of the technology in which they are involved. The cost, particularly to those functioning in direct
services, of being managed by a person who did not exhibit a
familiarity with the necessary formal knowledge and training

would, in most cases, probably prove too great. And although a manager without such knowledge might be correct about a specific method of increasing optimization or service effectiveness, it is unlikely that he or she could generate the necessary support and cooperation. The manager's ability to base managerial authority on professional ability would be severely limited, and managerial initiative in the technological realm based on hierarchical position is a prescription for furthering the dysfunctions of the organization, rather than alleviating them. At the level of the planning organization, where less direct contact with practitioners exists, this would probably tend to be less true. It does seem apparent, however, that familiarity with human service technology is necessary in order to perform many of the functions that the concept of management presented in this book requires.

It is clear, however, that many individuals who hold management positions in human service organizations, particularly at the planning level, have no formal training in the specific human service technology utilized in their organization. Many pivotal positions are held by those whose backgrounds are in law, in business, public administration, or economics. This kind of training tends to emphasize the *process* of management and public service rather than the *outcome* from the perspective of service delivery. The resulting orientation can often omit questions of service quality and particularly the integration of managerial process and service outcome. Management is often viewed as a generic process that is applicable to a variety of organizational contexts. The result is an overemphasis on efficiency and other aspects of maintenance management, which is aggravated in times of scarce resources, when cutbacks and consolidation can become ends in themselves. A manager does not need formal credentials but does require knowledge about human service technology. He or she must understand the technology's potentials and limitations and must be prepared to integrate service management with maintenance management. If maintenance management is not to predominate by default, it seems clear that considerations of technology and the quality of care need to be included in graduate programs that ultimately produce individuals who manage in the human services. This is an issue that requires consideration in schools of public administration, business, law, and so forth if the rationality and effectiveness of management in human services is to be enhanced.

The identity of the human service manager at either the delivery or planning level needs to be closely intertwined with the technology of the service with which the organization or domain is involved. Like the clinician, the manager must develop a professional commitment to ensure the highest quality of service through the use of technology. It is this commitment that makes management in the human services different from management in other organizational contexts. Although the maintenance functions in other fields may be similar to those in the human services, the character of the service function is unique.

HUMAN SERVICE MANAGEMENT AND SOCIAL WELFARE

Perhaps the ultimate measure of a society lies in what it can offer those of its members who suffer from the social problems of its time. The social welfare institution in the United States represents society's organized attempt to meet the human needs of its population. Yet the social welfare institution is affected by periods of varying commitment on the part of the government and public. In some periods, social welfare is generously supported; in other times there is extensive criticism. The success or failure of social welfare in solving or alleviating social problems is a key factor in the degree of support it can command. Therefore, much depends on the ability of human service organizations to provide service that is recognized as effective and beneficial. Talcott Parsons has written: "A formal organization . . . is a mechanism by which goals somehow important to the society, or to various sub-systems of it, are implemented and, to some degree, defined."[1] These "goals somehow important to society" in the context of the human services are what we have termed the official goals. Society has, in effect, sanctioned the social welfare institution in general, and the human service organization specifically, to pursue these official goals in an attempt to alleviate social problems. The overall intent of the social sanction thus gets translated through the social welfare institution into the broad official goal of each human service organization, and little reward for society exists unless the organization can effectively deliver the service.

The present period and the immediate future pose a significant threat to the social welfare institution and the organizations that compose it. Political attitudes reflect skepticism; economic conditions ensure frugality.[2] The social welfare institution is in danger, and, as a result, there is less opportunity in our society for the compassion Americans hold for one another to be realized. This trend in attitude and condition needs to be reversed by a pragmatic effort that achieves convincing results.

Recent criticisms of social welfare advocates have ranged from the claim that they are "throwing money at problems" to characterizations such as "soft" and "bleeding heart." From the perspective of effectiveness and accountability, some of this criticism has been justified. As a result, political capital and economic support have been lost. Yet the suffering remains, the needs continue, and the effects of our social problems gnaw at the fabric of society. We need to reexamine our social welfare institution from the perspective of "what works." The answer does not lie in cutbacks or in the pursuit of efficiency and consolidation, for taken alone, these steps do not aid social welfare but dismantle it. We cannot afford to accept the argument: "The programs are not working, so the problems must be insoluble." We need to examine the approach, but we cannot ignore the task. A new pragmatic approach is necessary in relation to social welfare; an approach reflecting improvement not reduction, enrichment not abandonment. The kind of managerial approach stressed throughout this book can provide an instrument to those who would take the lead in this endeavor.

A pragmatic examination of the social welfare institution must lead us to the question: Why do programs fail? Three problem areas provide insights: (1) The technological approach that is used; (2) the degree of organizational co-optation that is present; and (3) the level of funding that is available.

(1) *The technological approach.* Throughout this book, we have stressed the importance of human service technology as the basis of service effectiveness. All human service organizations utilize some kind of technological approach—knowledge, assumptions, and techniques—which form the core of the service it delivers.

Sometimes this is a uniform approach, sometimes it is a mix. Sometimes its nature is purposive, emerging from deliberation; sometimes it is ritualistic, arising from "the way things are done here." Because of their importance, technological assumptions require constant and systematic scrutiny from manager and service practitioner alike. Such scrutiny must be probing and honest and not merely pro forma. If the technology is primitive that fact needs to be recognized and accepted, and technological improvement sought. The organization's use of available technology must also be questioned. Are technological decisions made and approaches adopted because they are correct or because they are traditional? Does a professional hierarchy hinder the quality of a technological approach? Are innovative approaches disregarded because there is a professional or ritualistic stake in the old? We need, then, to continually examine the premises of service, and to the limits of our knowledge try to determine whether the approach we are using is actually working. Do community residences, for example, provide better, more effective care than an institutional setting? If so, where and why? Is Alcoholics Anonymous more effective than professional care? Is methadone maintenance the best treatment for heroin addiction? Does employment counseling ultimately end in employment? Programs which do not have the appropriate service premises will ultimately fail.

(2) *Organizational co-optation.* We have also stressed the dynamics of organizational co-optation—how the functioning of a human service organization (the throughput process) can reduce the effectiveness of its service to recipients. At issue is the inability of many human service organizations, both on the planning and delivery levels, to function in ways that maximize their service resources. Therefore, these organizations do not provide acceptable levels of effective service to their clients. Those who are concerned with social welfare and responsible for its delivery need to examine carefully the difficult question regarding how the functioning of a human service organization affects the quality of its service. We have attempted in this book to indicate pivotal points of organizational functioning that lend themselves to such an examination. How is organizational optimization or co-optation a product of these dynamics in the functioning

of a human service organization? The answer lies in the inter-relationships of the level of its technology, the patterns of decision making, the maintenance of goals and its structure of authority and compliance. These factors in combination determine the nature of everyday activities such as hiring and firing, budget preparation, the dispersal of maintenance resources, trade-off mechanisms, personnel appraisal, the relationship between supervisor and practitioner, interorganizational relationships, the relationships between practitioner and client, accountability relationships, and so forth.

If those in management do not consider the effect of daily functioning on service quality, if management is confined to maintenance, and if there is no component of an organization that focuses on the manner in which organizational functioning affects the quality of care, then increased co-optation is the probable result. Part I of this book, in a sense, was a guide to the dynamics of such co-optation. The dynamics presented are not inexorable, but if ignored they will strongly affect the direction in which a human service organization is likely to drift. Given the necessity in social welfare for highly functional organizations, organizational co-optation needs to be reduced and human service management must take such reduction as its principal task. If through the application of management, optimization of service resources can be increased throughout the social welfare institution, then, surely, the ends to which that institution is dedicated will be served.

(3) *The level of available funding.* There is always more need than there is service. If two social workers are counseling a total of 40 students per week who suffer from emotional disorders interfering with their high school education, then whatever good which is being achieved and whatever the level of effectiveness, it can probably be doubled if there are sufficient funds for four social workers to see 80 students. In this instance, if funding were available for two more positions, society would presumably benefit through the treatment and alleviation of this kind of social problem. Funding is vital; without it there can be no service, and it is funding and its so-called waste that provides the leverage for opponents of social welfare.

What is crucial is the definition of waste—waste brought about by unnecessary duplication or by expenditures that do not contribute to service is unacceptable. Is it wasteful however to spend money on a program that is characterized by efficiency, but which fails to be completely effective due to inadequacy of technological development? It is impossible that every dollar invested in the human services will result in 100 cents of service effectiveness. The question is: What level of return is politically necessary? It is a matter of value. Some maintain that anything under "90 cents worth of effectiveness" is "social experimentation and a waste of taxpayers' money." Others may believe that even 20 cents "worth of effectiveness" in the alleviation of human suffering is money well spent. Here the focus is on the 20 that produces results rather than on the 80 that does not. Obviously, such quantification is impossible; the point is not one of numbers but one of general public perspective. In the 1960s, a program generally presented to be about 30 percent effective might have support; now 60 percent effectiveness might be a necessity. Yet, problems of technology and co-optation make such success difficult, and this is the dilemma facing social welfare. Demonstrations of efficiency are required and successful maintenance management is a necessity. Public support cannot be counted on if "waste" actually does exist, but ultimately effectiveness is the best "salesman" for social welfare and effectiveness cannot be achieved unless the problem areas of technology and co-optation are confronted.

Can human service management attain success in confronting the problems of appropriate technology, of organizational co-optation, and of funding; can service effectiveness actually be improved? The problem leads us beyond the perspective of the individual human service organization and its management to the structure of the whole social welfare institution itself. The management of individual human service organizations can achieve only so much; it is often limited by the *structure* of the social welfare institution in which it operates. In short, *the organizational structure of the social welfare institution needs reexamination from the perspective of its contribution to service effectiveness.* The tangled interrelationship of funding and administrative procedures on the federal, state, regional, and local levels of government requires exploration.[3] Can this structure be improved so as to facilitate more effective application of human service technology and less organizational co-optation? At present there are many problems.[4] Since the mid-1960s, a myriad of different programs have been established in response to a variety of recipient groups. Such programs were often initiated with little regard for the relationships between organizations charged with the planning and delivery of service, and for the overlap among recipient groups. Because so many programs were developed more in response to individual groups as each new need was identified than to technological capabilities and the need for rational, coordinated delivery systems, they often created conflicting political domains. Thus, programs for aging, youth, alcoholism, mental health, minorities, women, poverty, and housing came into being without sufficient integration on the federal, state, regional, and local levels. Next came the "umbrella" agencies, charged with coordinating programs on a local level. The official goals of these organizations often overlapped with other agencies responsible for coordination of different services in the same community. For example, a program serving poor alcoholics might be caught between the conflicting coordinating efforts of a poverty program's "umbrella" agency and an alcoholism services coordinating council. At times the only solution appears to be the creation of an agency for coordinating coordinative agencies!

The problem of fragmentation is compounded by the varying degrees of local autonomy granted by each state. These structures have emerged from tradition, the interplay of political forces, and a multitude of funding patterns. Competing interests, rather than integrated service, are often the result. Political interests in, for example, aging, mental retardation, mental illness, and so forth may conflict with concerns about youth. Much management energy is expended to deal with these political exigencies and the victim is the quality of care. Fragmentation has also resulted in a single agency having multiple funding sources, making it simultaneously accountable to several external bodies. Different regulations, for monitoring and accountability, tax limited staff and divert energies from programmatic objectives. Quality care again is the victim.

As in an individual human service organization in which the

throughput functioning can have an enormous influence on service outcome, so, too, can the overall structure of program implementation adversely affect the intent of policy. The point to determine is what kind of structural arrangement is most likely to ensure the quality of care in service delivery. There is no question that youth, the aging, the mentally ill, and many others need services; the issue is how these services can best be organized to bring about effective results.

Answering these questions requires structural planning within the social welfare institution itself. This planning, based on a realistic assessment of service capability, must focus on fashioning a structure that will maximize the use of service capability and minimize co-optation arising through dysfunctional interorganizational relationships.

Although the social welfare institution in the United States is decentralized and is thus not amenable to sweeping uniform changes, several alterations could improve the quality of service delivery and service outcome. These are (1) improved policy initiation; (2) improved linkages; and (3) centralized accountability for program effectiveness.

(1) IMPROVED POLICY INITIATION

Despite decentralization of *implementation*, policy *initiation* has traditionally been from "the top down" in social welfare. Such initiation is often vague with technological considerations lost in the process. Theodore Lowi, in discussing bureaucratic digression at the lower levels of implementation has noted that

> There is nothing in the clauses of the statutes and official records that even the most legally minded bureaucrat can feel guided by. There is no guidance because all the appropriate categories are open-ended. There are lists always introduced with "not limited to" or "such as. . . ."[5]

When policy is initiated at the national level, thereby creating or altering human services, far more attention needs to be paid to (1) human service technology and capability; (2) the organizational structures that will deliver the service; and (3) the relationship of new service structures to those already in existence. Too often policy has been made at the national level without sufficient consideration of these three factors.

The ability of the human service organization to function effectively is the ultimate test of the efficacy of the social welfare institution. Yet the dynamics of co-optation and optimization in human service organization may depend on the nature of the policies that create them. If those policies are not informed by appropriate technological and structural considerations, then the beginnings of co-optation and service ineffectiveness are planted even before the organization begins to operate. The making of social welfare policy may, in effect, be characterized by noncongruent decision making on a large scale. Politics and values may well have come to eclipse the rational consideration of service capability, and the result is the creation of a vast network of highly ineffective organizations. In the policy process, consideration may be given to politics, economics, timing, administrative factors, and legal questions and human needs, but they must be weighed in terms of the three issues raised above: (1) Given current knowledge, what program approaches or combination of approaches will work best? (2) What kind of organizational structure might best implement this approach? (3) How, given the approach chosen, can the organizational structure be coordinated with structures already in place? In short, more needs to be done than to state official goals, create an organization, and appropriate funds. The implementation of effective human service in the complexity of postindustrial society requires far more of the policy process. Program assumptions need to be questioned *before* programs are enacted. For example, if the official goal is the elimination of poverty, then the approach of the Community Action Program—the dispersing of money to a multitude of communities across the country with little accountability for effectiveness and with vague guidelines—may not be sufficient for the task. Technology will seldom guarantee program results—we have often referred to the primitiveness of human service technology—but there is an obligation to use available knowledge as much as possible as a means of evaluating service methods. This assessment process needs to play a far greater role in policy making.

What is required is a formalized component which can channel considerations of human service technology and organizational structure into the policy-making process. Staff work, which currently informs the creation of policy, needs to include these considerations, both in the legislative and executive areas of government. Many ideas designed to achieve this end have been advanced. Among these are the establishment of governmental institutes of social policy analysis and the creation of "social reports," which portray the social health of the nation and indicate where policy and program require improvement. These and similar ideas require further exploration.[6]

(2) IMPROVED LINKAGES

Policies are implemented through a network of organizational linkages. As noted in Chapter Twelve, much can be achieved by improving these linkages at all levels of human service organizations. These linkages need to be characterized by *the interchange of issues and concerns regarding technology, service capability, and service outcome*. Issues of maintenance need to be closely integrated with questions of service, but not be permitted to virtually displace them. In some cases, existing linkages must be altered to allow for more service considerations, by changing the functions of staff responsible for interorganizational relationships. In others, structural attention, such as regionalization, may be necessary; in still other cases, the elimination of bureaucratic layers may prove to be the best approach. Just as in the individual human service organization, there needs to be some aspect in the linkage between organizations, which is responsible for the promotion of the quality of care. Such a component must possess the authority to intervene when interorganizational structure causes organizational co-optation and when there is a significant opportunity for optimization. Several kinds of linkages are appropriate.

(a) *The linkages within one focal domain.* The first set of linkages involves the relationships between the planning organization and the delivery organization. Attention needs to be focused on whether these relationships facilitate the reduction of co-optation and the enhancement of optimization, and whether structural alteration can help bring this about. Practitioners of management have observed that delivery organizations do not communicate information about procedures and approaches that could be of help to other organizations facing similar problems with similar client populations. As noted in Chapter Twelve, the planning organization should assume the initiative in encouraging such formalized linkages;[7] much freedom exists within the legal structure of many human service networks for the establishment of structures of communication. For example, shared activities by appropriate numbers of service delivery organizations in areas such as budget preparation, program evaluation, staff development, community relations, and so forth could help in the development of a more coordinated substantively oriented organizational interaction within a focal domain. Increased service management and decreased fragmentation would result. Much managerial effort is required in this regard, but the payoffs for social welfare are significant.

(b) *Linkages between planning organizations.* This is a very fertile area for human service management. State departments of corrections, youth, and mental health, for example, may function in isolation. Yet the actual technological content of their effort from a service perspective may be very similar with shared procedures, approaches, and client problems. The duplication of effort, and the "falling between the cracks" on the part of service recipients is often a result of the manner in which these services are structured. The barriers between planning organizations in different areas and their respective delivery organizations need to be analyzed and eliminated.[8] Such effort needs to be achieved on the basis of technology and capability—"what works and works best together." This may well require the participation and direction of top governmental levels whose power supersedes the various human service departments—for instance, the Bureau of the Budget (or similar state-level component) or the office of the governor. Such reorganizations are often attempted, but the impetus has usually been to save money—rarely to improve the quality of service. What has occurred between focal domains is that the relationships have been guided by political interest, tradition, and budgetary competition, rather than technological and service considerations. Often when the meetings end and the squabbling subsides, the issue of the quality of care has received little attention and even less action. The potential for human service management in this area is enormous, and the benefit for the social welfare institution is significant.

(c) *Community linkages.* The third type of organizational linkages concerns the community that surrounds a human service delivery organization. Most important are those organizations that deliver similar or the same services, but, because they function under different auspices, have no formal relationship. For example, a local department of mental health that is part of a governmental structure may have no formal relationship with a private family counseling agency funded through United Way or Community Chest. Yet the clients they serve and the technologies they employ are similar, and a formalized linkage between them could improve service. Such linkages are often difficult to achieve because no formal mechanism often exists that can relate public and private agencies. Yet the opportunity for mutual benefit is certainly present. This is most likely on the local delivery level, although planning level organization needs to relate more consistently with the private sector social welfare to facilitate such beneficial linkages.

(d) *Input linkages.* Finally, linkages are needed between human service organizations and the places in society where developments and innovations in human service technology are being developed. As has been previously noted, many delivery and planning organizations are not open to technological innovation and others ritualistically "do things the way they've always been done." But the service resources, or input, of human service organizations can be improved by the ongoing injection of new techniques, knowledge, and perspective, thus aiding in achieving organizational optimization. The social welfare institution lacks such formalized input. Linkages need to be established between the planning and delivery organizations, on the one hand, and universities, hospitals, and research locations, on the other. These linkages should ensure that the transmission of technological development is more than serendipitous and informal, with a resulting payoff in service effectiveness.

In discussing the dynamics of patterns of service effectiveness, the enhancing of the input is the most important activity in leading an organization to optimization. The often-ignored activity of providing organized mechanisms for the transmission of new human service technology requires managerial attention. Governmental bodies with national perspective, such as HHS, need to assume leadership in this regard.

(3) CENTRALIZED ACCOUNTABILITY

If the goal of structural change is the improvement of service quality, then improved policy formulation and the establishment of interorganizational linkages reflecting the substance of service provides an important but not sufficient step. There needs to be far more accountability on the part of organizations throughout the social welfare institution. As with linkages, such accountability needs to be for *service outcome*, not merely for maintenance. It must result from program evaluation, not from reporting systems, and focus on the alleviation of social problems, not on the proficient keeping of the books. The mere advocacy of such accountability is not sufficient; trade-offs must be built into the structure of social welfare that motivate human service organizations toward the pursuit of such accountability.

The predilection for local autonomy and decentralization in this country is strong and appropriately so. However, at the present stage in the development of social welfare, given scarce resources and the need for effectiveness, excessive decentralization may be costing too much in terms of the quality of service outcome. Accountability that provides incentives for service effectiveness cannot be achieved without some shift toward more centralized human services. Although service delivery must remain decentralized and locally based, accountability needs to be closely tied to the deployment of fiscal resources to the delivery organizations. In short, to the degree possible, resources need to be granted on the basis of actual results. This is true accountability, which presumably is what the public would support. This kind of accountability will help the recipients of service, and that will ultimately strengthen social welfare. There is some risk in more centralized accountability, which could result in the greater concentration of power and authority in fewer governmental locations. However, is it rational to have more than 4,000 separate departments of public welfare throughout the country, each with some autonomy to provide income and services to the poor in 4,000 separate ways, none of which is formally accountable for actual program quality? The same holds true in lesser numbers in many of the other human services. It is unlikely that a business could be run this way, with effective results. It is also unlikely that other governmental endeavors, such as defense, could be organized effectively if every locality maintained its own department of defense with a significant degree of autonomy for both organization and delivery.

Given the urgent need for increased effectiveness, there seems little alternative for social welfare but to move toward more centralized accountability. This can be achieved through changes in the legal structure that create agencies and their relationships. It also be achieved through fiscal relationships. For example, each agency in a given service area could be required to set aside a certain percentage of its budget for the evaluation of its programs and the results of such evaluation utilized in program improvement. There is more leverage in some human service areas than in others for the application of centralized authority, but the idea needs consideration throughout the social welfare institution if its effectiveness is to be augmented.

It is important to distinguish centralized accountability from centralization. Centralization would mean the elimination of 10,000 local departments of welfare, and a direct relationship between HEW and the recipient, as in Social Security. Social Security has local offices but they are federal offices that are not controlled by localities. In the area of income policy, such as the income maintenance aspect of public welfare, centralization does seem more appropriate for reasons of equity. In the service areas, the issue of whether the employees of a local office are under the administrative auspices of federal, state, or local levels of government is less important than the quality of care that is being provided. Accountability for the quality of service is the issue, not what level of administration controls the organization. If effectiveness can be improved through centralized accountability, then that would be preferable to increased centralization, although the latter may ultimately require consideration if the former fails.

The functioning of the social welfare institution can thus be improved through a technologically informed policy process, through the initiation of specified kinds of linkages and through more centralized accountability. This is neither a panacea nor a blueprint; it is, rather, a perspective, which, by concentrating upon program approach and program delivery as a way of achieving some effectiveness and gaining public support for social welfare, offers a viable alternative to dismantling social welfare—a direction in which we may be heading.

The kind of human service management discussed in this book will accomplish less if it is practiced in a vacuum. Structural changes in the institution are required and ideally should occur in concert with the efforts of human service management at the delivery and planning levels. Organizations such as HHS need to play a far more active role in bringing about these changes, for the problems are national in scope.

These departments need to move in two directions, reflecting the service management conception of this book. First, they must attempt, through the use of finding incentives, changes in guidelines, and alterations of program procedures to stimulate the performance of service functions inside human service organizations. Incentives or the establishment of integrated programs of budgeting, program evaluation, community relations, and staff development need to be created to a far greater extent than has been the case in the past. Should a program of counseling, for example, be supported which does not demonstrate evidence of program evaluation or effort to improve staff skills? Should some degree of funding be based on the pursuit of these and other functions? Secondly, federal departments need to help institute changes in the institutional structure of social welfare. Organizational reform, such as establishing the needed linkages, increasing centralized accountability, and creating a technologically informed policy process, needs to be directed from the national level.

In short, departments such as HHS need to complement their current role as a grantor and monitor of funds, with far more involvement in issues regarding the quality of care which such funds are intended to achieve. This can be achieved without new money, but not without pain. The vested political interests of current bureaucratic entrenchment often appear inexorable in the face of proposed reform. Yet, if effectiveness is to be achieved and support for social welfare gathered, there is no choice.

Less tangible than such structural changes, but equally as significant in relationship to social welfare is national political leadership. In the first chapter of this book, it was noted that American attitudes toward social welfare vary with the times. One influence on shaping these attitudes is the view of social welfare communicated by national political leaders. Neglect can foster apathy: negativism can bring about opposition; inaction can ensure despair. On the other hand, if government leaders communicate a sense of the possible, it can engender support for the social welfare institution. The federal government has assumed such leadership in the past, particularly during the years of the New Deal and the Great Society. Both policy and message, however, need to be tempered by contemporary reality. The compassion of the American people for groups who need special social programs, and their self-interest as program recipients themselves, form the basis of national support for social welfare. This can only be brought forth and sustained by demonstrations of program effectiveness. In Chapter Eleven, the concepts of education and advocacy were presented as important tasks of human service management in individual organizations. Similar approaches are possible at the national level. Education about social problems and about the services designed to alleviate them is a necessity. So too is advocacy stressing the value of such services and the unacceptable cost of leaving the problems unsolved. We live in a society of specialized and powerful interest groups; social welfare needs similarly aggressive representation.

As we have argued in this book, there is need for a new perspective in human service management. Most would agree that the social welfare institution needs to be better managed. In the period of the next few years, the nature of that management may well be decided. It appears that because of the manner in which management has been traditionally conceived in the United States, the human services are moving toward the wholesale adoption of the procedures and techniques of business management and public administration. Little attention has been given to the factors that distinguish human service management from management in these other spheres. This book has confronted that issue. Throughout the social welfare institution, we need human service managers who will pursue the compassionate ends that their organizations were designed to achieve; who will be pragmatic in the pursuit of these ends; who understand the technology of the service in which their organization is involved; who will perceive service effectiveness as their ultimate goal, and who will strive to improve and augment service, not to eliminate it. We need human service managers who understand the dynamics of their organization as those dynamics influence service effectiveness. We need managers who understand the relationship of maintenance functions and service functions, and can help create a system of managerial process that represents a balance between the two. We need managers who can understand the nature of trade-offs and can utilize them in the achievement of service effectiveness. We need managers who are concerned with the welfare of their community, as well as with the organization to which they are accountable. And we need managers who can help plan and implement the structural changes required to improve the social welfare institution.

The ultimate strength of social welfare, both in terms of political support and fiscal survival, lies in the development of a managerial perspective that can bring about more *effective* use of resources. The more *efficient* use of resources, although important, needs to be viewed only as an important accompaniment to effectiveness. Efficiency itself may provide short-term protection, but not long-term durability, and certainly not an answer to human need. It is superficial to maintain that the programs of the 1960s failed to build a lasting constituency among the public because these programs squandered resources and were inefficient. More to the point, *they did not work;* and because they were not effective, they did not provide a sufficient measure of official goal achievement. It is effectiveness that compels attention and should form the nature of our perceptions about social programs, and it is effectiveness that should define the questions we ask about social programs—questions that do not center on issues such as:

> How many recipients went through a Job Corps program? And at what cost? And what were their demographic characteristics?

But rather:

> How many recipients hold full-time jobs at adequate wages one year after participation in the program?

Not on questions as:

> How many patients are seen per therapist in a mental health program? What are the demographic characteristics of the patients?

But rather:

> How many patients are functioning better and to what degree after participating in the program?

Not:

> How many community meetings were held during the past year at a local OEO office?

But rather:

> Has poverty been alleviated in that community?

We return, then, to the point at which we began in the introduction. Those who are concerned with the survival and growth of social welfare must examine the conduct of our human service programs. For it is a lack of management, management as we have described it throughout the book, that has caused, and will continue to cause, difficulties for the institution and its organizations: difficulties in goal achievement and in alleviating human need, difficulties in gaining political consensus and social sanctions, and difficulties in obtaining financial resources. These difficulties are manifested and aggravated when human service organizations display a high degree of organizational co-optation. They are augmented, too, when organizations do not forge interorganizational linkages from complementary service capabilities; when opportunities for public education and explanation are not sought; when there is little or no program evaluation; when maintenance predominates in the budgetary process, in staff development, and in community relations; and when important elements of technology and personnel that can improve service quality are not brought in to the appropriate components of an organization because there is no functioning mechanism with which to do so.

The confrontation and successful treatment of these problems is both subtle and demanding; the specific tasks involved, the balance between functions that must be struck, the personnel to be included, and the multiplicity of interests and trade-offs needing consideration, all provide imposing challenges. Yet no purpose as important as the alleviation of social problems and human need can go unmanaged and unplanned. Increased effectiveness in human services need not await the development of a perfect technology, nor does it demand technological intricacy; rather, it requires the intelligent and realistic use of the technology available. In the final analysis, those concerned about the survival and development of the social welfare and human services need to help conceive, implement, and deliver service programs and concepts that work, and meet human needs. Those in human service management are in a unique position to assume a role of leadership in this endeavor.

NOTES

1. Talcott Parsons, *The Social System* (New York: Free Press, 1952), p. 286.
2. For a presentation of accumulated disbelief in political solutions to our problems see R. E. Miles, *Awakening From The American Dream* (New York: Universe Books, 1976).
3. James Sunquist et al., *Centrally Planned Change: A Re-examination of Theories and Concepts* (Urbana: University of Illinois Press, 1974).
4. Alfred J. Kahn, "Perspectives on Access to Social Services," *Social Work*, vol. 15, no. 2, April 1970, pp. 95–101; Winfred Bell,

"Services for People: An Appraisal," *Social Work*, vol. 15, no. 3, July 1970, pp. 5–12.

5. Theodore Lowi, *The End of Liberalism* (New York: W. W. Norton, 1969), p. 236.
6. See for example, *Toward a Social Report* (U.S. Department of HEW, Washington, D.C., 1969), under the direction of Mancur Olson.
7. Downes, Anthony, *Inside Bureaucracy* (Boston: Little Brown & Co., 1967), p. 315.
8. For problems inherent in this process see Herbert Kaufman, "Administrative Decentralization and Political Power," *Public Administration Review*, vol. 29, Jan.–Feb. 1969.

Bibliography

Administrative Science Quarterly. (special issue) 3(3) (December 1958.)

Aiken H. and J. Gage. "Organizational Interdependence and Intra-Organizational Structure." *American Sociological Review,* 33(6), 1968, 912–30.

Aldrich, Howard. "Technology and Organizational Structure: A Re-examination of the Findings of the Aston Group." *Administrative Science Quarterly,* 17 (March 1972), 26–43.

Anderson, Wayne, Bernard J. Freeden and Michael J. Murphy (eds.) *Managing Human Services.* Washington, D.C.: International City Management Association, 1977.

Anderson, Theodore and Seymour Workow. "Organization Size and Functional Complexity: A Study of Administration in Hospitals." *American Sociological Review,* 20(1), 23–28.

Argyris, Chris. *Integrating the Individual and the Organization.* New York: John Wiley and Sons, 1962.

———. "Interpersonal Barriers to Decision-Making." *Harvard Business Review,* 44 (March-April 1966), 84–97.

———. *The Applicability of Organizational Sociology.* Cambridge (England): Cambridge University Press, 1972.

Arkava, Morton L. and E. Clifford Brennen (eds.) *Competency-Based Education for Social Work: Evaluation and Curriculum Issues.* New York: Council on Social Work Education, 1976.

Azumi, Koya and Jerald Hage. *Organizational Systems: A Text Reader in the Sociology of Organizations.* Lexington, Mass.: Heath Publishing Co., 1972.

Beck, Walter E. "Agency Structure Related to the Use of Staff." *Social Casework,* 50 (June 1959), 341–46.

Bell, William. "Obstacles to Shifting from a Descriptive to an Analytical Approach in Teaching Social Services." Journal of Social Work Education (Spring 1969), 5–13.

———. "Staff Education in Systems Change." *Social Casework,* 53(4) (1972), 236–42.

Bell, Winifred. "Services for People: An Appraisal." *Social Work,* 15(3) (July 1970), 5–12.

Berliner, A. K. "Curriculum: Education for Mental Health Administration." *Administration in Mental Health* (Summer 1974), 77–85.

————. "Some Pitfalls in Administrative Behavior." *Social Casework* 52(9) (1971), 562–66.

Berne, Eric, M.D. *Games People Play: The Psychology of Human Relationships*. New York: Grove Press, 1964.

Biggerstaff, Marilyn A. "The Administrator and Social Agency Evaluation," *Administration in Social Work* 1(1), 71–78.

Blau, Peter M. *The Dynamics of Bureaucracy: A Study of Interpersonal Relations in Two Government Agencies*. Chicago: University of Chicago Press, 1955.

————. "A Formal Theory of Differentiation in Organizations." *American Sociological Review* 35 (April 1970), 201–18.

————. "The Hierarchy of Authority in Organizations." *American Journal of Sociology* 73(4), (1968), 453–67.

————, Wolf V. Heydebrand, and Robert Stauffer. "The Structure of Small Bureaucracies." *American Sociological Review* 31 (April 1966), 179–91.

————, and Richard Schoenherr. *The Structure of Organizations*. New York: Basic Books, 1971.

————, and W. Richard Scott. *Formal Organizations: A Comparative Approach*. San Francisco: Chandler Publishing Co., 1962.

Blonney, Norman and Lawrence A. Streicher. "Time-Cost Data in Agency Administration: Efficiency Controls in Family and Children's Service." *Social Work* 15 (October 1970), 23–31.

Bloom, Martin. "Analysis of the Research on Educating Social Work Student." *Journal of Education for Social Work* (Fall 1976) 12(3), 3–10.

Bobbie, Richard and Robert Schaffer. "Mastering Change: Breakthrough Projects and Beyond." *American Management Association Management Bulletin No. 120*, 1968.

Bocchino, William. *Management Information Systems: Tools and Techniques*. Englewood Cliffs, N.J.: Prentice-Hall, 1972.

Boehm, Werner W. "Social Work Education: Issues and Problems in Light of Recent Development." *Journal of Education for Social Work* 12(1) (Winter 1976), 20–27.

Brady, R. H. "MBO Goes to Work in the Public Sector." *Harvard Business Review* (March 1973), 65–74.

Brager, George A. and Steven Holloway. *Changing Human Service Organizations: Politics and Practice*. New York: Free Press, 1978.

Braybrooke, D. and Charles E. Lindblom. *A Strategy of Decision: Policy Evaluation as a Social Process*. Glencoe, Ill.: Free Press, 1963.

Brenner, Melvin N. "The Quest for Viable Research in Social Services: Development of the Ministudy." *Social Service Review* (September 1976), 426–44.

Brewer, J. "New Dimensions on Employee Development: A System for Career Planning and Guidance." *Personnel Journal* 54 (April 1975), 228–31.

Brody, Stanley, Harvey Finkle, and Carl Hirsch. "Benefit Alert: Outreach Program for the Aged." *Social Work* 17(1) (January 1972), pp. 14–23.

Brown, D. S. "The Management of Advisory Committees: An Assignment for the 70's." *Public Administration Review* (July–August 1972), 334–42.

Brown, R. G. S. *The Management of Welfare: A Study of British Social Service Administration.* London: William Collins, 1975.

Bucher, R. and J. Stelling. "Characteristics of Professional Organizations." *Journal of Health and Social Behavior* 10(1) (March 1969), 3 ff.

Burns, Tom and G. M. Stalker. *The Management of Innovation.* London: Tavistock Publications, 1961.

Butterfield, Anthony. "An Integrative Approach to the Study of Leadership Effectiveness in Organizations." Doctoral dissertation: University of Michigan, 1968.

Buttrick, Shirley M. and Vernon Miller. "An Approach to Zero-Base Budgeting." *Administration in Social Work* 2(1) (Spring), 1978.

Callahan, James J., Jr. "Obstacles and Social Planning." *Social Work* 18(6), (November 1973), 70–79.

Carlson, Norman A. "Designing and Selling a Staff Training Program: A Case Study." *Public Administration Review* (November–December 1971), 632–36.

Caro, Francis G. (ed.) *Readings in Evaluation Research.* New York: Russell Sage Foundation, 1971.

Carter, G. W. "The Challenge of Accountability—How We Measure the Outcomes of Our Efforts," *Public Welfare* 29 (1971), 267–77.

Catherwood, H. R. "A Management Information System for Social Services." *Public Welfare* 32(3) (1974), 54–61.

Cheek, Logan. *Zero-Based Budgeting Comes of Age.* New York: AMACOM, 1977.

Chommie, Peter W. and Joe Hudson. "Evaluation of Outcome and Process." *Social Work* 19(6) (1974), 682–87.

Churchman, C. West. *The Systems Approach.* New York: Delta, 1968.

Coursey, Robert D. et al. *Program Evaluation for Mental Health: Methods, Strategies and Participants.* New York: Grune and Stratton, 1977.

Craig, R. L. and L. Bittel (eds.) *Training and Development Handbook*. New York: American Management Association, 1971.

Cressey, Donald. "Achievement of an Understated Organizational Goal." *Pacific Sociological Review* 1(2) (1958), 43–49.

Crowfoot, J. E. *Planning and Social Systems: Organizations as a Special Case*. Ann Arbor, Mich.: University of Michigan, Center for Research on Utilization of Scientific Knowledge, 1972.

Cruthirds, C. T. "Management Should be Accountable Too." *Social Work* 21(3) (1976), 114–20.

Cumming, John and Elaine. "Social Equilibrium and Social Change in the Large Mental Hospital." In *The Patient and the Mental Hospital*, M. Greenblatt, D. Levinson and R. Williams (eds.) New York: Free Press, 1957.

Cutlip, Scott M. (ed.) *Public Opinion and Public Administration*. Montgomery, Ala.: University of Alabama Bureau of Public Administration, 1965.

————, and Allen H. Center. *Effective Public Relations*. Englewood Cliffs, N.J.: Prentice-Hall, 1971.

Cutt, James. *Program Budgeting for Welfare: A Case Study of Canada*. New York: Praeger Publishers, 1973.

Dales, Sophie, "Federal Grants to State and Local Governments, 1970–71." *Social Security Bulletin* 35(6), 29–38.

Denhardt, R. B. "Bureaucratic Socialization and Organizational Accommodation." *Administrative Science Quarterly* 13(3) (1968), 441–50.

————. "Leadership Style, Worker Involvement, and Deterrence to Authority." *Sociology and Social Research* 54 (1970), 172–80.

De Woolfson, Bruce H., Jr., "Public Sector MBO and PPBS: Cross Fertilization in Management Systems." *Public Administration Review* 35 (October 1976), 523–28.

Dimock, Mildred. *Administrative Vitality*. New York: Harper & Row, 1959.

Donahue, J. H. et al. "The Social Service Information System." *Child Welfare* 53(4) (1974), 243–56.

Drezner, S. M. "The Emerging Art of Decision-Making." *Social Casework* 54(1) (1973), 3–12.

Drucker, Peter F. "Managing the Public Service Institution." *The Public Interest* No. 33, Fall, 1973, 43–60.

————. *Management: Tasks, Responsibilities, Practices*. New York: Harper & Row, 1974.

Dudley, J. R. "Is Social Planning Social Work?" *Social Work* 23(1) (January 1978), 37–41.

Duet, C. P., Jr. and J. W. Newfield. "Sources of Information for the

Development of Training Programs." *Personnel Journal* 54 (March 1975), 162–64.

Duncan, Robert B. "Characteristics of Organizational Environments and Perceived Environmental Uncertainty." *Administrative Science Quarterly* 17 (September 1972), 313–27.

Eaton, Joseph. "Symbolic and Substantive Evaluative Research." *Administrative Science Quarterly* 6 (March 1962), 421–42.

Elbow, M. "On Becoming an Executive Director." *Social Casework* 56(9) (November 1975), 526–30.

Elkin, R. "Systems Approach to Managing Welfare Programs." *Social Work Practice, 1968*. Selected Papers, 95th Annual Forum, National Conference on Social Welfare, 159–74.

———— and D. J. Vonwaller. "Evaluating the Effectiveness of Social Services." *Management Controls* 19(5) (1972), 104–11.

Emery, J. C. "Overview of Management Information Systems." *Management Review* 63 (July 1974), 44–47.

Enblow, A. J. and W. C. Weston. "Cooperation or Chaos: The Mental Health Administrator's Dilemma." *American Journal of Orthopsychiatry* 42(4) (1972), 603–09.

Encyclopedia of Social Work, (2 vols.) Washington, D.C.: National Association of Social Workers, 17th Ed., 1977.

Engel, Gloria. "The Effects of Bureaucracy on the Professional Autonomy of Physicians." *Journal of Health and Social Behavior* 10(1), 30–41.

Epstein, I. and T. Tripodi. *Research Techniques for Program Planning, Monitoring and Evaluation*. New York: Columbia University Press, 1977.

Etzioni, Amitai. "Authority Structure and Organizational Effectiveness." *Administrative Science Quarterly* 4 (June 1959), 43–67.

————. *A Comparative Analysis of Complex Organizations: On Power, Involvement and their Correlates*. New York: Free Press, 1961.

————. "Mixed Scanning: A 'Third' Approach to Decision Making." *Public Administration Review* 27(5) (1967), 385–92.

————. *Modern Organizations*. Englewood Cliffs, N.J.: Prentice-Hall, 1964.

————. "Alternative Conceptions of Accountability: The Example of Health Administration." *Public Administration Review* 35 (May–June 1975), 279–86.

————, (ed.) *The Semi-Professions and Their Organization*. New York: Free Press, 1969.

Evan, William. "Toward a Theory of Inter-organizational Relations." *Management Science* 11 (August 1965), 217–30.

Fallon, K. P., Jr. "Participating Management: An Alternative in Human Service Delivery Systems." *Child Welfare* 53(9) (1974), 555–62.

Fanshel, David (ed.) *Research in Social Welfare Administration: Its Contributions and Problems.* New York: National Association of Social Workers, 1962.

Feldman, Saul. "Budgeting and Behavior." In *The Administration of Mental Health,* Saul Feldman, (ed.), Springfield, Ill.: Charles C Thomas, 1973.

Fellin, P. "Issues in Making Decisions on a Merger of Agencies." *Child Welfare* 51(5) (1972), 280–86.

Fischer, Joel. "Is Casework Effective: A Review." *Social Work* 18(1) (January 1973), 5–20.

Fisher, William, Jr. "Social Agencies: A New Challenge for Public Relations." *Public Relations Quarterly* 4 (April 1959), 14–21.

Fordyce, Jack. *Managing with People: A Manager's Handbook of Organization Development Methods.* Reading, Mass.: Addison-Wesley Publishing Co., 1971.

Frank, Andrew G. "Goal Ambiguity and Conflicting Standards: An Approach to the Study of Organizations." *Human Organization* 17 (Winter 1959), 8–13.

Franklin, J. L. and J. H. Thrasher. *An Introduction to Program Evaluation.* New York: John Wiley and Sons, 1976.

Frey, L. A., E. Shatz, and K. Katz. "Continuing Education—Teaching Staff to Teach." *Social Casework* 55(6) (June 1974), 360–68.

Friedlander, Frank and Hal Pickle. "Components of Effectiveness in Small Organizations." *Administrative Science Quarterly* 13(2) (1968), 289–306.

Friedman, I. J. "Psychiatric Administration." *New York State Journal of Medicine* 74 (1974), 884–86.

Fullan, Michael. "Industrial Technology and Worker Integration in the Organization." *American Sociological Review* 35 (December 1970), 1028–39.

Galbraith, John Kenneth. *Economics and the Public Purpose.* New York: Houghton-Mifflin, 1973.

Georgopoulos, Basil and Floyd Mann. *The Community General Hospital.* New York: Macmillan, 1962.

Gerth, H. H. and C. W. Mills. *From Max Weber: Essays in Sociology.* New York: Columbia University Press, 1976.

Gibson, F. K. and C. E. Teasley. "The Humanistic Model of Organizational Motivation: A Review of Research Support." *Public Administration Review* 33(1) (1973), 89–96.

Gilbert, Neil and Harry Specht. *Dimensions of Social Welfare Policy.* Englewood Cliffs: Prentice-Hall, 1974.

———. "The Incomplete Profession." *Social Work* 19(6) (November 1974), 665–74.

———. *Planning for Social Welfare: Issues, Models and Tasks.* Englewood Cliffs, N.J.: Prentice-Hall, 1977.

———. "Quantitative Aspects of Social Service Coordination Efforts: Is More Better?" *Administration in Social Work* 1 (Spring 1977), 53–61.

Gilbert, Neil, Armand Rosenkrantz, and Harry Specht. "Dialectics of Social Planning." *Social Work* 18(2) (March 1973), 78–156.

Gil, David. *The Challenge of Social Equality: Essays on Social Policy, Social Development and Political Practice.* Cambridge, Mass.: Schenkman Publishing Co., 1976.

———. *Unravelling Social Policy.* Cambridge, Mass.: Schenkman Publishing Co., 1973.

Gillespie, David F. "Discovering and Describing Organizational Goal Conflict." *Administration in Social Work* 1(4) (Winter 1977), 395–408.

Glennester, H. *Social Service Budgets and Social Policy: British and American Experience.* New York: Barnes and Noble, 1976.

Goffman, Erving. *Asylums.* New York: Doubleday, 1961.

Golembiewski, Robert. *Renewing Organizations: The Laboratory Approach to Planned Change.* Itasca, Ill.: F. W. Peacock Publishers, 1972.

———, and Frank Gibson, (eds.) *Managerial Behavior and Organizational Demands: Management as a Linking of Levels of Interaction.* Chicago: Rand McNally, 1967.

Goode, William J. "Encroachment, Charlatanism and the Emerging Profession: Psychology, Sociology and Medicine." *American Sociological Review* 25 (December 1960), 902–14.

Gortner, Harold F., *Administration in the Public Sector.* New York: John Wiley and Sons, 1977.

Granwald, Donald K. "Supervision by Objectives." *Administration in Social Work* 2(2), 199–209.

———. "Supervisory Style and Educational Preparation of Public Welfare Supervisors." *Social Work Administration* 1(1), 79–88.

Greenwood, Ernest. "Attributes of a Profession." *Social Work* (2) 3 (July 1957), 45–55.

Gronbjerg, Kirsten A. *Mass Society and the Extension of Welfare,* Chicago: University of Chicago Press, 1977.

Grosser, Charles F. *New Directions in Community Organization: From Enabling to Advocacy.* New York: Praeger, 1973.

Gruber, A. R. "The High Cost of Delivering Services." *Social Work* 18(4) (1973), 33–40.

Gruber, Murray. "Total Administration." *Social Work* 19(5) (September 1974), 625–36.

Gummer, Bert. "A Power Politics Approach to Social Welfare Organizations." *Social Service Review* 52(3) (September 1978), 349–61.

Hage, J., and M. Aiken. "Routine Technology, Social Structure and Organizational Goals." *Administrative Science Quarterly* 14 (1969), 366–76.

———. *Social Change in Complex Organizations.* New York: Random House, 1970.

Hall, Richard. "Some Organizational Considerations in the Professional Organizational Relationships." *Administrative Science Quarterly* 12(3) (1967), 461–78.

———, J. Eugene Mass and Norman J. Johnson. "Organizational Size, Complexity and Formalization." *American Sociological Review* 32 (December 1967), 903–12.

Hanson, M. C. "Career Development Responsibilities of Managers." *Personnel Journal* 56(9) (September 1977), 443–45.

Hartog, N. and J. Weker. *Boards of Directors.* Dobbs Ferry, N.Y.: Oceana Publications, Inc., 1974.

Hasenfeld, Yeheskel and Richard A. English (eds.,) *Human Service Organizations: A Book of Readings.* Ann Arbor, Mich.: The University of Michigan Press, 1974.

———. "People Processing Organizations: An Exchange Approach." *American Sociological Review* 37 (June 1972), 256–63.

Hawkins, J. David and Donald Sloma. "Recognizing the Organizational Context: A Strategy for Evaluation Research." *Administration in Social Work* 2(3) (Fall 1978), 283–94.

Heilbroner, Robert L. and Peter L. Bernstein. *A Primer On Government Spending.* New York: Random House, 1971.

Herzberg, Frederick. *Work and the Nature of Man.* Cleveland, Ohio: World Publishing Co., 1966.

Hicks, Herbert. *The Management of Organizations: A Systems and Human Resources Approach.* New York: McGraw-Hill, 1971.

Hickson, David J., D. S. Pugh and Diana C. Pheysey. "Operations Technology and Organization Structure: An Empirical Reappraisal." *Administrative Science Quarterly* 14 (September 1969), 378–97.

Homans, George C. *Social Behavior, Its Elementary Forms,* revised ed. New York: Harcourt Brace Jovanovich, Inc., 1974.

Hoshino, G. "Social Services: The Problem of Accountability." *Social Service Review* 47 (1973), 373–85.

Hudson, Walter. "Elementary Techniques for Assessing Single-Client/ Single-Worker Interventions." *Social Service Review* 51(2), 315–26.

Huntington, Harris. "Community of Interest—A Concept of Public Relations." *Quarterly Review of Public Relations* 6 (Spring (Spring 1961), 2–8.

Irwin, P. H. and F. W. Langham. "The Change Seekers." *Harvard Business Review* 44 (January–February 1966), 81–92.

Jacobs, J. "Symbolic Bureaucracy: A Case Study of a Social Welfare Agency." *Social Forces* 47(4) (1969), 413–22.

Janowitz, Morris. *Social Control of the Welfare State.* New York: Elsevier Scientific Publishing Co., 1976.

Johnson, B. S. and Brown, V., "The New Approaches to Training the Alienated Worker." *Public Welfare* 30(2) (1972), 54–58.

Johnson, Lyndon Baines. *The Vantage Point,* 1st ed. New York: Holt, Rinehart, and Winston, 1971.

Jones, L. H. "How Time and Cost Analysis Can Be Used to Improve Agency Management." *Child Welfare* 49 (1970), 395–99.

Jun, Jong S. "A Symposium on Management by Objectives in the Public Sector." *Public Administration Review* 26 (1976) 36(1), 1–45.

Kadushin, Alfred. "Supervisor-Supervisee: A Survey." *Social Work* 19(3) (May 1974), 288–97.

———. "The Knowledge Base of Social Work." in A. J. Kahn (ed.) *Issues in American Social Work.* New York: Columbia University Press, 1959, pp. 39–80.

———. *Supervision in Social Work.* New York: Columbia University Press, 1973.

Kahle, J. H. "Structuring and Administering a Modern Voluntary Agency." *Social Work* 14(4) (1969), 21–28.

———. "Assessing Executive Performance." *Social Casework* 52(2) (1971), 79–85.

Kahn, Alfred J. "Perspectives on Access to Social Services." *Social Work* 15(2) (April 1970), 95–101.

———. *Social Policy and Social Services.* New York: Random House, 1973.

Kahn, Robert, Donald Wolfe, Robert Quinn, and J. D. Snoek. *Organizational Stress; Studies in Role Conflict and Ambiguity.* New York: John Wiley and Sons, 1964.

Kaluzny, A. D. and J. E. Veney. "Attributes of Health Services as

Factors in Program Implementation." *Journal of Health and Social Behavior* 14 (June 1973).

Kamerman, Sheila B. and Alfred J. Kahn. *Social Services in the United States: Policies and Programs.* Philadelphia, Pa.: Temple University Press, 1976.

Kaplan, B. H. "Notes on a Non-Weberian Model of Bureaucracy; the Case of Development Bureaucracy." *Administrative Science Quarterly* 13(3) (1968), 471–90.

Kast, Fremont and James Rosenzweig. *Organization and Management: A Systems Approach,* 2nd Ed. New York: McGraw-Hill, 1969.

Katz, R. L. "Skills of an Effective Administrator." *Harvard Business Review* 52 (September–October, 1974), 91–102.

Kaufman, Herbert. "Administrative Decentralization and Political Power." *Public Administration Review* 29 (January–February, 1969).

Kelley, H. H. et al. "A Comparative Experimental Study of Negotiation Behavior." *Journal of Personality and Social Psychology* 16(3) (1970), 411–38.

Kendall, M. G. (ed.) *Cost-Benefit Analysis.* New York: American Elsevier.

Kidneigh, J. C. "Administration and Community Organization in Social Work." *International Social Work* 11(3) (1968), 17–22.

Kirkpatrick, D. "Determining Training Needs, Four Simple and Effective Approaches." *Training and Development Journal* 31(2) (February 1977), 22–25.

Klimoski, R. J. and W. J. Strickland. "Assessment Centers—Valid or Merely Prescient?" *Personnel Psychology* 30(3) (Autumn 1977), 353–61.

Koch, Louise. "Facilitating Program Development by Staff Study." *Social Casework* 53(4) (April 1972), 224–35.

Kolb, L. C. "Who Should Administer Psychiatric Facilities?" *Hospital and Community Psychiatry* 20(6) (1969), 170–73.

Kopple, Frances A. "An Administrator's Evaluation." *Social Casework* (April 1972), 214–17.

Kotin, I. and M. Sheraf. "Management Succession and Administrative Style." *Administration in Mental Health* (Summer 1974).

Kraut, A. I. "Developing Managerial Skills via Modelling Techniques: Some Positive Research Findings." *Personnel Psychology* 29(3) (Fall 1976), 325–28.

Lasagna, J. B. "Make Your MBO Pragmatic." *Harvard Business Review* 49 (November 1971), pp. 64–69.

Lauffer, Armand. *Doing Continuing Education and Staff Development.* New York: McGraw-Hill, 1978.

Lawrence, P. R. "How to Deal with Resistance to Change," *Harvard Business Review* 47 (January–February, 1969), 14–22, 166–76.

Lefton, Mark and William R. Rosengren. "Organizations and Clients: Lateral and Longitudinal Dimensions." *American Sociological Review* 31 (December 1966), 802–810.

Leiby, James. "Social Welfare: History of Basic Ideas." *Encyclopedia of Social Work* 15 ed., New York: National Association of Social Workers, 1977.

Lerman, P. "Evaluative Studies of Institutions for Delinquents: Implications for Research and Social Policy." *Social Work,* 1969 (13:3), 55–64.

Levine, A. "Cost-Benefit Analysis and Social Welfare Program Evaluation." *Social Service Review* 42, (1968), 173–83.

Levine, Sol and Paul E. White. "Exchange as a Conceptual Framework for the Study of Interorganizational Relationships." *Administrative Science Quarterly* 5(4), (1961), 583–601.

Levinson, Perry. "Evaluation of Social Welfare Programs: Two Research Models." *Welfare in Review* 4(10), (1966), 5–12.

———. 'Goal Model and System Model Criteria of Effectiveness." In *Planning, Programming, Budgeting.* ed. F. Lyden and E. Miller. Chicago: Markham, 1972.

Levitan, Sar and Robert Taggert. *The Promise of Greatness.* Cambridge, Mass.: Harvard University Press, 1976.

Levy, Charles. "The Ethics of Supervision." *Social Work* 18(2) (March 1973), 14–21.

Leyendecker, Gertrude. "A Comprehensive Staff Development Program." *Social Casework* (December 1965), 607–13.

Lippitt, Ronald, J. Watson and B. Westley. *The Dynamics of Planned Change.* New York: Harcourt Brace Jovanovich, 1958.

Litvak, Eugene and Lydia Hylton. "Interorganizational Analysis: A Hypothesis on Coordinating Agencies." *Administrative Science Quarterly* 6(4), 395–420.

Litvak, Eugene and Henry J. Meyer. "A Balance Theory of Coordination Between Bureaucratic Organizations and Community Primary Groups." *Administrative Science Quarterly* 2 (June 1966), 31–58.

Loeb, R. "A Tentative Classification of Decision-Making." *Sociological Inquiry,* 44(1) (1974), 41–46.

Lowi, Theodore. *The End of Liberalism.* New York: W. W. Norton, 1969.

Lynn, L. E. and J. M. Seidl. "Bottom-Line Management for Public Agencies." *Harvard Business Review* 55(1) (January 1977), 144–53.

Lindblom, C. E. "The Science of Muddling Through." *Public Administration Review,* (Spring 1959), 214–29.

Lippett, M. E. and K. MacKensie. "Authority-Task Problems." *Administrative Science Quarterly,* 2194 (December 1976), 643–60.

Long, Norton E. "The Local Community as an Ecology of Games." *American Journal of Sociology.* 64:3 (November 1958), 251–61.

Lyden, F. and E. Miller. *Planning, Programming, Budgeting.* Chicago: Markham, 1972.

Maccoby, Michael. *Gamesmen, The New Corporate Leaders.* New York: Simon and Schuster, 1977.

March, James G. (ed.). *Handbook of Organizations.* Chicago: Rand McNally and Co., 1965.

——— and Herbert Simon. *Organizations.* New York: Wiley, 1958.

Marrett, C. G. "On the Specification of Interorganizational Dimensions." *Sociology and Social Research* 56(1) (October 1971), 33–42.

Martin, A. R. "Morale and Productivity: A Review of the Literature." *Public Personnel Review* 30(1) (1969), 42–45.

Martino, R. L. *Project Managment.* Wayne, Pennsylvania: Management Development Institute, 1968.

Marwell, Gerald and Jerald Hage. "The Organization of Role Relationships: A Systematic Description." *American Sociological Review* 35 (Ocober 1970), 884–900.

Maslow, Abraham. *Motivation and Personality.* New York: Harper & Row, 1954.

Mathlesen, T. *Across the Boundaries of Organizations: An Exploratory Study of Communication Patterns in Two Panel Institutions.* Berkeley, California: Glendessary Press, 1971.

Mayer, M. F. "Program Evaluation as a Part of Clinical Practice: An Administrator's Position." *Child Welfare* 54 (June 1975), 379–94.

Mayo, Elton, *The Human Problems of Industrial Civilization.* New York: MacMillan, 1933.

Mechanic, David. "Organizational Power of Lower Participants." *Administrative Science Quarterly,* 7 (December 1962), 349–64.

Meld, Murray B. "The Politics of Evaluation of Social Programs." *Social Work,* 19(4) (July 1974), 448–55.

Melvin, Herman and Michael Munk. *Decision-Making in Poverty Programs: Case Studies from Youth Agencies.* Columbia University Press, New York: 1968.

Melzer, A. E. and M. Haug. "Staff Development and Differential Development." *Social Work,* 19 (1974), 467–76.

Mencher, Samuel. *From Poor Law to Poverty Programs: Economic Security Policy in Britain and the United States.* Pittsburgh: University of Pittsburgh Press, 1967.

Merewitz, Leonard and Steven H. Sosnic. *The Budget's New Clothes.* Rand McNally College Publishing, Chicago, 1971.

Merton, Robert. *Social Theory and Social Structure.* New York: Free Press, 1968.

Meyer, Carol. "Frameworks and Knowledge: The Content of Social Work Practice." *Social Work Practice,* (2 ed.), New York: Free Press, 1976.

Meyer, Carol. *Staff Development in Public Welfare Agencies.* New York: Columbia, 1966.

Michels, Robert. *Political Parties.* New York: Dover, 1959.

Miles, R. E., Jr. *Awakening From the American Dream.* New York: Universe Books, 1976.

Miller, Seymour M. and Pamela Roby. *The Future of Inequality.* New York: Basic Books, 1970.

———. "The Study of Man: Evaluating Action Programs." *Trans-Action,* (March–April 1965), 38–39.

Mills, C. W. and Gerth. *Essays in Sociology from Max Weber.* New York: Columbia, 1976.

Miringoff, Marc L. "Incomplete Technology and the Organizational Dynamics of a State Mental Hospital." *Administration in Mental Health* 3(2), (Spring 1976).

———. "O.E.O.: The Formulation of Poverty Policy: A Study of the Relationship Between Social Analysis and Social Planning." Ph.D. dissertation, University of Chicago, School of Social Service Administration, September 1972.

Mo, Linn. "Coordination of Social and Medical Services: An Issue in Norway." *Social Service Review,* (5294), (December 1978), 632–43.

Mokler, R. J. "A Situational Theory of Management." *Harvard Business Review* 49, (May–June 1971), 146–51.

Monsky, Mark. *Looking Out For No. 1.* New York: Simon and Schuster, 1975.

Montagne, Paul D. "Professionalization and Bureaucratization in Large Professional Organizations." *American Journal of Sociology* 74(2) 1908, 134–45.

Morris, John A. Jr. and Martha N. Ozawa, "Benefit-Cost Analysis and the Social Service Agency: A Model for Decision-Making." *Administration in Social Work* 2(3), (Fall 1978), 271–82.

Morris, Robert and A. Binstock. *Feasible Planning for Social Change.* New York:

Morrissey, George L. *Management by Objectives and Results.* Reading, Mass.: Addison-Wesley Publishing Co., 1970.

Mott, Paul. *The Characteristics of Effective Organizations.* New York: Harper & Row, 1972.

Moynihan, Daniel. *Maximum Feasible Misunderstanding.* New York: Free Press, 1969.

Nance, K. N. and J. B. Pillsbury. "An Evaluation System for Decision-Making." *Public Welfare* 34, (Spring 1976), 45–52.

Neugeboren, B. "Developing Specialized Programs in Social Work Administration in the Master's Degree Program; Field Practice Component." *Journal of Education for Social Work* 7(3), (1971), 35–47.

Newman, Edward and Jerry Turem. "The Crisis of Accountability." *Social Work* 19(1), (January 1974).

Newman, Emmanuel and William H. Wilsmack. "Measurement of Effectiveness of Social Services." *Public Welfare,* (January 1970), 80–83.

O'Brien, George. "Interorganizational Relations." in *Mental Health Administration,* (Saul Feldman, ed.), Illinois: Charles C Thomas, 1973.

O'Connell, Brian. *Effective Leadership in Voluntary Organizations: How to Make the Greatest Use of Citizen Service and Influence.* New York: Association Press, 1976.

Odiorne, George. *Management By Objectives—A System of Managerial Leadership.* New York: Pitman Publishing Co., 1965.

Oliva, G. and D. Adams. "Utilization of Informal Leadership in Mental Health Hospital Change." *The Social Worker* 40(2) (1972), 86–92.

Ozawa, Martha N. "Taxation and Social Welfare." *Social Service Review* 18(3), (May 1973), 6–76.

Palumbo, Dennis "Power and Role Specificity in Organization Theory." *Public Administration Review* 29(3), (May–June 1969), 237–218.

Parsons, Talcott. *The Social System.* New York: Free Press, 1952.

———. *Structure and Process in Modern Societies.* New York: Free Press, 1953, 16–96.

Patti, R. "Organizational Resistance and Change: The View from Below." *Social Service Review* 48(3), (1974), 367–74.

——— and Philip Osborne. *Management Practice in Social Welfare: An Annotated Bibliography.* New York: Council on Social Work Education, 1976.

————— and Herman Resnick. "Changing the Agency From Within."
Social Work 17(4), July 1972, 48–57.

————— and H. Revnich. "The Dynamics of Agency Change." *Social
Casework* 53, (1972), 243–255.

Perlman, Robert and Arnold Gurin. *Community Organization and
Social Planning*. New York: John Wiley, in cooperation with the
Council on Social Work Education, 1972.

Perlmutter, F. "Systems Theory and Organization Change: A Case
Study." *Sociological Inquiry* 42(2), 1972, 109–122.

Perrow, Charles. "A Framework for the Comparative Analysis of Organizations." *Administrative Science Quarterly* 32(2), 194–208.

—————. "Hospitals: Technology, Structure and Goals." In March,
J. G. (ed.) *Handbook of Organizations*, Chicago: Rand McNally,
1965.

—————. *Organizational Analysis: A Sociological View*. Belmont, California: Wadsworth Publishing Co., 1970.

—————. "Organizational Prestige, Some Functions and Dysfunctions."
American Journal of Sociology 66(4), (1961), 335–41.

—————. "The Analysis of Goals in Complex Organizations." *American
Sociological Review* 26(6), (1961), 854–66.

Pettigrew, Andrew M. *The Politics of Organizational Decision-Making*. London: Tavistock Publications, 1974.

Pfeffer, J. and G. R. Salavch. "Organizational Decision-Making as a
Political Process: The Case of a University Budget." *Administrative Science Quarterly* 19(2), (1914), 135–51.

Pigou, Arthur Cecil. *The Economics of Welfare*, 4 ed., New York:
A.M.S. Press, 1978.

Piliavin, Irving and Thomas McDonald. "On the Fruits of Evaluative
Research for the Social Services." *Administration in Social Work*
1(1), 63–70.

Pines, Ayala and Ditsa Kaffrey. "Occupational Tedium in the Social
Services." *Social Work* 23(6), (November 1978).

Polsky, Howard. "From Cliques to Factions: Subgroups in Organizations." *Social Work* 23(2), (March 1978), 93.

Prince, G. M. "Creative Meetings Through Power Sharing." *Harvard
Business Review*, 50, (July–August 1972), 47–54.

Pruger, Robert. "The Good Bureaucrat." *Social Work* 18(4), (July
1973), 26–32.

Public Welfare Directory 1978/79. Vol. 39, Washington, D.C.:
American Public Welfare Association.

Pugh, Derek S. et al. "A Conceptual Scheme for Organizational Analysis." *Administrative Science Quarterly* 8 (December 1963),
289–315.

Raider, M. C. "A Social Service Model of Management by Objectives." *Social Casework*, (October 1976), 523–28.

Reid, D. M. "Human Resource Planning: A Tool for People Development." *Personnel* 54(2), (March–April 1977), 15–25.

Reid, Dolores B. and Merle E. Springer. "The Formulation and Integration of a Staff Development Program in a Public Child Welfare Agency." *Public Welfare* 28(3), (1970), 291–96.

Reid, P. N. "Reforming the Social Service Monopoly." *Social Work* 17(6), (1972), 44–54.

Reid, William. "Interagency Coordination in Delinquency Prevention and Control." *Social Service Review* 38(4), (December 1964), 186–94.

Rein, Martin. *Social Policy: Issues of Choice and Change.* New York: Random House, 1970.

Rice, R. M. "Organizing to Innovate in Social Work." *Social Casework* 54(1), (1973), 226.

Richman, Barry M. and Richard Farmer. *Management and Organizations.* New York: Random House,

Ringer, Robert J. *Winning Through Intimidation.* (2d ed.), L.A. Book Publisher Co., 1974.

Rivlin, Alice. *Systematic Thinking for Social Action.* Washington, D.C.: Brookings Institution, 1971.

Robins, A. J. "Administrative Process Model for Community Mental Health Centers." *Community Mental Health Journal* 8(3), (1972), 208–217.

Roby, Pamela (ed.), *The Poverty Establishment.* Englewood Cliffs: 1974.

Roethlisberger, Fritz. *Management and Morale.* Cambridge: Harvard University Press, 1955.

Rogers, D. L. "Towards a Scale of Interorganizational Relations among Public Agencies." *Sociology and Social Research* 59(1), (October 1974), 61–70.

Romonyshyn, John M. *Social Welfare: Charity to Justice.* New York: Random House, 1971.

Rose, Stephen M. *Betrayal of the Poor.* Cambridge, Mass.: Schenkman Publishing Co., 1972.

Rosenberg, Marvin L. and Ralph Brody. "The Threat or Challenge of Accountability." *Social Work* 19(3), (May 1974), 344–50.

Rosengren, William. "Communication, Organization, and Conduct in the "Therapeutic Milieu'." *Administrative Science Quarterly* 32(3), 237–47.

——— and Mark Lefton (eds.). *Organizations and Clients.* Columbus, Ohio: Charles E. Merrill Publishing Co., 1970.

Ross, Murray. *Community Organization: Theory and Principles* (2d ed.), Harper & Row, 1971.

Rossi, Peter H. and Walter William. (ed.). *Evaluating Social Programs: Theory, Practice and Politics.* New York: Seminar Press, 1972.

Rothman, Jack. *Planning and Organizing For Social Change: Action Principles From Social Science Research.* New York: Columbia University Press, 1974.

———. "Three Models of Community Organization Practice." *Social Work Practice,* New York: Columbia University Press, (1968), 16–47.

Rummler, G. A. "Human Performance Problems and Their Solution." *Human Resource Management* 11(4), (Winter 1972), 2–10.

Ruthman, Robert and Ann R. Perucci. "Organizational Concerns and Professional Expertise." *Administrative Science Quarterly* 15, (1970), 282–94.

Samuel, Yitzhak and Bilka F. Mannheim. "A Multi Dimensional Approach Toward a Typology of Bureaucracy." *Administrative Science Quarterly* 15, (June 1970), 216–28.

Schatz, H. A. (ed.). *Social Work Administration: A Resource Book.* New York: Council on Social Work Education, 1970.

Schick, Allen. *Budget Innovation in the States.* Washington, D. C.: Brookings Institution, 1971, Ch. 7, 192–218.

———. "The Road to PPB: Stages of Budget Reform." *Public Administration Review* 26(4), (December 1966), 243–258.

Schmidt, Frances and Harold N. Weiner (eds.). *Public Relations in Health and Welfare.* New York: Columbia University Press, 1960.

Schneiderman, Leonard. "Collaboration Between the Health and Social Services in England." 23(3), *Social Work,* (May 1978), 192–97.

Schwartz, Edward. "On Macro-Social Work: A Practice in Search of Some Theory." *Social Service Review* 51(2), (June 1977), 207–227.

Selltiz, Claire et al. *Research Methods in Social Relations.* New York: Holt, Rinehart and Winston, 1976.

Sherwin, D. S. "Strategy for Winning Employee Commitment." *Harvard Business Review* 50, (May–June 1972), 37–47.

Schichor, D. and L. T. Empey. "A Typological Analysis of Correctional Organizations." *Sociology and Social Research* 58(3), (April 1974), 318–34.

Shubik, M. (ed.). *Readings in Game Theory and Political Behavior.* New York: Doubleday, 1954.

Silverman, Herbert A. "A Beleaguered Welfare Program: A Case

Study in Organizational Response." *Social Service Review* 45(2), (June 1971), 147–58.

——— and F. Perlmutter. "CMHC: A Structural Anachronism." *Social Work* 17(2), (March 1972), 78–84.

Simon, Herbert A. *Administrative Behavior* (2d ed.), New York: Free Press, 1965.

———. "On the Concept of Organizational Good." *Administrative Science Quarterly* 9, (June 1964), 1–22.

Simpson, Richard L. and William Gulley. "Goals, Environmental Pressures and Organizational Characteristics." *American Sociological Review* 27(3), (1962), 344–51.

Sleeman, John F. *The Welfare State: Its Aims, Benefits and Costs.* London: Allen and Unwin, 1973.

Smith, C. "A Comparative Analysis of Some Conditions and Consequences of Interorganizational Conflict." *Administrative Science Quarterly* 10(4), (1968), 504–29.

———. *Social Work and the Sociology of Organization.* London: Routledge and Kegan Paul, 1970.

Smith, Neilson F. "A National Experiment in Staff Development." *Social Casework* 48(9), (November, 1967), 556–62.

Solomon, L. N. and B. Berzon. *Employee and Team Development.* La Jolla, Calif.: University Associates, 1975.

Spergel, Irving. *Community Problem Solving.* Chicago: University of Chicago Press, 1969.

Spindler, A. "Management by Crisis of Management or by Plan." *Public Welfare* 30, (1972), 44–47.

———. "On Decision-Making and the Social and Rehabilitation Programs." *Public Welfare* 29(2), (1971), 307–315.

Stanton, E. *Clients Come Last: Volunteers and Welfare Organizations.* Beverly Hills, Calif.: Sage Publication, 1970.

Steers, R. M. "When Is an Organization Effective? A Process Approach to Understanding Effectiveness." *Organizational Dynamics* 5(2), (Fall 1976), 50–63.

Stein, Herman D. et al. "Assessing Social Agency Effectiveness: A Goal Model." *Welfare in Review* 6(2), (March–April 1968), 13–18.

Steiner, Richard. *Managing The Human Service Organization.* Beverly Hills: Sage Publications, 1977.

Streiss, Alan Walter. *Public Budgeting and Management.* New York: D. C. Heath and Co., 1972.

Stinchcombe, Arthur L. "Bureaucrats and Craft Administration of Production: A Comparative Study." *Administrative Science Quarterly* 4 (September 1965), 167–87.

Studt, E. "Fields of Social Work Practice." *Social Work,* (October 1965), 10(4), 156–65.

———. "Social Work Theory and Implications for the Practice of Methods." *Social Work Education Reporter* 16(2), (June 1968), 22–24, 42–46.

Suchman, Edward A. *Evaluative Research: Principles and Practice in Public Service and Social Action Programs.* New York: Russell Sage Foundation, 1967.

Sundquist, James et al. *Centrally Planned Change: A Re-examination of Theories and Concepts.* Urbana, Illinois: University of Illinois Press, 1974.

Sutherland, J. W. *Managing Social Service Systems.* New York: P.B.I., 1977.

Taylor, Frederick W. *Scientific Management.* New York: Harper & Row, 1947.

Terreberry, Shirley. "The Evolution of Organizational Environments." *Administrative Science Quarterly* 12(4), (March 1968), 590–613.

Thomas, Edwin J. "Role Conceptions and Organizational Size." *American Sociological Review* 20(1), (1959), 30–37.

Thompson, J. B. *Organizations in Action: Social Science Basis of Administrative Theory.* New York: McGraw-Hill, 1967.

——— and William McEwan. "Organizational Goals and Environment: Goal Setting as an Interactive Process." *American Sociological Review* 23 (February 1958), 23–31.

Thompson, J. D. and A. Tuden. "Strategies, Structures and Processes of Organizational Decision." In J. D. Thompson (ed.), *Comparative Studies in Administration,* Pittsburgh:

Thompson, Victor. "Hierarchy, Specialization and Organizational Conflict." *Administrative Science Quarterly* 5(4), (March 1961), 485–521.

Thurow, Lester C. *Poverty and Discrimination.* Washington, D. C.: Brookings Institution, 1969.

Titmuss, Richard. *A Commitment to Welfare.* New York: Pantheon Books, 1968.

———. *Introduction to Social Administration in Britain.* New York: Hillary House Publishers, 1969.

———. *Social Policy.* London: Allen and Unwin, LTD. 1974.

Townsend, Peter, and Brian Abel-Smith. *The Poor and the Poorest: A New Analysis of the Ministry of Labour's Family Expenditure Surveys 1953–54 and 1960.* London: Bell. 1965.

Trattner, William. *From Poor Law to Welfare State: A History of Social Welfare in America.* New York: The Free Press, 1974.

Trecker, Harleigh B. *Social Work Administration: Principles and Practices.* New York: Association Press, 1971.

Tripodi, Tony, Phillip Fellin, and Irwin Epstein. *Social Program Evaluation: Guidelines for Health, Education and Welfare Administrators.* Itasca, Ill.: F. E. Peacock Publishers, Inc., 1971.

Tropp, Emmanuel. "Expectation, Performance and Accountability." *Social Work* 19(2) (March 1974), 139–48.

Turem, Jerry S. "The Call for a Management Stance." *Social Work* 19(5) (1974), 615–23.

Turk, Stuart A. "Denying or Delivering Services?" *Social Work* 19(4) (July 1974), 439–47.

U.S. Department of Health Education and Welfare. *Toward a Social Report.* Washington, D.C.: U.S. Government Printing Office, 1969.

Vyterhoeven, H. E. R. "General Managers in the Middle." *Harvard Business Review* 50 (March–April 1972), 75–85.

Warham, Joyce. *An Introduction to Administration for Social Workers*, Rev. Ed. Atlantic Highlands, N.J.: Humanities Press, 1975.

———. *An Open Case: The Organizational Context of Social Work.* London: Routledge and Kegan Paul, 1977.

Warren, Donald J. "Power, Visibility and Conformity in Formal Organizations." *American Sociological Review* 31(6) (1968), 951–70.

Warren, Roland L. "The Intraorganizational Field as a Focus for Investigation." *Administrative Science Quarterly* 12(3) (December 1967), 396–419.

Wasserman, Harry. "The Professional Social Worker in a Bureaucracy." *Social Work* 16(1) (January 1971), 89–95.

Wasserman, Paul and Fred S. Silander. *Decision-Making: An Annotated Bibliography.* Ithaca, N.Y.: Cornell University Graduate School of Business and Public Administration.

Wax, I. "Power Theory and Institutional Change." *Social Science Review* 45(7) (September 1971), 274–88.

Weber, Shirley. "Goals for Staff Development." *Public Welfare* 29(3) (Summer 1971), 255–61.

Weirich, Thomas W., Felice D. Perlmutter and Willard C. Richen. "Interorganizational Behavior Patterns of Line Staff and Services Integration." *Social Service Review* 51(4) (December 1977), 674–89.

Weiss, Carol H. "Alternative Models of Program Evaluation." *Social Work* 19(6) (1974), 675–81.

———. "Evaluation of Staff Training Programs." *Welfare in Review* 3(3) (March 1965), 11–17.

Weissman, H. *Overcoming Mismanagement in the Human Service Profession*. San Francisco: Jossey-Bass, Inc., 1973.

Wetson, Kenneth W. "Differential Supervision." *Social Work* 18(6), (November 1973),80–88.

Whatcott, Weston E. "Bureaucratic Focus in Service Delivery." *Social Work* 19(4) (July 1974), 432–47.

Whitehead, T. N. *The Industrial Worker*. Cambridge, Mass.: Harvard University Press, 1938.

White, Ralph and Ronald Lippet. *Autocracy and Democracy*. New York: Harper and Row, 1960.

Wiehe, Vernon R. "Management by Objectives in a Family Service Agency." *Social Casework* 54(3) (March 1973), 142–46.

———. "Role Expectations Among Agency Personnel." *Social Work* 22(1) (January 1978), 26–30.

Wilcox, Clair. *Toward Social Welfare: An Analysis of Programs and Proposals Attacking Poverty, Insecurity and Inequality of Opportunity*. Homewood, Ill.: R. D. Irwin, 1969.

Wildavsky, Aaron. "The Political Economy of Efficiency: Cost-Benefit Analysis, Systems Analysis and Program Budgeting,: In Leyden, Fremont, and Ernest Miller (eds.) *Planning, Programming and Budgeting: A Systems Approach to Management*. Chicago: Markham Publishers, 1968, pp. 393–97.

———. *The Politics of the Budgetary Process* (2d ed.). Boston: Little, Brown and Co., 1974.

———. "The Self-Evaluating Organization." *Public Administration Review* 32 (1972), 509–20.

Wilensky, H. L. *Organizational Intelligence: Knowledge, Government and Industry*. New York: Basic Books, 1967.

——— and Charles N. Lebeaux. *Industrial Society and Social Welfare: The Impact of Industrialization on the Supply and Organization of Social Welfare Services in the United States*. New York: Russell Sage Foundation, 1958.

Wood, Katherine M. "Casework Effectiveness: A New Look at the Research Literature." *Social Work* 23(6) (November 1978), 437–60.

Woodard, Joan. *Industrial Organization Theory and Practice*. London: Oxford University Press, 1965.

Worthy, James C. "Organizational Structure and Employee Morale." *American Sociological Review* 15(2) (April 1950), 168–79.

Wright, Neil. "The States and Intergovernmental Relations." *Publius* 1 (Winter 1972), 7–68.

Young, David W. and Brant Allen. "Benefit Cost Analysis in the Social Services—The Example of Adoption Reimbursement." *Social Service Review* 51(2), 249–64.

Zald, Mayer. "Comparative Analysis and Measurement of Organizational Goals: The Case of Correctional Institutions for Delinquents." *Sociological Quarterly* 4 (Summer 1963), 206–30.

————. *Occupations and Organizations in American Society.* Chicago: Markham Pub. Co., 1971.

————. "Demographics, Politics and the Future of the Welfare States." *Social Service Review* 51(1) (March 1977), 110–24.

————. "Organizational Control Structures in Five Correctional Institutions." *American Journal of Sociology* 68 (November 1962), 451–65.

Zalaznik, Abraham. "The Human Dilemmas of Leadership." *Harvard Business Review* (July-August 1963), 49–55.

Zimbalist, Sidney. "A Comparison of Social Welfare Values: A Semantic Approach." 23(3), *Social Work* (May 1978), 198–202.

INDEX

Effectiveness of service (*cont.*)
149, 151, 153, 154, 165, 166, 167, 174, 175, 176, 177, 187, 188, 192, 193, 194, 195, 196, 198, 200, 201, 204, 205, 206, 208, 209, 211
Efficiency of service, 3, 8, 9, 10, 96, 97, 115, 125, 132, 135, 187, 193, 198, 209
Evaluation, *see* Performance appraisal; Program evaluation
Exchange theory, 99, 105; *see also* Trade-off mechanism
Experimental design, 136–37, 138, 144
Expressive management style, 108–11, 154, 155

Federal government, 3, 7, 165, 199, 200, 205, 206, 207, 208
Focal domain, 173–77, 185, 188, 202–203
Funding, 2, 3, 8, 26, 95, 97, 98, 115–25, 130, 133, 134, 163, 178, 186, 187, 195, 197–99, 205–208

General accountability audits, 132, 134, 144
Goals, 12, 32, 51–63, 72, 73, 75, 85, 86, 95, 104, 110, 115, 122, 131, 133, 138, 140, 141, 143, 145, 149, 150, 164, 165, 177, 183, 184, 194, 199, 201, 209
Government, *see* Federal government; State government
"Great Society," 2, 208

Hawthorne Study, 109
Health and Human Services, Department of (HHS) (formerly Dept. of Health, Education and Welfare), 7, 8, 205, 206, 207
Homans, George C., 99–102

Initiation of policy, 200–202
Input, 17, 19–21, 25–27, 39, 74–75, 77, 78, 79, 81, 95, 131, 149, 150, 153, 156, 177, 204–205
Instrumental management style, 108–11
Interorganizational relations, 164–70, 174–88, 197, 199; *see also* Linkages, interorganizational

Least Effective Service, Propositions of, 80–81, 167
Linkages, interorganizational, 166, 175–76, 177, 178, 183, 188, 200, 202–204, 205, 207, 211

Maintenance management, 8–9, 10, 11, 19, 27, 91, 94–99, 105, 110, 115, 118, 119, 130, 132, 134, 135, 144, 147–149, 156, 159, 164, 165, 167, 169, 177, 186, 187, 193, 194, 197, 202, 209, 211
Maintenance resources, 19, 20, 26, 73, 95, 105, 163, 197
Management By Objectives (MBO), 119, 123–25
Management styles, 108–11, 154, 155
Merton, Robert, 53
Most Effective Service, Propositions of, 79–80

New Deal, 1, 208

Official goals, see Goals
Operative goals, see Goals
Optimization, organizational, 72–75, 82, 85, 86, 98, 103, 105, 111, 115–25, 130, 131, 132, 133, 134, 140, 142, 144, 150, 151, 152, 154, 155, 169, 185, 197, 200, 201, 202
Outcome, 20, 26, 27, 33, 40, 87, 95, 97, 98, 105, 125, 129, 130, 131, 133, 135, 138, 144, 153, 154, 163, 166, 170, 174, 184, 185, 193, 202, 205
Output, 17, 26, 74, 75, 77–78, 80–81
Outreach to clients, 160, 162–163, 164, 168, 170

Performance appraisal, 150–51, 154, 168, 197
Perrow, Charles, 20
Planning, 12, 120, 122, 200
Planning organizations, 4, 6–7, 11, 71, 173–88, 193, 202–203, 204
Policy initiation, 200–202
Political elements in decision-making, 33, 35, 36–37, 38–39, 40, 46–47, 97, 103, 124, 139–40, 165, 166, 175, 201
Political leadership, 208
Program budgeting, see Program Planning Budgeting System
Program evaluation, 12, 94, 99, 115, 125, 129–32, 134–37, 143–45, 147, 149, 150, 156, 159, 167–68, 178, 179–85, 188, 203, 205, 206, 207
Program Planning Budgeting System (PPBS), 119, 121–122, 123, 124, 125, 168, 185
Public relations, 159–64, 170, 174–78, 188

Reporting systems, 129–30, 131–32, 134, 135, 144, 145, 186, 205
Resources, see Funding; Maintenance resources; Service resources
Reward system, 105–107